P9-CNB-273

DATE DUE

BROKEN

BROKEN

MY STORY OF ADDICTION AND REDEMPTION

WILLIAM COPE MOYERS

with Katherine Ketcham

VIKING

VIKING

Published by the Penguin Group

Penguin Group (USA) Inc., 375 Hudson Street, New York, New York 10014, U.S.A. • Penguin Group (Canada), 90 Eglinton Avenue East, Suite 700, Toronto, Ontario, Canada M4P 2Y3 (a division of Pearson Penguin Canada Inc.) • Penguin Books Ltd., 80 Strand, London WC2R ORL, England • Penguin Ireland, 25 St. Stephen's Green, Dublin 2, Ireland (a division of Penguin Books Ltd) • Penguin Books Australia Ltd, 250 Camberwell Road, Camberwell, Victoria 3124, Australia (a division of Pearson Australia Group Pty Ltd) • Penguin Books India Pvt Ltd., 11 Community Centre, Panchsheel Park, New Delhi – 110 017, India • Penguin Group (NZ), Cnr Airborne and Rosedale Roads, Albany, Auckland 1310, New Zealand (a division of Pearson New Zealand Ltd) • Penguin Books (South Africa) (Pty) Ltd, 24 Sturdee Avenue, Rosebank, Johannesburg 2196, South Africa

Penguin Books Ltd, Registered Offices: 80 Strand, London WC2R ORL, England

First published in 2006 by Viking Penguin, a member of Penguin Group (USA) Inc.

10 9 8 7 6 5 4 3 2 1

ISBN 0-670-03789-3

Printed in the United States of America
Designed by Katy Riegel

To my mother and father,
who have made the journey with me
every step of the way

A disciple asks the rebbe, "Why does Torah tell us to 'place these words *upon* your hearts'? Why does it not tell us to place these holy words *in* our hearts?"

The rebbe answers, "It is because as we are, our hearts are closed, and we cannot place the holy words in our hearts. So we place them on top of our hearts. And there they stay until, one day, the heart breaks and the words fall in."

—FROM "THE POLITICS OF THE BROKENHEARTED," BY PARKER J. PALMER

Contents

BROKEN

Prologue

OCTOBER 1994

THERE WAS A sharp rap on the door, followed by a muffled but unmistakable command from a voice outside in the hallway.

"We want the white guy, just the white guy. We know he's in there. He comes out now and there's no trouble for anyone later."

I was the "white guy." I knew in that instant that my family's desperate search to track me down had ended at this decayed two-story apartment in a violent pocket of Atlanta's inner city. Terrified, I rushed around the room, trying to warn the other crack heads to sit still and keep quiet.

"Don't panic," I whispered. "They'll go away." But nobody was listening because everybody was as high and as scared as I was. We bumped into one another as we tried to find a way out, but there was nowhere to go, nowhere to hide. We were like wild animals trapped by a wind-whipped forest fire.

Who was out there banging on the door? Was it my father? My mother? My wife? My mind flashed back to the morning four days earlier when I left my house in suburban Atlanta. I remembered kissing four-month-old Thomas and two-year-old Henry good-bye. It was a Sunday afternoon, and I told Allison I needed to run some errands before dinner. I drove to the parking lot on the corner of Boulevard and Ponce de Leon, approached a drug dealer with a thick scar running from his left ear to the corner of his mouth, and paid him one hundred dollars for six marble-sized rocks of crack cocaine. I held them in my hand and thought, "These will keep me going for a day or two." They were gone in four hours.

The knocking became a relentless pounding that shook the door frame. I thought about escaping out the back porch door to the vacant lot and just running, running, running. But where could I go? They would find me, just like they had in Harlem and St. Paul. I'd been running for five years. Now I had run out of options.

I sat down at the old wood table in the kitchen, the place where the deals were made, the pipe was fired up, and the crack was consumed. I couldn't run anymore—my legs felt weak and shaky. I couldn't hide—there was no place left. I couldn't think, but I could still react, and with the instincts of the addict I did the only thing that was left to do. I reached into my sock and pulled out the cellophane cigarette wrapper with the rocks carefully stored inside like precious stones. My hands were shaking and I noticed for the first time that the tips of my fingers were scorched and blistered from lighter burns. I loaded the pipe, flicked the lighter, and inhaled deeply.

The sizzle of the crack and the euphoric rush exploding inside my head were suddenly all that mattered to me. The banging on the door was like thunder on the horizon. I heard the warning, but I didn't feel threatened anymore because I was back in my element, that faraway place where nothing on this earth could touch me. The rush hijacked my brain, and the knocking, scurrying, and fear disappeared. The memories of my wife and children were gone. I was gone.

I tried to grab on and hold tight to the high, and for a few moments time stood still. I was a Roman candle on the Fourth of July, bright colors and showers of sparks. This, I thought, is what it's all about—stopping time, going higher and higher, explosions of light and heat, one after another after another. The rapture filled me for a minute or two, and then it began to fade, the sparks died down, the flame became a dying star far, far away.

I folded my arms over my chest, longing for comfort, for peace. I was so sick. So sick and tired of it all. In that moment I realized the hopelessness of my situation, and in a sudden, brief flash of clarity, I asked myself: *Now what?* I stared at the filthy wood floor littered with half-empty beer cans, cigarette butts, and used syringes. The answer wasn't here in this room anymore. It was all over. I was done.

I stood up and made my way past BJ, the Old Man, and the other addicts with whom I was living and slowly dying for the last four days. My steps were deliberate but out of my control as I walked into the hallway and out the front door, flanked by the two armed off-duty policemen who were part of the intervention team hired to get me out of the crack house and back into treatment.

A hard, steady rain was falling as we approached the gray van parked at the curb. The sliding door opened, and I collapsed into the backseat.

My father was sitting in the front passenger seat. Turning around to look at me, he saw a thirty-five-year-old crack addict who hadn't shaved, showered, or eaten in four days. A man who walked out on his wife and two young children and ditched his promising career at CNN. A broken shell of a man, a pale shadow of the human being he had raised to be honest, loving, responsible. His firstborn son.

Silence.

"You're angry," I said. I didn't know what else to say.

"That's hardly the word for it." His voice was harsh and cold, like the rain outside.

More silence.

"There's nothing more I can do," he said. "I'm finished."

All these years later, he tells me that's where the conversation ended. But whether I imagined it or not, I heard him say something else.

"I hate you."

And I remember looking in his eyes and speaking my deepest truth.

"I hate me, too."

1

Heaven

WHEN I THINK back to the time in my youth when happiness was all around me, inside and out, I think of Wilmer, Texas. In Wilmer, the sun was always shining and a steady wind blew across the fields, keeping everything in motion. My playmates were horned toads, chicken snakes, white scorpions, and crayfish that I would try to catch with a piece of my grandmother's leftover bacon tied to a string dangling in the waterlogged ditch by the side of Goode Road. My playground was the earth and the sky, every day was filled with adventures of my own creation, and nothing ever happened except what I wanted to happen, when I wanted it to happen.

"Was Wilmer as perfect as I remember it?" I asked my mother recently. She grew up on the farm in Wilmer, where four generations of her family had lived on the land with the rolling cotton fields and the creek running alongside.

"It was the perfect place," my mother said. "I think the love and longing for that place is in our genes, William, I really do."

Every summer and most holidays Mom would take me and my younger brother and sister to visit her parents at their farm twenty miles south of Dallas. The days always began in the kitchen. My grandmother's real name was Eula Dendy, although everybody in town called her Miss Judy. She was Nana to me, and she always wore an apron over her homemade dresses and hummed Baptist hymns as she piled piping hot biscuits covered in lumpy white gravy and thick, chewy bacon onto our plates. It seemed like every one of Nana's recipes required an *"and"*: chicken *and* dumplings, gravy *and* biscuits, pecan pie *and* vanilla ice cream hand-churned in a metal container packed in ice *and* salt.

We ate at a round oak table in the kitchen, where we'd look out the back window at the ruby-throated hummingbirds stabbing at the orange flowers on the sprawling trumpet vine my grandparents had planted decades before. Purple Martins circled the yard catching mosquitoes while mockingbirds—so named, my grandfather told me, because they could mimic the sound of all the other birds and even the screeches of my grandparents' cats—made a ruckus. The giant pecan tree created an umbrella of shade over the backyard and beyond that a stretch of Bermuda grass led to the back forty.

I loved walking through those fields. During corn season, I'd lose myself in the maze, running fast and hiding in distant rows to avoid the searching eyes of my brother and sister, who tried their best to keep up but never could. When the fields were planted with cotton, I'd wait until no one was watching and pluck the thick soft bolls, flipping them heavenward, watching the fluffy white clouds take off in the wind.

But my favorite time of all was when the fields were fallow, for that's when the hard soil offered up its most tantalizing secrets. Animal bones, broken pottery, square nails, and old marbles lay scattered like lost treasure. Roaming those fields where five generations of my mother's family had lived and died, I felt intimately connected with ancestors I knew only from stories and faded photographs. My grandfather, Henry Joseph Davidson, was born in the two-story wooden house, and my mother, Judith, grew up there. A half mile south a stand of crooked elms and pecan trees marked the original homestead where my great-great-grandparents lived until the house burned down on Christmas Day, 1930. My roots were firmly planted in the black dirt.

In the hottest part of the day, I'd head for the old pecan tree on the northwest corner of the property. It was as old as the homestead, and from one of its stout arms hung a homemade swing that was my elevator to the clouds. I'd spend hours with those clouds, imagining they were magic carpets that I could ride anywhere I wanted, even all the way to the Red River at the Oklahoma border. But the big black mushroom clouds that piled up one on top of the other were my favorites. Lying under that tree, gazing up at the dark underbellies of those clouds, I'd pretend that wild little monsters hid in those towering thunderheads, lashing out with electric fingers of forked light across the sky. I liked to imagine that I could scale those towers, finding a grip or toehold in the ridges and crags as I searched for them. I was always fascinated but never afraid of the power of these storms, not even when a spike of lightning struck the field across the road and made the whole earth tremble.

Even the ordinary took on a life of its own in Wilmer. The place was thick with stories waiting to be discovered and told. In the middle of one field there was an uneven patch of rocky soil and knee-high grass out by the "farmer's tree," where generation after generation of farmers sought refuge from the sun, and one day I took a shovel out there and started digging. In a few minutes I'd unearthed a complete skull filled with sharp, pointed teeth, and I had no doubt I'd discovered the first saber-tooth tiger's skull ever to be found in Texas. My mother didn't tell me until many years later that generations of her family had used the grassy area under the farmer's tree as a cemetery for their favorite pets and the skull I'd found probably belonged to Duster, the dog she'd had as a little girl.

Another day I was poking around in the dirt outside the old garage when I spied a half-buried rusty chain with a small key and something shiny and oval-shaped attached. I rubbed off the dirt to find my grandfather's name, H. J. Davidson, stamped on the metal. They were Pa Pa Joe's dog tags and the key belonged to his Navy duffel bag. He had worn the chain around his neck for two years of duty in the Pacific in World War II and then come all the way home to Wilmer and lost it. When I found that old chain, it was as if the attached key unlocked his memories. From that day on until he died in 1972, Pa Pa Joe never tired of telling me his war stories, no matter how many times I begged to hear them again. He even gave me a Japanese hand grenade that he had picked up after a battle on a tropical island. It was empty of gunpowder but still had the pin in it, and I used it to attack imaginary enemy soldiers hiding in the cornfields.

One of Pa Pa Joe's favorite stories featured a skirmish that happened right in his own backyard—and this one I witnessed with my own eyes. The moon was rising one summer night when we heard strange scratching sounds underneath the back porch. Armed with flashlights and big sticks, Pa Pa Joe and I searched for the source. With a sudden, terrifying grunt, an armadillo scurried out from under the house and ran right at me.

It might as well have been a charging Triceratops. I jumped straight up and tried to go in opposite directions at the same time, one leg to the left, the other to the right, hanging in the air for what seemed like forever as the bony creature scuttled below me and vanished into the dark with a final "urgggh" victory cry. When I finally came back to earth, Pa Pa Joe was bent over in hysterical laughter. I thought he was going to fall over he was laughing so hard. He loved telling people the story about the night the crazy armadillo tried to attack me and I went "two ways and no way" all at once.

Pa Pa Joe and I were kindred spirits, my mother tells me. He was a big talker who loved to tell jokes and saw the humor in everything. His favorite author was Mark Twain. He was also a history buff (especially of the Civil War) and an avid newspaper reader who loved politics. When I was about a year old, Pa Pa Joe was elected mayor of Wilmer, and in the years that followed, I will never forget sitting in the passenger seat, laughing at his jokes or listening intently to his stories as he steered around the potholes in the gravel roads on our way to city hall, a one-story brick building with a flagpole out front. He'd plunk me down on a counter and go about his business while I'd hold court, king of the world, with the town clerk and, sometimes, the chief of police.

Wilmer was heaven, the perfect place where I always wanted to be, the only place where I felt comfortable just being myself. I never wanted to leave and every time we did, I cried. Now, looking back from a distance of nearly four decades, I can see that Wilmer seemed like heaven because it stood in such direct contrast to the rest of my life. Back home in the suburbs of Washington, D.C., and later when we moved to Long Island, the days rushed by so fast that I sometimes felt like I could barely catch my breath.

The whirlwind began in 1960 when I was not quite a year old (Dad was twenty-six) and Lyndon Baines Johnson, then Senate majority leader, asked my father to help him with his campaign for the Democratic nomination for president. We moved to Washington, D.C., in January 1960, and seven months later John F. Kennedy won on the first ballot at the Democratic National Convention. In a surprise move, Kennedy selected Senator Johnson as his vice-presidential running mate and LBJ, in turn, asked Dad to serve as his executive assistant. Less than a year later, Dad asked President Kennedy for a leave so that he could help organize the Peace Corps. Within eighteen months, President Kennedy appointed him deputy director of the Peace Corps.

"The Peace Corps embodied the idealism personified in Kennedy's call to ask not what your country can do for you but what you can do for your country," my father wrote to me many years later. "It created an opportunity for moral teamwork with an exciting and talented array of people drawn by the same challenge. It placed our lives in a larger narrative than we had lived until then. When I traveled the country to research my book *Listening to America*, a desperate and alienated young fellow once told me, after riots had torn his campus apart, 'I'm just as good as I am bad. I think all of us are. But nobody's speaking to the good in me.' The Peace Corps appealed to the good in us: 'You matter, you can signify, you can make a difference.'"

The assassination of President Kennedy changed everything. On November 22, 1963, my father joined Lyndon Baines Johnson and Jackie Kennedy on Air Force One as the plane sat on the tarmac at Love Field and witnessed the swearing-in of the new president. For the next three years he served as a speech editor, policy coordinator, press secretary, and trusted friend to the most powerful man in the world. President Johnson loved my father as his own son and often affectionately referred to him as "mah Baptist preacher." One of my favorite stories about my dad and LBJ took place at LBJ's Texas ranch on Thanksgiving Day. Dad was saying grace when the president interrupted him and told him to speak up. "I wasn't speaking to you, Mr. President," my father said.

I was four years old when President Kennedy was killed, and while I have no clear memory of the assassination or its immediate aftermath, I was aware of the fact that our lives had been upended. Suddenly Dad was away all the time—even more than during his Peace Corps days—spending weeks at a time traveling the country and the world, working fifteen-hour days, six days a week, usually leaving the house before we woke up and coming home after we'd gone to bed. I remember watching the news on television and yelling out, "There's Dad!" and sure enough, there he was, talking to the press corps or standing near the president in the Rose Garden.

Newspaper reporters, government officials, and complete strangers would call at all times of the day and night. The telephone never stopped ringing. Dad even had a phone in the official government car that he used, but there was no way my mother was going to allow a phone in the family car, as it would disrupt what little precious time we had together. LBJ, frustrated that he couldn't reach my father on Sundays, tried to go over my mother's head and ordered the Signal Corps to install a phone in our car. When they showed up at our house in McLean, Virginia, they knocked on the door and explained to my mother what they had come to do.

"The president has told us we must install this phone in your car," they told my mother. She told them the car was in the shop being repaired and they would have to come back another time. The next time they showed up at the house, she told them the car had been loaned to a neighbor. We never did get a phone in our family car.

Life was always interesting and the older I got, the more exciting it became. There were Easter egg hunts on the South Lawn of the White House, trips on Air Force One, weekends spent at Camp David or at the president's ranch in the Texas hill country, and dinner parties at our home in suburban Washington where President Johnson was the guest of honor. But I was less interested in what was going on around the table than in sneaking around outside and trying to find the Secret Service agents hiding in the shrubs or behind trees.

It wasn't long, though, before I began to realize that my world was different from most everyone else's. At home, at school, and even at the store, people would stare or point at us, especially when Dad was with us. We were in the newspaper a lot and my sister even appeared in *Look* magazine, modeling the latest children's fashions in a photo shoot at the White House. Life was in constant motion and, for the most part, it was fun and exciting. From the outside, everything might have seemed perfect, but inside I had a growing sense that something wasn't quite right.

My most painful memory isn't something I can even remember but nonetheless remains fresh in my mind through the stories of others. They say I was five or six years old, flying on an air force jet somewhere to meet up with Mom and Dad. The plane made a scheduled refueling stop in some small midwestern town, and I stepped off the plane to a welcoming committee made up of the mayor, a high school band, and community leaders gathered on the tarmac to greet the famous Bill Moyers. Apparently they were as surprised as I was. The awkward moment lingered until I was ushered back on board the plane and flew on to Texas or Washington or wherever I was going. I remember nothing about that day, yet my emotions around those events are still strong. Although I always laughed along with everyone who ever told or heard the story, I felt a deep sense of shame knowing that I had disappointed an entire town.

When I was seven my father's picture appeared on the covers of *Time* and *Newsweek* magazines in the same week. THE MAN IN CHARGE OF EVERYTHING proclaimed the headline running across the *Time* cover. The inside story included a photograph of the Moyers family (originally published in *Life* magazine), in which Dad looked fondly at my mother, while my baby brother, John, sat on his lap playing with a toy and Mom smiled at two-year-old Suzanne perched on the dining room table. Only I am outside the family circle, one foot on the windowsill, arms spread wide, staring out the window, seemingly oblivious to the photographer and the set scene behind me. Even after all these years, I have a good sense of what I was thinking that day: "Let me out of here!" I was literally climbing the walls.

I could be reading too much into that photo. Maybe I was just an active kid, curious about everything and unable to sit still for very long. My mother always said I was "born with the gift of wonder." Whenever we'd take a walk or go for a drive in the car, I'd always be calling out, "Look, look, there's a red barn!" (Or a horse, a train, a thundercloud, whatever happened to catch my eye at the time.) Telling the story decades later, my mother smiled in a nostalgic kind of way. "You just wanted everyone else to share in your excitement," she told me.

But there's something about that family picture that proves what I knew even back then, before I could explain it. I wasn't comfortable in my own skin, and I was constantly trying to get attention to soothe some deep ache inside. My report cards as far back as kindergarten reveal the same truth.

"He needs to learn that he shouldn't talk out in the classroom whenever he wants, as this is disturbing to the rest of the class," wrote Mrs. Bavry, my first-grade teacher at Churchill Road School in Fairfax County. "He needs improvement in exercising self-control."

A year later Mrs. Birge, my second-grade teacher, reported that I had made some improvement. "He has been trying to exert more effort on his self-control and work more quietly. I hope he will continue to work on this."

"What can I do to help him learn self-control?" my mother wrote on the back of the report card.

When my behavior improved during the next reporting period, my mother was clearly relieved. "He appears to be developing some self-control, thank goodness," she wrote.

But on the back of my next report card, she wrote this note: "I am disappointed that his behavior has regressed."

That was the year the school principal called my parents to report that I had given away my collection of nickels during recess. ("You were always passing out nickels," my father recalls.) I don't remember what Mom or Dad said, or if they even disciplined me, but I clearly remember my classmates gathering around to thank me and pat me on the shoulder. Some yearning deep inside, something I couldn't name or understand, was satisfied for the time being.

I don't remember being aware of this concern about my behavior at school, although I do remember feeling that something was missing from my world. But what could it be? I had everything any child could possibly want—a big house in a safe, friendly neighborhood, good teachers who appreciated my enthusiasm even as they tried to quiet my energy, loving babysitters and au pairs (and, a few years later, Pricella, our live-in housekeeper who I came to love with all my heart), a new bicycle at Christmas, my mother's homemade birthday cakes, summer vacations out west, and parents who loved me beyond any doubt. What was wrong with me?

I don't know when the truth hit me, but one day I realized that I hadn't done anything to deserve all the good things in my life. Everything had been given to me—I hadn't earned any of it. I watched my father work eighty to ninety hours a week, and I thought I should be working that hard, too. He was successful, and everybody loved him—maybe if I was successful, people would love me that much, too. Slowly, over a long period of time, I convinced myself that there was really only one way for me to be truly happy—I had to do more than my father. I needed to *be* more than my father. Anything less and my life would be a failure.

So I started to push myself. I figured that if I talked louder, acted smarter, worked harder, practiced longer, behaved myself (or didn't get caught), did my chores, got a job, played sports, always said "Yes, sir," "No, ma'am," "Please," and "Thank you," went to church and faithfully believed in a loving God, success would be mine. All I had to do was be all that I could be and a little bit more.

I couldn't wait to grow up and prove myself. When my father's photo appeared on magazine covers, I made a solemn promise to myself that someday my face would be on the cover of major news magazines. When the president called my father early in the morning or late at night, I'd fantasize about the day when someone important would call me at my home. When Dad became a big-time newspaper publisher, I decided I'd become a journalist and write stories that would make the whole world stand up and take notice. When Dad's first book hit the best-seller lists, I told myself I'd write an even better book that would sell even more copies. When people told me how proud I should be of my father, I silently vowed that someday he would be more proud of me than I was of him. One day I would be his hero.

These thoughts became even more focused and intense when we visited my father's parents in his hometown of Marshall, Texas, just twenty miles from the Louisiana border. Marshall was ten times the size of Wilmer, and everybody there, it seemed, either already knew or wanted to know Bill Moyers. From the moment we arrived at my grandparents' two-bedroom house on Nathan Street, the sounds of the phone and the doorbell were a constant presence—the ringing in the background never stopped. Friends, neighbors, cousins, and members of the Central Baptist Church dropped by in what my mother laughingly called a "parade." Wanda from the *Marshall News Messenger* called to get the latest gossip so she could put a paragraph or two about my famous father in her "Wandering with Wanda" column. By the time everyone came to visit with their plates of cookies and brownies, the whole day was gone.

"We'll only stay a few minutes," everyone promised, but they always lingered long enough to eat a piece of my grandmother's homemade chocolate cake covered with an icing so rich that the sugar crunched like sand between your teeth. The cake itself was a good enough excuse to visit Miss Ruby and Mr. Henry, as my grandparents were known in town, but we all knew the visitors were really dropping by to say hello to the small-town boy who had made it big.

Marshall was the grand community stage where every six months or so Henry and Ruby Moyers got to be king and queen for the day, Dad was the reigning crown prince, and all the rest of us were treated like royalty. At Sunday services at Central Baptist Church where Pa Pa Henry was an usher (and proud of it), the congregation seemed much more interested in staring at us or leaning across the church pews to whisper greetings than in listening to the fire-and-brimstone sermons. When we went out to eat, either at the Lake O' the Pines, where we'd feast on fried catfish and hushpuppies, or Neely's Brown Pig BBQ, where we'd chow down on pork and coleslaw sandwiches called Brown Pigs, old friends would pull up a chair and strangers would stop by to shake my father's hand.

During every visit to Marshall, we'd make sure to stop by the old brick courthouse set on the picturesque town square with a Confederate soldier standing guard over his beloved South. In the courthouse museum an exhibit honored my father's life. (Today, the courthouse exhibit includes Marshall's other two famous citizens, Y. A. Tittle and George Foreman.) I'd been to plenty of museums in my life and spent lots of time staring at dusty old dinosaur bones, Civil War mementos, and Native American artifacts, but I always felt weird looking at memorabilia of a man who was not only my father, but also still alive. I remember thinking that I'd need to become famous, too, so that one day I could have my own exhibit in a museum.

When we walked down the street in Marshall, people waved at us from their cars or stopped for a few minutes to talk. I was a minor celebrity in my own right thanks to the fact that I was named after Millard Cope, the publisher of the *Marshall News Messenger*, who gave Dad his first job as a newspaper reporter when he was just sixteen. It was Millard Cope who told my dad to get in touch with Texas senator Lyndon B. Johnson for a summer job, and it was Millard Cope who wrote the senator a letter praising young Billy Don Moyers's prodigious energy, strong moral values, and uncommon skill with words.

When my parents named me William Cope Moyers and then dropped the "William" to call me "Cope," my nickname might as well have been "Marshall." People in Marshall were immensely proud of Millard Cope and Bill Moyers, and my name honored them both. But not everyone was pleased. Rumor had it that LBJ was furious that my dad didn't name his firstborn son after him.

Lyndon might have been better. I hated my name because it made me feel different, not in the sense of being special or unique, but odd and out of place. Not one of my friends or classmates had ever heard of someone named Cope, so the kids would tease me and make up little taunting phrases like "Cope is a dope." In high school when I ran for the student council, my opponent came up with the slogan, "There's no hope with Cope." When I wasn't being teased, people young and old were always asking me about my name. "No, I am not Cole or Coke or Coat," I'd explain, always careful to keep a polite smile on my face. "I'm Cope. And yes, I can cope."

But I couldn't. Long before most kids ever have to face what it means to "cope" with life, I was painfully aware that I couldn't cope with much of anything. When people asked me where I got my name, I felt obliged to tell them the story of my father's humble beginnings and Millard Cope's role in shaping his career. Telling the story over and over, it soon became as much a part of me as my own shadow, but it was my father's shadow, not mine, that everyone seemed interested in. After a while I didn't know who I was apart from him—my life was so inextricably intertwined with his that I couldn't figure out where he ended and I began. I was Bill Moyers's son, and that's all I ever could be.

Maybe that's why Wilmer was the perfect place, because nothing every happened there. I had the clouds, scorpions, and crawdads to play with, Nana's biscuits and gravy and Pa Pa Joe's stories to nourish my body and soul, and the wind to keep me company. I loved the wind most of all. I can still see it whipping dry Nana's billowing white sheets on the clothesline, giving life to the homemade curtains in the front bedroom where I took afternoon naps, shaking pecans from the limbs of the giant tree, and stirring up little dust devils in the fields that I'd run through just for the sheer thrill of it, even though I always ended up with grit in my nose, mouth, and eyes. When I faced the wind, turning my body so it hit me full-force, it filled my ears with wild sounds that drowned out my own thoughts. When I turned around to create a tailwind, I felt its hand on my back, steering me to the places I wanted to go.

All these years later the wind moves through my memories, reminding me that before everything fell apart there was a place where I fit in and felt whole, just the way I was.

2

The Death of Faith

"GOD IS GREAT, God is good, and we thank Him for our food. Amen."

It didn't matter if the flaky homemade biscuits were hot out of the oven, the fried chicken still sizzled on the platter, or the *CBS Evening News with Walter Cronkite* was about to start on the black-and-white television on the kitchen counter—dinner was served but never eaten until we recited this prayer.

Heads bowed, holding hands around the table, we took turns saying grace. When the duty fell to my sister, brother, or me, the words spilled out pretty fast. Sometimes we'd peek at one another through squinted eyes trying to get a laugh, or I'd squeeze my little brother John's hand to make him yelp. When it was Mom or Dad's turn, though, the mood was much more serious, and the prayer was amended to include thoughts about the war in Vietnam that was tearing the nation apart, family members facing illness or distress, or loved ones who were no longer with us. I kept my eyes shut and tried hard to sit still, but all I was really thinking about was the food heaped on the plate in front of me.

Besides, I didn't need to think very long or hard about those fourteen words because I knew God was great and good. I had been taught that everything on the table and all the good things in my life were there because of God, and I believed in Him with all my heart. God *was* great—not great like my favorite football team, the Dallas Cowboys, or Charles Lindbergh, my flying hero, or even my dad, Bill Moyers. God was great because He had the power of knowing it all, past, present, and future. The Cowboys, Lindbergh, and the Moyers family were on this earth because God wanted them to be there and had some kind of plan for them. In my small world, God had the power to do anything He wanted to do.

I remember the first time I saw an image of what I thought God's greatness actually looked like. I was in Sunday school one morning when I found a children's picture book that used simple, colorful illustrations to highlight the Bible's parables. In the chapter about heaven I saw a giant man with big hands, a bald head, and a long white beard that matched his flowing white gown. He was surrounded by a bunch of angel musicians playing trumpets and strumming harps. Angel families sat on clouds with weird smiles on their faces gazing out over a landscape that wasn't like any place I'd ever seen because there weren't any trees, houses, cars, or even the familiar golden arches of McDonald's.

Those angels really spooked me. Unlike God, who looked human enough to resemble my grandfathers if they'd grown beards and worn long robes, the angels were definitely from another world. Their plastic smiles were strange enough, but those pigeonlike wings attached to their shoulders made them look like the flying monkeys in *The Wizard of Oz*. The angels were even scarier than the monkeys because they were in the Bible and I'd been taught that everything in the Bible was real. The monkeys were only extras in an old movie.

Besides, the angels lived in heaven forever and that was a long time, so I imagined things got boring up there after a while. It was scary to think about living forever with nothing to do. My life on earth was busy and exciting, and I liked it that way. I had a lot of friends, interesting vacations, school was okay, Pricella's home-cooked food was the best in the whole world, and I liked sleeping in my own bed. Love was everywhere. "I love every hair on that boy's head," Pa Pa Henry was fond of saying. My grandmother Mimi scratched my back until my skin was red, Pa Pa Joe spent countless hours teaching me to drive his orange Vega before I was old enough to get a driver's license, Nana sang Baptist hymns to put me to sleep, my dad loved to toss the football with me and talk about the Giants or the Cowboys, and my mother was always eager to accompany me on the piano while I played the trombone ("Beautiful Isle of Somewhere" was our favorite duet). I didn't need to go to heaven when I had everything I needed on earth. Those strangers with wings and harps and robes and weird smiles could love somebody else—I was spoken for already.

Heaven was also for people who had died, usually because of bad things, and that scared me, too. Pa Pa Henry told me about the time he saw a tornado hit a farmhouse and pick up a mattress with a man and child on it and throw them into a ditch, killing them. Pa Pa Joe let me look at his *Life's Picture History of World War II*, which had a lot of photographs of dead people. Once Dad took me to Arlington National Cemetery for the funeral of a young soldier killed in Vietnam, and I remember thinking the wet grass smelled like blood seeping from his coffin into the ground. But tragedies like death always seemed just beyond what I could grasp, because they happened to other people, not me. I comforted myself with the knowledge that God wasn't mean or angry or bad and thus He couldn't be blamed for the bad things that happened in the world. As long as God watched over me, I was safe.

Still, at times I felt threatened. Once I was playing hide-and-seek and burrowed into the sheets on my parents' queen-sized bed at home in McLean. Underneath my mother's pillow I discovered a little white box and inside was a derringer pistol, no bigger than my hand. A gun, in my parents' bed? What could be so bad, so threatening, that my mother would sleep with a gun under her pillow? I put it back in the box, covered it up with the pillow, and ran out of the room. I didn't want to know about the gun, and I never uttered a word about it. But I always wondered. Decades later my mother told me that she put the gun (a gift to my father from LBJ) under her pillow one night because my father's life had been threatened and she was alone in the house with us kids and our nineteen-year-old au pair. The McLean police advised her to keep the clip separate but to have both the gun and the clip handy in case of an emergency. When my father returned the next day, she put the gun back in the case and never had reason to take it out again. For some reason, I just happened to look under her pillow on the only night she ever put a gun there.

Then there was Pa Pa Henry's big black Bible, which he kept on the nightstand by his bed in Marshall. In the front of that book someone had written down the birth and death dates of my dad's three sisters and his older brother, James. Dad's sisters died in infancy of "childhood illnesses," but that was all I knew, because nobody ever talked about them and I never saw any pictures either. Uncle James was only thirty-nine when he died. I was seven, and I remember my father telling me that his brother died of cancer. Decades later I would learn the real story and realize how much Uncle James and I had in common.

We had some shadowy characters in our family, too. My mother's sister was married to an alcoholic who at times became violent when he drank, and my great uncle Ralph, my grandmother's brother, had what everyone called "a drinking problem." I only met Uncle Ralph a few times, but he seemed like a nice man, kind, quiet, unassuming. He was always down on his luck, and he died as he had lived, a lonely, seemingly helpless alcoholic.

So I knew bad things happened, and I even felt them lurking around the edges of my life. But they hadn't happened to me, and for that I thanked God at the dinner table when we said grace and in bed at night when I said my prayers. *God is great, God is good. And we thank Him for our food (and everything else). Amen.* A simple prayer to sum up my simple faith.

That all changed the summer after my twelfth birthday when we headed off for our annual vacation roaming around the western United States. My father loved to take us out west where he said the vista, sky, and mountains all gave him a sense of something grand about nature and humbling about our place in it. While he had a special place in his heart for the humid pine forests of eastern Texas where he grew up, he once told me the trees filtered the light, trapping and hiding more than they revealed. Out west he felt liberated from the closeness of the small-town life he led in those woods. The sheer vastness of it all was about the future, not the past, he said, adding that "the future is always a good place to visit."

The West was my father's playground and early on in my childhood it became mine, too. We stayed at a dude ranch in the Rocky Mountains, watched the rodeo at Frontier Days in Wyoming, climbed ladders to explore the cave ruins of Mesa Verde in southern Colorado, floated on a raft down the Snake River, and walked the battlefield near Little Big Horn River in Montana where Custer made his last stand.

In the summer of 1971, a friend of Dad's from his seminary days offered us his two-room log cabin located at an altitude of 9,500 feet in the Sangre de Cristo Mountains near Red River, New Mexico. The cabin was built in 1958, the year before I was born, some twenty feet from a trout stream in a beautiful valley of blue spruce and shimmering aspen trees. Of all the places we had ever visited out west, that cabin on the Red River promised to be my favorite. Black bears raided the hummingbird feeders just outside the bedroom window. Eagles soared overhead in playful duels. Trout seemed eager to jump right into the frying pan that we had set up over a campfire on the banks overlooking the river.

The days were warm and sunny, but almost every afternoon the mountain winds picked up, pushing the clouds together to create towering thunderheads. I knew I could always count on a good afternoon thunderstorm with cooling rains and lightning flashing in all directions. We were usually in town when the storm started, buying groceries, getting an ice cream cone, or tagging along behind my parents as they shopped for antiques.

One day the winds suddenly picked up when we were packing up the rental car with groceries to head back to the cabin. I looked up at the sky and saw that this anvil-shaped cloud was different—it was bigger and blacker, a real monster of a cloud, and even as the winds began to push and pull the air around us, the cloud didn't move from its position. As I studied the roiling mass, I realized it stood between the town and our cabin, which was several miles away. We were going to have a fun ride home.

"Big storm coming, Dad!" I announced in eager anticipation. Dad looked up at the clouds, all black-and-white against the graying sky, and gave a low whistle to confirm my observation. Although Mom always checked the groceries to make sure nothing had been forgotten, this time she skipped the routine. She looked worried as she guided us into the backseat with a firm nudge of her hand on our backs.

I put my nose right up against the backseat window, craning my neck to look up at the sky. I loved any kind of storm—ice storms, hurricanes, blizzards, tornados—but thunderstorms were my favorites. I liked to count the seconds between the sudden flashes of light and the pounding drums of thunder, and the best thrill of all was when the flash and the clap came together in the same moment.

We drove right into the heart of the storm. Rain and hail rattled the roof of the car and the tall pines swayed back and forth in the wind with such force that I thought they would snap. Leaning forward in my seat, I could see my father's hands tense, white-knuckled on the steering wheel, as he tried to negotiate the narrow dirt road in the driving rain. A blinding bolt of lightning flashed right in front of us, so close that it looked like a twisted strand of pale blue yarn with fibers of energy wrapped around inside it. It hit the ground just beyond where the road disappeared over the next hill.

Suddenly Dad hit the brakes hard to avoid a huge rock that had washed down the side of the mountain into the road and at almost the same moment a car came at us from the opposite direction with its lights flashing. I could just barely hear the car's horn honking through the sound of the rain and the booming thunder that shook the car.

"They're going to warn us about the rocks in the road, Dad," I said, leaning over my father's shoulder from the backseat. "Wow, I'll bet we can't get back to the cabin! I bet we have to turn around!"

Dad didn't say a word as the car pulled up next to us and he rolled down the window. The woman in the other car was shouting to him, straining to be heard above the storm. I caught only a few words. *Family. Lightning. Dead.*

"What happened?" my mother asked in a terrified voice.

Dad kept his voice low. "Six people were hit by lightning," he said. "Four of them are in a grove of trees ahead, and two more are in the back of her car. We need to go up there and wait until help arrives."

As Dad drove on, I began to scream. My sister and brother—not quite sure what was happening but following their older brother's lead—started to scream, too, and then they were sobbing next to me. My mother leaned over into the backseat and tried to calm us down, but I couldn't hear her words because I couldn't stop screaming. Death was in the air, all around us; it felt like it was pushing against the windows and trying to get to us, too.

When we stopped, I stared out the side window, trying to see through the thick curtains of water. A pine tree towered over us, a narrow strip of its bark peeled away to reveal the white flesh of wood running down it in a spiral like a barber pole. A woman leaned up against the tree, holding something in her hand; her legs were black, like charcoal. Nearby a man sat on the ground slumped against a red dune buggy. Lumps of clothing were scattered around the campsite, like piles of dirty laundry. *Why don't they get out of the rain?* I wondered, but then I realized they weren't moving. I started screaming again.

When the rain began to let up, I could see arms and legs poking out of the piles on the ground. A boy lay huddled under a tarp he had used for shelter from the rain. A girl, her mouth open, could have been napping, except that her eyes were staring off into nothing. The people just lay there quietly, silent, mouths and eyes open. There were four all together. With the two people in the back of the lady's car that made six.

Six people. It was the family from Texas. We didn't know their names or much else about them, but they had been camping not far from our cabin. Just hours before, like we did every afternoon when we headed into town, we had waved to them and they had waved back. They were alive then, and now they were dead. The woman held a Coca-Cola bottle in her hand. I wondered when her hand would open and the bottle would fall to the ground. My brother and sister were sobbing, begging my father to drive back to the cabin where everything would be all right again, but I couldn't take my eyes off those dead people. They didn't move.

I heard Dad say something about the wolves and how we had to stay until help came. Then I understood. We had to stay there so that scavenging wolves didn't eat the dead people. I imagined wild animals tearing the clothing apart, dragging the parents and their children into the forest. I stared intently at the bodies, as if my steady focus could make them move again, get up and start their day all over. I searched their faces, trying to get to know them, wanting to understand who they were and how they had lived the last moments of their life on my earth. Were they afraid? Did they have any idea what was about to happen? Why did they pick that tree for a place to wait out the storm? Didn't they know what I knew, that no tree is safe in a storm? What did it feel like to die—did they suffer or was it all over in a sudden blue flash?

Another bolt of lightning shot through the sky. Did they believe in God? With that question, my search for answers spun upside down. This was no longer just about the dead people at the campsite—this was about me and God. Either His power couldn't stand up to the storm or the storm was His power, which meant that He allowed it to happen. *God isn't good.* The words echoed inside my head. *God is bad. He let this happen. He made this happen.*

I don't remember much about the rest of the vacation except that it seemed to go on forever. I think we stayed at the cabin for another week. I remember all five of us fishing in front of the cabin and my brother John and I feeling a little put out because Mom and Suzanne caught most of the fish. We must have roasted marshmallows over the campfire, laid on our backs at night trying to connect the dots in the sky to constellations, fed the chipmunks that lived under the cabin, and watched for bears raiding the hummingbird feeder outside the window, just like we had done before.

But everything had changed. Every sound made me jump, and I no longer felt safe wandering deep into the pine forest, out of sight of the cabin. Late in the afternoon when thunder rumbled through the trees and bounced off the mountains, I ran inside, pretending not to care but terrified because I feared what was coming. At night when I turned off the light and tried to sleep, I imagined the bears clawing their way into the cabin and eating me alive.

We stopped going to town every afternoon, but at least once before we left we all packed into the car to go to the grocery store. The only way into town was the dirt road that passed the tree where the people died, and I remember my mother turning around in the front seat, trying her hardest to distract us with games or stories. It didn't work, of course. I looked up at the top of the tree where the strip of freshly peeled bark began its long run to the ground, and I followed the strip all the way down to the bottom where it stopped. In my mind I could still see the woman leaning against the tree, the man sitting with his back against the dune buggy, and the children lying in little scattered heaps.

My father tried his best to help me. We'd sit and talk for hours, mostly at night when the noises outside the cabin stirred up my fear and intensified my grief. Dad talked to me about God, and the sound of his voice and expression on his face revealed his struggle to ease my pain and his own, as well.

"God doesn't send lightning bolts to earth," Dad said over and over that week at the cabin. "God doesn't send armies into battle or make airplanes crash or infect people with illness. God is a refuge for us when these things happen. God gives us relief from the pain and suffering, the fear and the loss that make up life every day."

I nodded my head, pretending to understand, but his words didn't comfort me. No matter what Dad said, no matter how many Bible passages he quoted or how many prayers he offered, I couldn't believe in a God who would strike down an entire family. I had never doubted God before, but now I couldn't even bring myself to say His name. I desperately wanted to believe, but I didn't know this God and if I didn't know Him, how could I believe in Him? I couldn't see His goodness anymore—all I could see were the faces of the dead people under the tree.

A few days before we left the cabin to go home, Dad and I went for a walk along the river, just the two of us. He had his arm around my shoulder.

"I want to be baptized," I said. "I want you to baptize me."

How many times in my father's life had he heard those words? After he was ordained but still a student in seminary, he spent weekends ministering to the needs of the men, women, and children who lived in Brandon, Shiloh, and Weir, all small Texas towns with tiny congregations. On Sundays, he'd give his sermons and my mother would play the piano in the simple wooden church. My parents had never baptized us because in the Southern Baptist faith people believe that baptism should only take place when you are old enough to understand what it means and are willing to make a firm commitment to live with love, honesty, humility, and forgiveness. Baptism symbolizes the end of an old life and the willingness to start a new life grounded in faith and good works.

"I want you to do it in Wilmer," I said. Dad nodded his head. He understood. I wanted to start over again, go back to being me again, and where else could I do that but Wilmer? I was angry with God, but at the same time I couldn't imagine living without Him. The thought of losing God was unbearable, but being close to God terrified me because I didn't trust Him anymore. Every night before we left the cabin I got down on my knees and prayed for forgiveness for doubting Him. I asked God to forgive me, but the reality was that I could not forgive Him. I felt dirty inside. I needed to be washed clean inside and out.

Two weeks later on August 1, 1971, I was baptized in the First Baptist Church in Wilmer. It must have been a big moment for everyone— my grandparents, Mom, my brother and sister, and, especially Dad and me. I'd like to be able to tell a rich and detailed story about being "born again" and making that decision all on my own, just twelve years into my life. I wish I could remember the look on my father's face as he put his arms around me and gently lowered me into the water and my emotions as I felt God's love lift me up and out of myself, folding me back into His good graces and He into mine. When it was all over, there must have been a scrumptious, home-cooked meal at Nana and Pa Pa Joe's house.

But I can't remember any of those details. All I remember are the dead spiders floating on the surface of the baptismal pool and a solitary black cricket swimming furiously to escape up the side wall. I remember standing up afterward and wondering if the congregation could see the bulge in my crotch or the outline of my underwear through the wet, white gown I had to wear. Then it was over. The day came and went. Summer ended, school started, and for a while life seemed to go back to the way it once was. I played touch football with John, Dad, and our neighbors in a big field on the grounds of the cathedral across the street from my house, listened to the Beatles on my headphones, rode my bike just about everywhere, tried to avoid the lessons of Pricella's wooden spoon on my backside when I did something I shouldn't, took over the lawn-mowing duties at home, and said my prayers at bedtime.

"God, where are you?" I'd whisper into the dark. I wanted Him back in my life, but I wanted the old God, that perfect God that existed before the lightning storm.

"Where are you?" I'd repeat. But He never answered.

3

Confirmation

THE EMOTIONAL SCARS from the lightning storm never disappeared, but like all wounds, the pain faded over time. I was twelve years old when I returned to Garden City on Long Island late that summer, and I was too busy growing up to think much about the dead people underneath the pine tree.

In the next year I grew six inches in six months to become the second tallest kid in my class. My classmates teased me with names like "Gawk" and "String Bean," but it didn't bother me because there were advantages to having long arms and legs. I was a good athlete, excelling in football, basketball, and most of all, track, where I lost only one race in the 440-yard dash and was undefeated in the long jump. With my long arms, I found it easy to reach the low notes at the end of the slide trombone that I played in the big band, orchestra, and jazz combo. Dancing with girls was a bit awkward, but since I didn't have a steady girlfriend in junior high school, I didn't have to worry about it much at the Friday night socials in the school cafeteria—not nearly as much as the shorter boys whose girlfriends towered over them.

I kissed a girl in seventh grade. Her name was Mary, and she was the prettiest girl in the world. She liked me, too.

On clear nights after I finished my homework, I searched the stars with my Tasco long-lens telescope, looking for Saturn's rings, Jupiter's big red spot, or the polar ice caps on Mars. My parents gave me a White's metal detector for Christmas when I was in eighth grade (I'd been begging them for it), and I spent every extra daylight hour searching the cathedral grounds with my metal detector, finding buttons from old military uniforms, jewelry, and rare coins that I kept in a yellow cardboard box by my bed. I thought a lot about the people who once owned these things, and wondered what I might leave behind when I died.

On weekends I spent several hours doing my chores. Besides mowing the lawn, it seemed like Mom and Dad always had a long list of household tasks for me, including pulling weeds, trimming the hedges, raking leaves, splitting and stacking firewood, and cutting ivy off the brick walls of our house. In ninth grade I got a part-time job at the 7th Street Stationery Store. Both my parents had jobs when they were teenagers, and they thought I should, too. I arrived at work just before dawn on Saturday mornings to begin the two-day job of putting together the Sunday *New York Times*. The entertainment, travel, and classified sections were always printed ahead of time, and I'd spend a few hours in the dark putting them in order so that on Sunday morning, when the hard news and sports sections arrived, I could finish the job and the paper would be all ready to go when the first customers arrived around seven a.m.

Hauling those massive Sunday papers around was like lifting sandbags, and by the time I was done my hands were covered in black newsprint and my whole body ached. I was starving, too, and every Sunday after work I went next door to the deli to order a bologna and butter sandwich on a hard roll, gulping it down with orange juice, and then riding my bike home to shower and get dressed for services at the Garden City Community Church.

The summer of 1974, just before my sophomore year in high school, I participated in a month-long wilderness experience sponsored by an Outward Bound offshoot for young people in the Pine Barrens of New Jersey. A solo experience capped the adventure. On the last three days and nights of the trip, I was alone with a notepad and pen, a tarp (I had to choose between a tarp and a sleeping bag and decided I'd rather stay dry than warm), nine matches, a tin can for heating water and a bag of sweetened cocoa mix. There was nothing to do and a lot to think about, especially after I spent a sleepless night huddled under the tarp in the midst of a violent thunderstorm like the one that had killed those people in New Mexico. Stuck in the middle of a forest of tall pine trees, there wasn't a thing I could do except try to pray and remind myself I was going home soon. When the sun rose the next morning I was overjoyed to be alive. I filled six pages of the notepad with gratitude (expressed with numerous misspellings) for everything my parents had done for me.

WHAT MY PARENTS MEAN TO ME

I look around today at my friends and neighbors. Many of them don't have both parents, but they say, "So what, I get away with much more having only one pair of eyes watching over me." They go out on Friday nights and get drunk, knowing their parents won't punish this person. Well, with me it's different. I have the best parents in the world. I enjoy spending weekends with them going to movies, playing games or just having them in my company. In the afternoons when I get home late, there's my mom cooking something extrodinary. A few minutes later my dad walks in from a hard day, or weekly trip, and again we are safely reunited. On cold winter nights when school is getting hard, my parents and I always sit in front of a cozy fire and talk. On Sundays my dad and I sit and watch football games. This means so much to me! My mom will come in with some hot chocolate and cookies and this adds to my pleasure. We go on many vacations, which is excellent.

When we go my parents and I do special things like fishing, swimming and dining at restaurants. I don't know if they know it, but this gives me great pleasure! Every morning my mom gets me up for school and cooks a fantastic breakfast. I don't know of any other familys mom doing this. The mothers of my friends just stay in bed and expect thier children to get a wholsome meal. Mom, I hope you know how well that food tastes. In a way it seems as though my parents have been parents before. They know just whats right and wrong. For example, we (children) are not generally alowed to watch T.V. until we've done our homework. I tell most kids that and they say, "Oh, your parents must be mean. I always watch T.V. when I get home in the afternoon." But these kids rarely get good grades or have a good relationship with thier parents.

My parents are extremly talented. By using thier talents they show me what I need to do when I get to be a parent. First, take my dad. When he was young, he worked hard in school and soon got a job at a local newspaper. Through the years he received respect and soon found himself deputy director at the Peace Corps. Soon he became Johnson's press secretary during the Johnson years. In 1967 he decieded to run a large newspaper where he could really put his talents to work. He was then offered to begin a weekly T.V. series. For three years this show was rated tops. He also wrote a book which was on the top ten for many weeks. I hope to be as succesful a man as my dad is, but I want to work at it like he has had to do. To help do this I need a trait my mom uses in her daily life.

My mom works hard. Not only around the house but out on the streets. When she was a kid, she was known as a hard worker. She was tops in her class all through school. You know, many women who have three children can't find the time to enjoy thier children, their husband and work on community problems. No way with my mom! She spends day after day helping we kids by making great foods, buying us clothes, and driving us to a movie. When ever my dad goes away on long, hard trips, my mom rarely falters. And if she does get depressed, she never, ever shows it! Somehow she manages to find time serving on the daycare council, being a trustee at Hofstra and leading N.C.C.J. You show me someone else like this, and I'll show you the *second* wonder woman of the world. She doesn't have to do all this, she could sit back and watch those silly soap operas all day. Or she could let Pricella do all the cooking while she talked on the telephone. But *my* mom won't ever do that!

TEN MEMORABLE EXPERIENCES WITH MY PARENTS

1. Going to St. Croix
2. Going to church with them and then out to eat
3. Playing and watching football on Sundays
4. Eating at the Yankee Clipper for my birthday
5. Going on a picnic in the mountains of Aspen
6. Going to Cooperstown

7. Eating lunch on Saturdays
8. Christmas time
9. Going to Texas each year
10. Being with them in a cozy room

Up until now, though I hate to say it, I hadn't really realized how good parents you were. I had taken you for granted
expecting you to do many, too many things for me. Now it's
different. I really look forward to spending snowy days with
you in a room with a fire, or helping you entertain guests, or
helping in the yard or around the house. By doing this I feel
our love for each other will be greater than before. I look forward to the years ahead. I may call on you when I have a
problem in school or when I need your fantastic advice.

To summurize these pages of writing into one sentence:

My parents are the eigth wonder of the world!

Your son,

Cope

When I returned from that trip, somehow I felt older and even a
bit wiser. I became much more interested in girls and less interested in
roughhousing with my brother or teasing my sister. I found time to
read more than just the sports pages of the newspaper. I began to
think about college and wonder what I might want to do with my life.
I started thinking about God again and discovered that I actually
liked going to church.

Church had always been the cornerstone of my parents' lives,
even before they met on the first day of college, and every Sunday
without fail the whole family attended services. The music had a profoundly peaceful effect on me, and I liked to sit next to my mother,
whose clear, fine voice reminded me for some reason of a cardinal
singing at the top of a tall tree on a spring morning. I even learned

something from Reverend Ahlberg's sermons and enjoyed discussing them with my parents when we went out to lunch after the service.

But my favorite part about church was socializing with my friends. I met Liz, my first girlfriend, in confirmation classes in the fall of 1975, and we were inseparable all through high school. Our parents sometimes let us sit together on Sundays—they probably figured it was good for our spiritual relationship. Maybe it was, but after the hanky-panky of our Saturday night dates, I'd sit in church with Liz and pray to God to forgive me if I'd gone too far. Liz always seemed okay with everything, so after the hot romancing of the night before, the cooling confessions of those Sunday morning services probably did us both a lot of good.

A few months before confirmation, Reverend Ralph Ahlberg asked me to be one of the speakers at the formal church ceremony on June 1, 1976. It was an honor I took very seriously, spending several weeks working hard preparing and revising my short talk all alone, without any help from my parents. I'll never forget standing up in front of a packed sanctuary on that hot, muggy Sunday in a new brown suit that felt itchy and stiff and stuck to my skin. The church pews were filled with familiar faces and even though I'd never stood at the pulpit before, much less given a talk in front of an audience, I wasn't nervous at all. The only thing that really worried me was sweating through the new suit my mother had bought me.

"When I started confirmation two years ago," I began,

> I never imagined that I would be one of the people to give the sermon on the day our confirmation group was confirmed.
>
> In the 9th grade I remember the first time I went to confirmation. My parents dragged me away from the TV and shoved me into the car. I didn't know what was going on but the next thing I knew I was sitting in a circle with the rest of the group explaining what I had done over the summer. Is

this what confirmation was going to be like? I thought we were here to learn about God.

Over the following weeks my views changed little. I just didn't like it. I remember one time my parents let me ride my bike to confirmation. Somehow I detoured around the church and found myself at 7-11 until 8:30 p.m., when confirmation ended.

For the remainder of that first year, I only went to confirmation when I had to go. I really wasn't interested in God or Jesus, even though I prayed at night before I went to bed— probably from habit.

This year in tenth grade, life and my enthusiasm took on a new approach. It wasn't enough for me to know the things that Jesus did. I had to know why. What did it mean that He died on the cross for my sins? What was meant by His resurrection? What is the purpose of His church and my part in it? These are some of the questions I knew this year I needed to answer.

I discovered this year that God is the One who can repair a torn life. God loves and forgives everyone, no matter what they have done. I'm really turned on when I realize that. I realized He is always with each of us and guides us through times of trouble. I don't expect Him to do everything for me, but I know He is always there.

One important thing I've learned concerns death. I have had the experience of having a death in my family. When my grandfather died, I put the blame on God. Why did he have to take my grandfather? Why couldn't He take the other kid's grandfather? Why mine? But I have learned now that God does not choose who lives and who dies. But He does console us in our time of grief and let us know, deep down inside, that our loved ones have everlasting life with God. My own experience tells me that, and confirmation helped me understand it.

But I've also learned that faith isn't a matter only of death; more importantly, it's the power to live. I have to accept God into my own life. I may have to sacrifice some things. I might be hesitant to. But I want to live the Christian life.

Whenever I think about Jesus, I get this great feeling all over. I know it's like nothing I've ever felt. I got this feeling when in confirmation class I learned more about why Jesus died on the cross. He died for me. It's hard to believe someone would die for my sins so that I might live. I know Jesus was a great man; what's more, He still is a great man. People are always saying how great He was, healing and helping many people. But He still *is* healing people, making them whole when they accept Him as Number One in their lives.

All of these things I have been helped to understand in confirmation this year. They have shaped my thinking and my life so that I even feel good just talking about God and Jesus.

I know that being confirmed today is by no means the end of my journey. It's just the beginning. There are and will be more questions that have to be answered. I have just taken a small step in the right direction. By being confirmed I am giving my life to God knowing that no matter what may happen, God will be by my side. This I have learned in confirmation, and I want to thank everyone who has helped me start on my way.

After Sunday dinner my father gave me a little blue book titled *Lincoln's Devotionals*. Abraham Lincoln's signature was embossed in gold lettering on the cover, and inside the front cover Dad had inscribed:

To Cope, on the day of your confirmation, June 1, 1975.
May your words and your life have the authentic simplicity
and power of this man who let God use him for good ends.

Tucked into the middle of the book I found a letter.

My Dear Cope:
I was quite proud of you today. You spoke from the heart,
with the clarity of a good mind. And people listened. As impressed as they may have been with you, they were impressed
with what you said. They *heard* you, and I think you felt the
joy, power and responsibility of *being* heard. It is a great thing,
to know people respond to your message, and it must be used
wisely and humbly, as you did today.

You have the talent, son, to be believed. You have the
ability to make people listen to what you say and to think
about what you are. I pray you will develop this talent. Train
your mind and enlarge your understanding of the world
around you and within you. Read, think and listen. Listen to
wise people and to the voice of God which is in you. Love the
language, and learn to choose the right word for the thought
you want to express. Many words seem to say the same thing;
one is always exactly the most powerful. Give yourself to large
purposes. Try to find out the facts. Seek truth. And leave
room for mystery—the truth that lies beyond our capacity to
know.

Be yourself. You are a fine human being whom God has
made. And I love you with all of my heart, all of my life.

Dad

Dad's words about loving the language and seeking truth seemed
important in some vague, distant way, but what really mattered was

that he was proud of me. I put his note back in the book and placed the book in my bookshelf, where it stayed untouched for nearly two decades.

That summer between my junior and senior year in high school we went to Aspen, where my parents moderated seminars at the Aspen Institute and I worked as a maintenance man, mowing the grass, pulling weeds, trimming trees, and enjoying my time off in the Rocky Mountains. I liked the hard physical labor, the pay was good, and there was always plenty of time left over for cookouts, Jeep trips through the wildflower meadows, and concerts at the Aspen Music Festival.

One day my coworkers and I were taking a break under a stand of aspen trees when Jerry, a year-round maintenance man in his late twenties or early thirties, rolled a joint. He inhaled deeply, held the smoke in his lungs, and with his head tilted slightly back, blew a steady stream of smoke into the deep blue sky.

"It's good," he said, offering it to me. "You should try this, man. It will blow your mind."

I hesitated for a moment, feeling a little bit like I did that night in Wilmer when the armadillo charged me. I didn't know what to do. Part of me wanted to run away—what if we got caught? The other part, enticed by the risk, wanted to stay.

I took the joint and tried to mimic Jerry's style, watching in fascination as the paper burned and crackled inches from my eyes. The smoke hurt my lungs, the back of my throat felt like it was on fire, my eyes watered, and I fought the urge to cough. Then I smiled, remembering something my health class teacher said just a few months before. "Marijuana usually doesn't affect people the first time." Boy, was she wrong! I felt lightheaded and dizzy, weird, like someone was spinning cotton candy inside my head. The purple and yellow wildflowers looked so pretty against the blue sky, and I noticed for the first time the dozens of dragonflies bobbing and weaving in the breeze. I was floating, and at the same time I felt firmly anchored in the most beautiful place on earth.

Wilmer, I thought. *This is just how I felt in Wilmer—free, unbounded, at home, at peace.*

Many years later, in treatment and in AA meetings, I came to understand that my experience that afternoon was anything but unique. When addicted people look back on the very first time they sipped a drink from the bottom of a parent's glass, swallowed a painkiller to ease the agony of a broken bone, or took a hit off a bong in a dorm room, they remember instant, intense feelings of freedom, rapture, and relief. Here's how Malachy McCourt, author of *A Monk Swimming*, remembers his first drinking episode, when he was an eleven-year-old boy guzzling beer in a Limerick pub.

A great feeling of peace and contentment floated out of the heavens and wrapped itself around my being, softly and lovingly clothing me in spiritual finery and the understanding that I was the best boy in the whole wide world, and there wasn't anything I couldn't be or do in this life.

For so many of us that first introduction to alcohol or other drugs becomes a lasting memory that defines the beginning of a torrid but doomed love affair. When I look back on the events of that day in the Rocky Mountain meadow, they are still as bright and vivid in my memory as if they happened yesterday, yet when I try to remember the night I first slept with my girlfriend later that same summer, I don't remember a thing.

Jerry gave me half a dozen joints that lasted the rest of the summer. I'd take a few hits and then stub out the joint, saving it for later. During the day, I liked to get high and lie on my back in a field of tall prairie grass and columbine watching thunderstorms build up over the mountains. The lightning and thunder didn't scare me anymore, no matter how close the storms came—the horror at the campsite in Red River, New Mexico, seemed as if it had happened to a different person in another lifetime.

Sometimes at night, after my parents had gone to bed, I'd sneak out to get stoned on the balcony, where I'd spend hours gazing at the stars, so bright and deep in the sky. Just before bed I'd put my headphones on and listen to a Beatles album. I liked to imagine I was right there in the studio with them as I eavesdropped on the chatter beneath the music, the sudden bursts of laughter, and the occasional off-key or missed note. As I listened to the words, it seemed like they were writing all about me and my life, the mysteries, the passions, and even the drugs. If the Beatles can get high, I thought, what's wrong with me doing the same?

The summer ended, and I started my senior year in high school back in Garden City. To everyone who knew me—my parents, my steady girlfriend, Liz, my teachers, even my closest friends—nothing had changed. I was still a good athlete, a decent trombone player, a responsible son always willing to help around the house, and a patient older brother. My grades weren't the greatest, but I kept a solid B average my senior year and, in 1977, I graduated number 210 out of 487 in my class.

On and off during that last year of high school, maybe once a week, I smoked marijuana. By this time I had a few friends who also liked to smoke pot, which had become the "cool" thing to do. We smoked at parties, in the school parking lot, and even under the stairwell outside the gymnasium. I liked flirting around the edges of authority—driving too fast, making out with girls, cutting an occasional class, and getting high were all part of growing up. Like most adolescents, I believed I was invulnerable and resilient—nothing could hurt me, at least not for very long.

Whenever I doubted myself or feared I wasn't good enough or just wanted to feel good or right or whole, I turned to marijuana, and it never failed to give me instant relief. Some people take aspirin for a headache; I took marijuana whenever my heart or soul ached. The pain only went away for the moment, but that was fine by me because the moment was all I lived for. I felt bad, I got high, I felt good. It was that simple.

Alcohol wasn't so magical, at least not in the beginning. In high school, I developed a taste for beer, but I don't remember ever getting drunk. I just liked the way alcohol mellowed me, softening the edges of my impossibly high ideals and releasing me from the need to play the part of the "good kid" from the "good family." Most of my friends liked to drink, and it was easy to buy beer back then because the drinking age in the state of New York was eighteen. My parents weren't overly concerned about me drinking a beer now and then, although hard liquor was definitely off-limits. I remember pleasant afternoons spent enjoying a beer with my parents on the terrace in our backyard, chatting about the day or discussing world events. I never drank more than one or two beers, and my parents rarely had more than one drink. I don't think I've ever seen either of my parents drunk.

My drinking habits changed the day I arrived for my freshman year at Washington & Lee University in Lexington, Virginia. The grain alcohol mixed with Kool-Aid at the opening class party tasted like fruit punch and within minutes my anxiety about school and classes disappeared, all the girls were beautiful, and every person I met was my best friend. Stumbling back to the dorm a few hours later, I threw up just outside the front door, a violent upheaval of alcohol and stomach acid that left a lasting stain on the cement. That was my initiation into the culture of college life, where alcohol was king and I, like so many others, was its loyal subject.

I managed to save my hard drinking for the Wednesday night fraternity parties and the weekend all-campus parties, but my infatuation with alcohol and marijuana definitely cut into my study time. Before the semester was even half over, I was placed on academic proba-tion. I took two "gut" courses spring semester—ROTC and Radio Broadcasting 101—and by the smallest decimal point, I slipped by.

Bad grades, bounced checks, bedtime strangers, blackouts, and killer hangovers—for most people such experiences eventually lead to the decision to stop or cut back on drinking, but not for me. Alcohol had become my new best friend, and I came to rely on it, need it, and love it just as much as the marijuana that I was smoking almost every day. Then, in the spring semester of my junior year, I discovered cocaine and LSD, "hard" drugs that offered a new and exciting fron-tier to explore and conquer. I set upon the task with absolute fearless-ness, wearing my frequent drug use like a badge of honor. Hang the consequences. When I had a severe case of strep throat, I didn't think about putting aside the bong for a few days until I felt better. After I wrecked my car driving drunk and under the influence of quaaludes—I told my parents that a farmer driving his tractor in the middle of the country road forced me to swerve off and hit a tree—I never seriously considered that it might not be safe to drive with a beer in one hand and pills in my stomach. When I went to History class af-ter eating psychedelic mushrooms and the professor became irritated with me, I thought the whole scene was hysterically funny. By the time I was twenty years old, I no longer knew what was normal and what wasn't.

Ironically, my grades began to improve my junior year when I de-clared a major in journalism. Encouraged by the As and Bs I was getting, my father often told me that I had a natural instinct and in-quisitiveness along with an eye for detail—traits that he considered essential for any journalist. My professors apparently agreed with him. I was most proud of the A I got in "Ham" Smith's class—considered the toughest journalism professor on campus, he told me he'd never be-fore handed out an A in an advanced reporting course.

I stayed active in extracurricular activities, too, anchoring a sports program on cable television and doing the play-by-play for the university's football and basketball teams. For three years straight I was the disc jockey for a popular Saturday morning radio show and no matter how much I drank or how late I partied the night before, I never missed a broadcast (even though I did plenty of shows stoned). I was a regular contributor to the school newspaper, and the highlight of my college journalism career was a widely discussed investigative series about drunk driving. No one suspected that much of my research was based on my own experience—except for the part about getting caught. I never got caught doing anything under the influence.

But that was about to change.

4

The Fish Market Incident

Seven digits seemed like seven hundred as my finger punched my home phone number at three a.m. on December 23, 1980.

A pause on the line. *Maybe they won't wake up,* I thought. Then I panicked. *What if they don't answer?* I felt as if I were suffocating. My lungs burned from the cigarette smoke in the bar, and my head pounded with the beginning of a horrendous hangover.

Dad picked up the phone on the third ring, his voice thick and groggy with sleep.

"Dad, it's me. This is Cope."

Silence on the end of the line. A second or two passed, and I had a sudden urge to hang up. I could picture my father at home, sitting up in bed and reaching for his glasses, jolted awake by a phone ringing in the darkness in the middle of the night, every parent's nightmare.

"Cope?" I could hear the fear rising in his voice. "Son, what happened? Where are you? Are you in the hospital? Are you okay?"

"I need you to pick me up," I said. "I'm in the county jail."

"What happened? Are you okay?" he repeated. His voice was stronger, and he even sounded relieved, now that he knew I wasn't lying in a bloody mess in some hospital emergency room.

If only it had been an accident, I thought. A broken leg. A totaled car.

"I'll tell you later, Dad, just please come pick me up."

A policeman led me to an empty jail cell and sat me down on the metal bench. The harsh overhead lights hurt my eyes, and I fought the urge to cry. What had happened to me? I put my head in my hands and forced myself to think back over the day, searching for where it had all gone wrong.

Everything started out so well. It was good to be home after a grueling first semester of my senior year and an even tougher week of final exams. Only three days left until Christmas! After a day spent visiting with my family and shopping for last-minute gifts, I drove to my friend Donald's house to watch *Monday Night Football*. The game wasn't very exciting, but we had fun finishing off a six-pack, smoking a joint, and talking about old times. Around eleven p.m. we decided to go to Leo's, a neighborhood watering hole where we hoped to meet up with our old classmates from Garden City High School. Our plan was to drink and have fun, then go home to bed.

Leo's attracted lots of college-age kids. We always had a good time there, and nobody ever seemed to get so drunk that they couldn't walk out of the place on their own two feet. Everybody got along and I never once witnessed an argument there, let alone a fight. A friendly, noisy place with a jukebox where we'd play rock-and-roll tunes for a dime, Leo's also served the best bacon cheeseburgers and fries anywhere in town, and it was the only place where you could find something to eat after midnight.

But no matter how good the food was, Leo's was a bar, bars were for drinking, and I was there to drink, which meant—to me—getting drunk. While I never began a night thinking, "I'm going out to get wasted," almost every time I drank, that's what happened. Like many young people, I kept drinking until I got drunk, but unlike most of my peers, I kept on drinking long after my friends decided they'd had enough. As long as I had money in my pocket or friends at the bar—and I always seemed to have enough of both—I drank until closing time.

That night at Leo's, I drank shots of Jack Daniel's Green Label Tennessee Whiskey chased with beer. I wasn't counting, but from what friends later told me, I tallied close to two dozen shots. The amount really didn't matter, though, because it was the effect I was after. Alcohol always made me feel good, and the more I drank, the better I felt. The string of Christmas lights draped across the long mirror behind the bar blazed like a rainbow in the dark. The young women on the barstools all looked friendly, willing, and able. The laughter of my high school buddies made me feel right at home.

In the days and weeks that followed that night, both my parents and I tried to explain what happened with a litany of excuses that on the surface made sense. It was the holidays and lots of people drink too much over the holidays. I'd been worried about my brother's recent surgery and my mother's flu. The pressure of final exams was intense. Most of the kids in the bar that night were drunk. The bartender should have stopped serving me when it was obvious I was drunk. And, of course, I should have known my limits.

Shortly before the bar closed, I had to go to the bathroom, but the line was too damn long and my bladder was stretched like a water balloon from all the whiskey and beer. I walked through the kitchen and out the back door into an alleyway that separated Leo's from the fish market next door. Standing against the brick wall of the fish market, I relieved myself and the thought crossed my mind that maybe I should go home and go to bed.

I looked up at a window about six inches above my head and in the next second I smashed the pane with my closed fist, reached through the broken glass to unlock the latch, raised the window, and climbed into the store. I knew exactly what I was doing, but I had no idea why I was doing it.

On my hands and knees, I crawled along a row of stainless steel counters where fish were cut up and packaged. *What the hell am I doing here?* I thought as I crawled on the floor. It was as if I were sitting in the front row at a theater watching myself in a skit, anticipating the next scene. "Don't do it. Turn around! Go back, get out of there!" I wanted to yell at the fool onstage, but I couldn't stop, even though I had no idea where I was going.

At the end of the counter, I found a pile of loose change just sitting there. I scooped up the coins and stuffed them in the front pockets of my blue jeans. I didn't realize it then, but somewhere along the way I'd lost my wallet with two twenty-dollar bills inside. I started back toward the window.

Outside in the alley, two squad cars and four Garden City policemen were waiting. A high school classmate who had been drinking with me had walked into the alley to relieve himself, just as I had, and when he saw someone disappearing through the broken window of the fish market, he thought it was a burglar and called the police.

Flashlights lit up the store from the outside. "Come out with your hands up!" someone yelled. I panicked and tried to squeeze underneath the counter, then scrambled like a cornered crab to a closet in the back of the store that was filled with empty fish-smelling boxes. I was trapped.

"You're surrounded," the voice said. "Come out now with your hands up!"

"I'm coming out! Please don't shoot me!" I yelled, walking toward the flashlights shining through the window. Crawling out through the window, I stood up to see the policemen standing in a semicircle, their guns pointed at me. Someone handcuffed me and pushed me into the backseat of the police car.

The policeman behind the wheel turned to look at me. "We know you're the guy who has been burglarizing stores around here," he said. "If you confess and admit what you've done, it will make it easier on you in the long run."

"I'm not a burglar," I protested, ashamed and angry at the same time. "I'm a college student. My parents live on Fourth Street."

One of the officers laughed and muttered something about stupid college students who think they can get away with anything. That made me even angrier. What were they trying to do, pin a bunch of crimes on me and get me to confess to things I hadn't done? They had it all wrong. I was a good kid. I volunteered at the Salvation Army. I went to church. I was the oldest son of Bill and Judith Moyers, two of Garden City's most respected citizens.

At the station they booked me, let me make my phone call, and put me in a holding cell. Terrified, dizzy, and sick to my stomach, I was suddenly overwhelmed by the enormity of my mistake. I was a thief and a criminal. I was stupid, worthless, pathetic. In one moment, I had wrecked my entire life.

When my father came to bail me out, I couldn't look him in the eye. As we walked past the front desk, I overheard the desk sergeant talking on the phone.

"You'll never guess who we got in here tonight," he said. My father looked straight ahead and kept walking.

Fat, wet snowflakes were drifting from a slate gray sky as my father drove me home. My head pounded, and I felt like I was going to throw up. The silence in the car was all I heard and it was deafening. There was so much I wanted to tell Dad, but how, what, why? Nothing I could say would change anything. The methodical sweep of the windshield wipers punctuated the unspoken thoughts between us.

A few blocks from home Dad stopped the car at a traffic light and turned to face me. The look on his face conveyed an anguish that was deeper than pain or anger.

"You know, Cope," he said in his soft, soothing voice, a voice that was commanding and pleading all at the same time, "we all make mistakes in life. Many years ago I made a mistake that I regret to this day. The only difference between what you did and what I did many years ago is that you got caught by the police."

I looked up at him, surprised. What could my father possibly have done that would compare to my crime?

He told me a story that I had never heard before, about when he was a young boy growing up in Marshall, Texas, and on a dare took money from the offering plate at the Central Baptist Church. A church deacon discovered the theft and made young Billy Don Moyers replace the stolen money.

"That was a shameful moment in my life," Dad confessed.

Something broke inside me, then, and I started to cry. In the moment of my deepest shame, his story pulled me closer to him than I had ever felt before. I always thought he was perfect, but here was a flaw, a rent in the seamless fabric of his life. We walked from the driveway to the house, his arm around my shoulder, the snow falling all around us. My mother was waiting at the door. She hugged me, but we didn't speak. What was there to say? I stumbled upstairs and lay down on my bed while images flashed through my head: those last innocent hours in Leo's laughing with my friends, the shots of whiskey lined up on the bar, the smashed window and stainless steel counters, my pockets bulging with change, the flashlights in the alley, my wrists tight in the handcuffs, the bright lights inside the jail cell. The images kept flashing until I ran into the bathroom and violently threw up into the toilet.

The next morning the phone woke me up and kept me up. It wouldn't stop. Listening to it, I felt as if I were drifting in space. Everything seemed so unreal. Did I imagine it? Maybe I had just gotten drunk and been knocked out in a fight. But the ringing phone brought me back to reality. People knew. I wanted to hide and never be found.

I had no idea, though, how many people knew. The police, it turned out, called their news sources and overnight the incident became national news. It led the morning national radio reports. The Associated Press and United Press wires carried it. Paul Harvey talked about it on his coast-to-coast ABC radio network show. *CBS Evening News* anchor Dan Rather and ABC News president Roone Arledge, both close friends of my parents, called to offer their consolation and condolences about it.

Lying in bed, wishing I could get back to sleep, I was completely unaware of the media frenzy. I just wanted that damn phone to stop ringing.

My father knocked on the door. "You have a visitor," he said. "Come downstairs."

"Who is it?" I asked.

"Mary."

I groaned. I first met Mary in sixth grade; she lived two blocks away from us in Garden City. She was the first girl I ever kissed and I always dreamed about dating her, but all through high school she had a boyfriend and I had a steady girlfriend. After high school we went our separate ways, although I did see her once during our sophomore year in college. She'd been injured seriously in a car accident, and when she was at home recovering, I brought her a dozen red roses. Now she had come to visit me when I was hurting. How did everyone find out so fast?

"Tell her I'm sick. I can't talk to her right now," I groaned.

"Cope." Silence. "You will come downstairs and talk to her. Now."

Mary was waiting in the living room. She looked so beautiful, so fresh and clean, and I felt so dirty, so ugly inside and out. We talked for a long time and she kept reassuring me that everything would be okay, it was a terrible thing, but I was a good person, and I just had to have faith that people would stand up for me. In a few months, she said, it would all be behind me.

"That wasn't really you who did that, Cope," Mary told me. "Everyone knows who you are and that's not the real you."

When she hugged me good-bye, I began to think that maybe I did have a future. Maybe I could put this fish market thing behind me. I felt such relief in that moment that I forgot to ask Mary how she had learned about my arrest.

For the rest of the day I tried to keep pace with my parents' detailed plan of action, doing what I was told and feeling scared to death. The first item on the to-do list that day was to apologize to my high school girlfriend, Liz, and her family. As I drove to her house, I turned on the car radio.

"Bill Moyers's son was arrested for burglary early this morning," the radio announcer said. I pulled over to the side of the road and leaned over the wheel, afraid I was going to be sick again.

"How could you do this to us, to me?" Liz said when she opened the door. Tears were running down her cheeks and her eyes were red from crying.

I lied. "It wasn't my fault, Liz," I said. "A friend tossed my wallet into the fish market as a joke, and I went in through an unlocked window to get it back."

Liz believed my story, just like my parents did, and when I left her house she told me she forgave me. My next stop was the lawyer's office—earlier that morning Dad wrote a five-thousand-dollar check to retain Stephan Scaring, one of the top criminal defense attorneys on Long Island. I lied to my new attorney, telling him about the friend who tossed my wallet into the open fish market window. But Scaring didn't make big money believing his clients unless he had all the facts. When I couldn't come up with a name for my phantom friend, he was done listening.

"Cut the bullshit," he said. "I want to know exactly what you were doing in there, what you were thinking."

I told him everything—how much I had to drink, how I broke the window and crawled along the counters, and how I found the pile of coins and stuffed them in my jeans.

"Whatever possessed you to steal a bunch of coins?" he asked me.

"I don't know," I answered, and this time I was telling the honest truth.

Church was my third and final stop that morning. I met behind closed doors with Reverend Ahlberg for more than an hour. We talked and prayed together, and he gently assured me that God's love and grace were greater than my sin.

"If you ask you will receive," he said. We got down on our knees and prayed for forgiveness, but I couldn't get past my own sense of shame. How could I ask for God's forgiveness when I couldn't forgive or, even worse, understand myself?

In the days and weeks that followed, it seemed like everyone in the world wanted to know how such a good boy from such a fine, upstanding family could do something so bad. Most of the news reports objectively stated the facts, as newspapers are supposed to do, but one Florida paper ran a two-inch story with a picture of my dad, smiling widely, with the headline: "While Bill Moyers drank, son burgled." My father wrote a letter to the editor chastising him for his "appalling journalism," setting the record straight ("I was at home in bed, asleep, when the incident happened"), defending me ("my son had never been involved in anything like this in his life"), and ending with a concern about what that article might be saying about the entire craft of journalism. Did the editor really consider such a distant and irrelevant event to be news, Dad asked, or did he decide to sensationalize the story because the burglar happened to be Bill Moyers's son?

Maybe this was the one time my father's journalism instincts got mixed up with his emotions, because whether the story was news or not, people all over the country paid attention to it. We got hundreds of phone calls and letters from friends and relatives who offered their comfort and support and reassured us that the incident was an aberration that surely wouldn't happen again. Many of the letters from strangers were written in the same spirit. But an uncomfortable number of people suggested that I might have a drinking problem. A few even went so far as to suggest I might need counseling, "treatment," or a program called Alcoholics Anonymous. I'd never heard of treatment or AA, and I remember feeling amazed that total strangers would leap to the conclusion that I might be an alcoholic based on one stupid mistake.

The only place nobody was really talking about the whole situation was right at home; we were all trying our hardest to cover the whole thing up. Mimi and Pa Pa Henry were staying with us for the holidays, and we did everything we could to shield them from the truth—Pa Pa Henry loved to read the newspaper, but he probably never noticed the cleanly cut hole in the "News Briefs" section of *Newsday* that chronicled my crime. My grandmother, always impossible to fool, knew something was up, but because she was too polite to ask, we didn't tell. Instead, we all talked about the weather, Christmas, the flu that was going around—anything but the "incident." At dinner one night my sister asked me why I looked so sad. For a moment I tried to deny that anything was wrong, but then I burst into tears, ran from the table, and hid in my room. For the next few days everyone tiptoed around the smelly mess in the house that was all about me.

When I wasn't in my room, I spent most of my time hunkered down in the basement where the "crisis" plan was launched. Taking directions from my parents, I set up a card table, an electric typewriter, a wastepaper basket, and typed letter after letter after letter. Dozens of them, all saying basically the same thing. I wrote to Reverend Ahlberg, the owners of the fish market, my father's colleagues at CBS

News, the principal of my high school, my professors at Washington & Lee University, and anyone else I could think of who had expressed support or was in a position to write a letter to the judge attesting to my good character. At times I felt like a naughty little boy whose teacher forces him to write, over and over again, "I'm sorry and I promise I will never do anything like this again." I typed until my fingers were numb.

"Dear Professor Smith," I began the December 28, 1980, letter to my favorite journalism professor at Washington & Lee.

> I cannot thank you enough for your phone call. Along with the many other people who called, your concern has given me the support to help face up to what I have done and know that in the end, everything will work out. I feel I owe you an explanation as to what happened last week.
>
> Because my brother had surgery Saturday and my mother came down with a severe case of the flu about the same time, I was forced to finish up my exams earlier than expected so that I could be home to help my father. Fortunately the operation was successful and my mother recovered before Christmas. Monday night I really had my first opportunity to go out and after drinking a few beers with an old high school friend, we went to a local bar where many of my cronies congregate. While at this bar, the spirit of Christmas, the happiness of seeing many old friends and the relief that my brother was going to be all right got the best of me. I drank too much beer and whiskey, impairing my judgment and leading to the incident for which I was arrested.
>
> The bar I was at was packed with people and using the bathroom inside was close to impossible, so I made frequent use of a back alley outside the bar. On one occasion, I saw an open window at a fish market behind the bar. It was dark, I

was drunk and before I thought about what I was doing, I found myself inside the store and taking $20.06 in coins from the store.

What happened next is difficult for me to remember because it happened so fast, but someone apparently heard me going into the store and called the police. They were there within minutes; I had climbed out the window and stood surrounded by them amidst the several people who had seen or heard the incident occur. I was arrested, photographed and fingerprinted, charged with burglary (a class A felony) and released without bond.

The next morning I was arraigned in Nassau County court and a preliminary hearing has been set for January 22. Ironically, the fish market is owned by a man whose son was a teammate of mine on the high school football team. He called my father to say that he would consider the matter a "college prank" because it was uncharacteristic of me.

Unfortunately it is now out of his hands and into the hands of the district attorney. We are hoping the charge will be reduced on January 22, provided my lawyer presents my previous pattern of behavior in a manner that will convince that court that what I did was done on impulse and does not exemplify my behavior. There is a good chance the charges will be reduced since this is the first time this has ever happened to me.

There is no excuse for my behavior and I take full responsibility for what I did. I regret any embarrassment I may have caused you. Again, thanks for your support. I will never forget it.

Sincerely,
Cope Moyers

The letter tidied everything up, making the whole incident seem like a strange but understandable drunken prank. I wrote with humility, accepted my responsibility, and rationalized what happened with all the excuses that would have made sense if only they were grounded in the fundamental truth none of us was ready to admit: I had a big problem with alcohol, and I needed much more than forgiveness. I needed help.

Even the owner of the fish market wanted the charges dismissed. Two weeks after the burglary, he sent a letter to my lawyer.

Dear Mr. Scaring:
I am speaking on behalf of my partners when I say that we have no desire to press charges against Cope Moyers.

We have agreed that the entire matter be dropped because it is so uncharacteristic of the Cope Moyers we know.

Knowing Cope, we are sure that it was an isolated incident. We all at sometime in our lives have done some prank that could have resulted in a similar situation.

We strongly urge that the entire matter be dropped because we feel that the grief and humiliation Cope has cast upon his fine family is punishment enough.

Everyone who knew and admired the Moyers family believed the incident was an aberrant action totally uncharacteristic of the Cope Moyers they knew. "Aberrant" and "uncharacteristic" were the two words repeated most often in the dozens of letters of support I received. My college professors, high school principal, pastor, employers, and old family friends described me as a polite, industrious, thoughtful, likeable, honest, gentle, ethical, honorable, hard-working, compassionate, generous, trustworthy young man "of the very highest moral character and impeccable integrity," as the dean of students at

Washington & Lee put it. I'd been punished enough, they argued; let bygones be bygones and allow the future to open up before me without saddling me with a felony that would be part of my record for the rest of my life.

I just wanted it all to go away. The basement and the constant clicking of the typewriter keys were my refuge, the place where I didn't have to think but just continued to type those same sentences, over and over again until I had memorized the letter and could type it by heart. Only once during the ten days before I returned to school did I come up for air. My parents insisted I accompany them to church on Christmas Eve. I had always loved that midnight service with hundreds of candles lighting the darkened sanctuary, the familiar faces, the traditional hymns, and the sense of peace and love that enveloped us all. But for the first time ever I didn't want to go to the service. How could I sing "Joy to the World" when there was no joy in my world, or wish people a "Merry Christmas" when this was my worst Christmas ever, or turn to the person next to me and "pass the peace" when I was at war with my own emotions?

As I walked down the center aisle of the church that night, I stared straight ahead. I didn't dare glance side-to-side, because I already knew everyone must be staring at me, and I felt as if the entire congregation could see right through the hole in my soul to the depths of my despair. Just a few years before in this very spot I had given the confirmation talk. Now I was on stage again, only this time I couldn't cover myself up with carefully crafted words and a new suit. I was stark naked—the real me was there for everyone to see, and I was not a pretty sight. I couldn't wait to get out of that place, flee Garden City, and escape the hell I had created. There was only one place to go, back to college where I could deal with this just like I did everything else— by getting stoned.

Just a few days after I returned to Washington & Lee I received a three-page, single-spaced, typed letter from my father. He spent the first long paragraph talking about the Cowboys-Falcons game and the upcoming Super Bowl. Then he got down to business.

I never did seem to find the time before you left to talk about all the things I wanted to talk about, but we'll have opportunities down the road. It will take time for all of this to sink in on us—for us to realize how close you came to a very crippling accident and for us to realize how fortunate we are that your whole life's record came to your rescue.

"Close to a crippling accident?" It seemed to me that I'd been involved in a head-on collision. But maybe Dad was right, maybe I had just barely avoided the worst and now I was back on track.

I was sitting in church thinking of all the lessons I've learned (or relearned) in the experience of the last ten days, scribbling on the bulletin. My notes, barely legible (it's hard to listen to the minister and make notes at the same time) read: "No one is immune to the potential power of drugs and alcohol to cause a good person to do bad things."

There it was—the idea that drugs make you do stupid things, make good people bad when they are under the influence and out of control. I liked that theory because it eased my conscience—under the influence, even good people do bad things. If I could just learn from what had happened, perhaps I could be better prepared the next time I got drunk. I didn't have to stop drinking, I just needed to exert more control, be a little more respectful of alcohol and what it could do to me.

A single mistake can jeopardize an otherwise exemplary life; on the other hand, an exemplary life can offset the damage of a serious mistake. "All we like sheep have gone astray"—

that's from the New Testament. "He that is without sin among you, let him first cast a stone"—that, too, is from the New Testament. "All things work together for good to them that love God"—you guessed it, the New Testament. The test of a man's character is not the mistakes he makes but the way he responds to them. We have so many friends who gave us the benefit of the doubt.

My father found solace for his own pain in the words of the New Testament, and with those simple phrases, he was trying to comfort me, too. Everyone makes mistakes. No one is perfect. Have faith in God and all will be well, goodness will be restored, and life will go on.

One day we'll have to compare the lessons we learned; I'll bet you can add substantially to that list. You never told me, for example, what went through your mind sitting in that room with the police, or being handcuffed on the way to the county jail, or waiting in that place. To this day I can remember the feeling in my stomach when the police picked me up thinking I had broken into a fire tower down at the Caddo Lake State Park. We'll have to talk about such feelings one day; experience (bad experience as well as good) unleashes some powerful ones.

What *had* happened at the Caddo Lake State Park? I had never heard that story. But even without knowing all the facts, our experiences were very different. Dad was falsely accused while I was caught in the act of burglary and hauled to jail. He was innocent—I was guilty as sin. He was anonymous, a little boy in the backwoods of eastern Texas—I was infamous because I was his son.

I think we're going to come out of this satisfactorily, having learned all of those and other lessons in the process. We're going to come out because you were honest, you stood up and admitted your responsibility, and you showed some courage in responding when you could have stayed home with your head under the pillow.

Now you mustn't dwell on the incident nor live nervously looking over your shoulder, but push on to do your best this semester and to make your way into the future.

Honesty, responsibility, courage—that's how you face your mistakes in life, and then you move on. No point in dwelling on "what was" because that only invited the potentially disastrous mistake of missing out on "what could be." Looking backward I would surely stumble. Now it was time to move on and look forward to the future.

But Dad wasn't letting me off the hook. Sensing that there might be something dark and disturbing lurking deep inside me, he urged me to see the campus psychologist.

In frank conversation with a professional it may become clearer that it simply was the result of mixing beer, alcohol, and pot—a lethal mixture—or that the combination was just a trigger to something down there waiting to get out. All of us have something in the basement always bumping to get out, and alcohol or drugs will slip the lock off to let it out. Was it just an appetite for a little adventure—to live dangerously for a moment? Are you fed up with being a straight arrow and subconsciously trying to tell Garden City or your folks or yourself something? Are you uncertain about trying to compete with your father in journalism—fearful of not being as lucky as he was or maybe luckier? I don't know; such thoughts may be pure nonsense, but this is a good time to look into yourself with the right kind of professional help, and I urge you to do so.

When it came to the demons lurking in the basement of my soul, Dad was on to something. But whatever was down there scared the hell out of me. I wanted to run away from whatever was "bumping" to get out and never think about it again. Escape was what I was after, not confrontation.

Dad closed his letter by encouraging me to pursue my dream of becoming a journalist and moving away from home so that I could escape his shadow and influence.

I think you are probably right in wanting at least for a couple of years to work on a newspaper, and I think that as much as I love having you around here—or close by—it's probably good for you to go off on your own. If you stay in this business, I believe there is a possibility that one day, in some capacity, we'll be collaborating on a project or two. But first you have to keep out of my reach; I can't stop being a father right now, and if you're around I'll be giving you too much advice, asking you to take on my priorities, putting a safety net under you too often to allow you to make your own mistakes, and generally do the things a father's here to do. But as the old prayer goes, "Lord, teach me to let go," and I can't let go as easily if you're in the house, or next door. As hard as it will be on us to have you so far away, we'll be able to get together, we'll meet for long weekends, and vacations, and we'll know all along that the purpose of the sacrifice now is for some important goal down the road.

Let me say again that despite the unexpected deviation, it was a good holiday. No one was really petty, I think we all enjoyed one another's company, and we learned that we can be a pretty good family when the going's rough and not just when it's easy.

I love you, Cope. And I want nothing more than for you to know it.

Dad

I kept thinking about those words—*the purpose of the sacrifice now is for some important goal down the road*—in the second-to-last paragraph of Dad's letter. Maybe I should be looking forward to the future rather than backward at the past. Maybe I had learned, through a lot of pain and suffering, a valuable lesson that would change my life in some unknown but positive way.

Maybe, in the end, this would all work out for the best.

5

Free Fall

WITHIN AN HOUR after arriving back at Washington & Lee, it was all good again. I got high and stayed that way, even as I was forced to face the consequences of my actions. At the end of January I appeared before a student committee in charge of deciding if my arrest violated the university's vaunted honor code, created by none other than Robert E. Lee right after the Civil War when he became president of the college. If they decided I was guilty, I would be expelled. It was a complicated case because the offense occurred at home during the holidays and the whole thing probably would have gone unnoticed if I hadn't been the son of Bill Moyers. After weeks of deliberation behind closed doors, my peers on the committee decided I could stay and graduate. I celebrated by getting drunk.

In February I flew back to New York to face the judge and the district attorney in a crowded courtroom. My mother stood by me through the whole ordeal and later told me that my face was "white as a sheet." I was terrified, no doubt about that, but I was also immensely relieved to be pleading guilty to a reduced charge of disorderly conduct, a misdemeanor. Apparently the judge was swayed by the dozens of letters he received attesting to my good character. It didn't hurt that some of those letters came from people like Dan Rather, the CBS news correspondent, who wrote that I was "the kind of honest, hardworking young man any parent would be proud to call their own."

The conditional discharge stipulated that I must agree to "avoid injurious or vicious habits, refrain from frequenting unlawful or disreputable places or consorting with disreputable persons and make restitution for damages." Because I was drinking or taking drugs every day, my whole existence depended on "vicious habits" and hanging around "disreputable" people and places, but I paid the hundred-dollar fine, signed the form, and was off the hook.

In March I had another near disaster. A fellow student, who also happened to be my drug dealer, was busted by undercover police in Lexington just hours after I bought $150 worth of marijuana from him. He had my money in his pocket when he went to jail, and for weeks afterward I lived in terror that he'd get squeezed by investigators and give them a list of his clients. But he was expelled from school, and I kept right on getting high.

I was still getting stoned when my brother arrived on campus in May, just a month before graduation. Fifteen years old and a freshman in high school, John was a great kid, smart, sensitive, and adoring of his older brother. During the day I showed him around campus, introduced him to my friends and professors, and gave him a tour of Lexington and Civil War sites. At night we partied hard, and I didn't see any reason why John shouldn't drink a few beers or smoke a joint with his older brother. I only hesitated for a moment before bringing out the cocaine.

"Have you ever tried this?" I asked John.

He shook his head no, but he looked curious and eager, and I was, too—curious to see if he'd like it as much as I did and eager to impress him with my knowledge. Cocaine was a recreational drug, after all, and wasn't the party all about having fun? Sharing cocaine with my brother seemed, at that moment, as routine as picking up the tab for a steak dinner at a fancy restaurant. It was my way of communicating a sense of healthy dominance to a boy who looked up to his older brother and enjoyed following him around. I was teaching John the ways of the world so that one day he too could experience on his own what he had first learned from me. What I did felt entirely natural and normal, almost like it was my duty as an older, more experienced person. I didn't want to let him down, and I wanted to show him a good time—that's all I was thinking about.

When John returned to Garden City, my parents must have suspected something because they kept asking him probing questions. According to John's version of the story, they asked him so many questions, worded in so many different ways, that he eventually tripped himself up with inconsistencies.

Early Monday morning, the phone in my apartment rang. My father didn't even say hello.

"How could you expose your younger brother to cocaine?" he said, his voice shaking with fear and fury. "Do you know the risks that you have exposed him to? Cocaine is a highly addictive drug and John is only fifteen years old—what were you thinking, Cope?"

Listening to my father's voice, normally so calm and controlled, I felt like a fool. It was a stupid move on my part, giving my little brother cocaine. He could have died of a heart attack or something. But much more powerful than my regret was a growing sense of anger, even fury. This wasn't any of Dad's fucking business. He was violating my space, interfering in the only place where I could be who I wanted to be and do what I wanted to do. What did he know about college life in the seventies or eighties? Everybody was getting high, snorting coke, smoking weed, drinking to get drunk—did he really think my brother had never been exposed to alcohol or other drugs?

How could he even begin to guess what life was like for me and my brother? How could he presume to judge me? Dad had always been a straight arrow, through and through. He married my mother when he was twenty and she was nineteen, worked a full-time job at a radio station while enrolled as a full-time student, and was twice elected president of his class. What right did he have to invade my world with his old-fashioned standards and expectations? I wasn't married, I wasn't the president of anything, and I certainly wasn't going to be at the top of my class—but I was tops in my class in drinking and drug use, and proud of it, too. My father knew nothing about drugs and I knew everything—that's one area where I had it all over him.

Mixed up with that weird pride in my ability to hold my liquor (and smoke a joint or snort a few lines at the same time) was a vague sense of foreboding. I drank too much, smoked pot all the time and, whenever I had extra money, snorted cocaine. Every once in a while after overdoing it, I'd feel so bad in the morning that I'd think about cutting down or even quitting for a while. But a toke on a joint, a few stiff Bloody Marys, or a couple of lines always silenced those thoughts. I never doubted that I could control my drug use, if I wanted to, and that was the point—I didn't want to quit or even cut down. I liked the feeling too much to give it up.

Besides, it was easy to label my drug use "adolescent experimentation" and "youthful indiscretion" because that's what everybody else called it. I'll never forget the letter I got from a big city newspaper editor, a good friend of my father's, who told me that he wasn't surprised when the judge agreed to reduce the charges against me. "While this may seem like a cavalier attitude," he wrote, "I wasn't surprised. Cope, this old world is not always fair, and injustices do occur. But in an amazing number of instances, things do turn out all right. I felt that this would be one of those times."

Twice in five months—my arrest in December followed by the drug-saturated weekend with my brother in May—alcohol and other drugs had ripped jagged holes in the fabric of my carefully stitched-together life, but the torn pieces were quickly sutured by a court system that agreed to view my behavior as a temporary aberration, friends who rallied to my cause, and my parents whose love, hope, fear, and ignorance about the symptoms and progression of chemical dependency blinded them to the truth. Even though Dad suggested in his letter that I might want to talk to a professional to find out what was bothering me, no one in my family or the criminal justice system ever mentioned the possibility of alcoholism or the need for an alcohol assessment. While it was clear that something might be wrong with me—most likely a problem such as minor depression, chronic anxiety, or general stress—few people could imagine that a clean-cut, well-mannered, church-going young man like me might have a serious alcohol problem. Denial took over because the truth was simply too strange and terrible to grasp.

Immediately after my graduation from Washington & Lee in June, my father wrote me another heartfelt letter. Looking back at the events of the past six months, he gently raised his concerns about my drinking and drug use but stopped short of suggesting that I might have a serious drug problem. As he did in all his letters, Dad expressed his deep love for me, almost as if he were trying to heal my underlying shame with words that affirmed my inherent worth. Although he framed the problem as a moral issue involving right and wrong, he was clearly motivated by concern that my drug use might kill me. Attached to his letter was a *New York Times* story linking a surge in deaths and illnesses to the heavy use of cocaine.

Dear Cope:
Until you are a father you cannot know how a man can both love his son deeply and yet reach the moment when,

because of that love, he must allow him to attempt his own passage.

I love you with all my heart and there is nothing I would not do for you anytime you need my help. But the fundamental decisions you face are those only you can now make.

One concerns your work. . . . When I was 22, I was sure I would be a minister. Everyone takes a fork in the road and in time it leads to another fork, and that one to another, and so on. All you can do is to face the immediate choices and from there go the way your heart leads you. Since you alone know your heart, you alone can decide.

The second decision you have to make concerns the risks you are prepared to take. All decisions involve risks; life is risk. But some risks are foolish, and I have particularly in mind the use of alcohol and drugs. I do not know the extent to which you are involved, but I worry about you because I love you. This is a matter of right and wrong, although your generation rationalizes drugs. It is a matter of right and wrong because of the law—you cannot afford another incident such as happened last December—and because foolish risks are wrong. Every young person says, "I know the worst might happen, but it won't happen to me." But that is the risk: it can. The dice can go against anyone, and with drugs, it is not money you lose when the dice come up wrong; it is the potential of life itself at stake.

The time to say no to such risks is now. And I pray you so choose.

Enjoy your summer. Keep your eyes open, take in all you see, and take care.

With all my love,
Dad

Reading that letter today I wonder how my life might have been different if my father had insisted I get professional help. He knew I was taking foolish risks, and he feared my life might be at stake. Was he hoping I would see the error of my ways and make an about-face on my own? He prayed I would say no to the risks associated with drugs, but I didn't know what risks he was talking about. I wasn't going to get hurt, and I was too young to die.

I don't blame my parents. What was true for them is still true today for a lot of parents, because all the cutting-edge science and groundbreaking research about addiction still can't overcome the shame and stigma that prevent families from seeing what is directly in front of them. It's so much easier and more socially acceptable to talk about a "problem" than an "addiction," a "mistake" than a pattern of out-of-control behavior, a "defiant act" rather than conduct that defies rationalization. When young people look healthy and relatively happy on the outside, how could they possibly be suffering from a chronic, progressive, inevitably fatal disease? If morals and values have been an integral part of their upbringing—if they come from a "good" family—aren't they protected against addiction and shouldn't they find the strength within themselves to turn their backs on drugs? And when families do suspect something more than what they see, where do they turn for help? In my case, the legal system responded with the same "he's a good kid, it's just a mistake" rationalizations. Why argue with that?

To this day I wonder how much agony might have been spared if, after I got busted, the judge, the prosecutor, the probation officer, or my own attorney had insisted on an assessment to determine if my temporary drug problem was actually a progressive drug addiction. We all sensed that something was wrong, but no one knew exactly what it was. Nobody could see or understand—not even me—that my "problem" wasn't so much about using drugs as it was about not being able to stop using drugs. *Wanting* to drink and use had meta-morphosed in a period of just a few years into *needing* to drink and use. I thought I could control my drinking and drug use—*I can stop anytime I want,* I kept telling myself—but the last thing on my mind was quitting because by this point my drug use was all mixed up with feelings of inadequacy and confusion about who I was and who I wanted to be. I drank to feel better about myself, and it worked instantly, miraculously. I smoked marijuana and snorted cocaine to forget my problems, and the drugs made my problems disappear for a few hours. I couldn't see that the more I used, the worse my problems became, because in the short run, in the moments and hours when I was high, I felt better. When I was high, my fears of inadequacy and unworthiness faded away. But they always came back.

My shame and my drug use ran along parallel lines until they eventually merged and became one. I drank because I was ashamed, and I was ashamed because I drank. Which came first, the drinking or the shame? I'm not sure I will ever know the answer to that question, but at some point "want" became "need" and I drank and used not to feel better but to feel normal. It wasn't just about lack of self-esteem, childhood trauma, right and wrong, or making bad choices—something deeper and more insidious was going on. I needed to get high and that need became so deep and strong that I was powerless before it. When want became need—and, truthfully, that transformation is only clear to me in retrospect—the nature of my problem changed from using too much and too often to not being able to stop using. From the outside, I still looked like a healthy, balanced, ethical young man. On the inside, however, I was raging against everything and everyone, especially myself. I didn't understand what was happening to me and because no one else could see it or name it for what it was, I was left alone with my tormented self. All my energy became focused on one goal—to keep the inside from showing on the outside, to hide the truth of my misery and my shame from others and even from myself.

I graduated from Washington & Lee with a 2.64 out of a possible 4.0 grade point average, a journalism degree, and a job at the *Washington Star* newspaper. Two weeks after I was hired and before I ever started work, the newspaper was pushed out of business by the mighty *Washington Post*, so I went to work as a researcher at a small television production company in New York City. I spent my days at the studio and the library, with plenty of time to take breaks and walk the streets looking for drugs. I had some scary encounters, too, like the day I bought a dime bag of pot from a street dealer at Union Square Park in Manhattan and suddenly found myself surrounded by five punks with knives who threatened to cut my throat if I didn't hand over the pot along with my cheap watch and Sony Walkman. The next day I was back at the park, looking for more.

Most of that time I was high—drinking a lot, smoking pot regularly, and spending sleepless weekends buzzed on cocaine. Nobody suspected anything was awry, not because I fooled them but because I had fooled myself into thinking that I was only doing what everyone else was doing. On the surface everything looked so normal, even exceptional by some standards. I was working full-time, lived in an apartment in New York City, jogged every day, volunteered at soup kitchens, and went to church. One day I ran into Mary, the first girl I'd ever kissed back in Garden City, and I asked her out on a date. A few months later we were living together in Manhattan. Seven months later, in April 1982, I moved to Dallas to work as a reporter at the *Dallas Times Herald*. After Mary and I were married in November, she joined me in Dallas, we bought a house, talked about having a family, and, in the meantime, got a golden retriever, who we called Dallas (Dally, for short).

Dallas was a two-newspaper town back then, and the competition to get the scoop or get scooped was intense. My beat was crime and criminal justice in the suburbs between "Big D" and Fort Worth, and I was constantly on the prowl looking for a headline story the other beat reporter wouldn't find. My big break came one sweltering August day when a disgruntled truck driver shot and killed nine coworkers at a warehouse in Grand Prairie before getting killed in a blazing shootout with the police. I was the first reporter on the scene, getting there before the shooting stopped, and that lucky break earned me a promotion to the main newsroom in downtown Dallas.

I had a pretty good nose for the news, as my father would have phrased it, and I knew how to use those good Texas manners my parents had instilled in me to squeeze information out of the secretaries at the cop shop and convince criminals to give me exclusive interviews. I earned a reputation for scooping the *Dallas Morning News* with front-page stories—gifted editors were integral to my success—and it wasn't long before I was being compared in Dallas to one of the nation's top journalists, Bill Moyers.

Those comparisons drove me crazy. What the hell was I doing in a profession where everything I did naturally invited references to my famous father who had set the bar so high I could never jump over it? For years my father, always sensitive to my fear of failure, had warned me about entering his chosen field.

"Are you sure you want to be a journalist?" he'd casually ask me during a game of catch in our front yard on a Sunday afternoon. "Have you ever thought about being an airline pilot or an archaeologist?"

"But I love the news, Dad," I'd say, reminding him that he was the one who introduced me to the exciting, adrenaline-packed world of journalism. He took me dog sledding in the High Rockies during the filming of a PBS documentary on Stuart Mace, the legendary dog musher. In 1976, when I was seventeen years old, I worked as a gopher for CBS News during the Republican Convention and was interviewed live on national television by reporter Mike Wallace. Six months later I accompanied Dad to Cuba and met Fidel Castro, whom he interviewed for a CBS documentary on the CIA. We rode around the streets of Havana in a Russian limousine in the middle of the night while the dictator lectured us on what was wrong with American democracy, and I even got to sip Castro's own stock of Cuban rum. Then there was the time Dad took me to a tree-lined street in Queens, New York, to film a protest by white residents who were upset that a black family was moving into their neighborhood. I stood in the street crying because that was the first time I'd seen the ugly face of racism.

Journalism was in my blood. Perhaps Dad really did hope that my lifelong passion for airplanes and history might lead me to a vocation that would spare me comparisons to his fabled career, but secretly I think he was pleased with my passion for words and facts. Journalism was his life and he considered it a noble profession, the very foundation of democracy. "If free and independent journalism committed to telling the truth without fear or favor is suffocated," he once said in a speech, "the oxygen goes out of democracy."

He was just as passionate about his profession when we talked privately. "My work is what gets me up in the morning," he'd say. "I've always looked on journalism as a calling, a public service that takes the reader or viewer as close as possible to the verifiable truth."

I'd been a reporter in Dallas for only a few months when Dad offered some personal and professional advice. He was always trying to make me feel better about myself, even to the point of confessing mistakes he had made in his own life.

You are off to a fine start in journalism, and everything you are doing will improve your skills as a professional and enable you in time to make more informed judgments about where you want to invest the major part of your work. Do not make the one mistake I made about which I have the most regret:

that I worked too hard and thought too much about my work in the beginning to go on long walks with my wife, or learn to grow roses, or watch the sun set, or spend time with good friends. There are some things the loss of which success doesn't compensate for, and one of them is just the accumulating joy of being with someone you love and in awe of life itself.

Dad sensed that my fledgling career was already starting to consume my private life and he attributed my restlessness and discontent to my relentless drive to prove myself by matching or even exceeding his accomplishments. He was concerned about my physical and emotional health, but I don't think he had any idea how much I was drinking or that I was snorting cocaine regularly. Only Mary saw that side of me, but I was even able to hide my drug use from her. Mary was a social drinker and after a few glasses of wine, she was done. Not me—I kept going, even after she went to bed. Although I used cocaine in front of her several times, I was soon covering up my drug use with a secret stash in the car and lines cut up and snorted behind the locked door in the bathroom.

Whenever I overdid it, Mary focused attention on my emotional issues with my father, which she believed drained my self-esteem. "You're a good man," she kept repeating every time I melted down in anxiety over a deadline, despair over not measuring up, or resentment toward my father. Almost every day I'd find little affirmations on pieces of paper she'd taped to the bathroom mirror or on the dashboard of my car when I went off to work. Searching for answers to my problem that was quickly becoming her problem, we spent a lot of time and money trying to make me feel better about myself—romantic weekend trips, marriage counselors, couples workshops on intimacy, a new car and a bigger house with a pool, dinner parties with movers and shakers, and a fertility specialist to help improve our chances to have a child. We tried everything, even attending Baptist, Methodist, and Unitarian churches all over the city, hoping that God might work when nothing else did. But every effort was doomed because we didn't understand the real problem. I was an alcoholic and a drug addict.

Early one morning, after an all-night marathon of drinking and drugging with a sports reporter at the newspaper, I dragged myself home to get showered and dressed for work. In the bathroom I found a note taped to the mirror. This note wasn't like all the others.

"Why can't you just be happy being who you are?" Mary wrote. "Just what are you trying to prove, and to who? You don't have to prove anything to me anymore."

For the first time I sensed her desperation. Those little notes started appearing all over the place after all sorts of embarrassing escapades. One evening at a dinner party at our house, I jokingly sucked a crawling giant beetle off the kitchen floor and into my mouth. I meant to just hold it there and then stick out my tongue to get a laugh, but I accidentally swallowed it and began choking. Up it came, along with two bowls of spicy homemade Texas chili and a pint of whiskey, right on the floor in front of my horrified guests.

On the job one day I mistakenly left a tiny brown glass vial of powdered cocaine on the bathroom sink outside the Dallas County district attorney's office before I interviewed him for a newspaper story. When I realized what I'd done, I excused myself for a moment to look for it. I stopped at the secretary's desk to ask if anyone else had been in the bathroom since I had used it. She looked at me suspiciously (maybe I was paranoid) and said no one had been in there, but when I locked the door and searched for the cocaine, it was gone.

Less than a week later, I was back in the D.A.'s office for another interview, carrying another glass container of cocaine and snorting it up in the bathroom. That time I remembered to put the vial back in my pocket.

Drinking cold beer after a hard day at work, sipping champagne and fine wine to mark birthdays and anniversaries, sucking on a joint to relax on lazy summer afternoons, snorting cocaine whenever I could score a gram or two—in the decade between my twentieth and thirtieth birthday, using drugs became an everyday ritual that achieved reliable results. Getting high, staying high, planning the next high were all part of the routine, as automatic and reflexive as breathing. I did it without even thinking about it. Only when I tried to stop for a few days did I face the baffling dilemma of figuring out how to live without the substances that made my life worth living. Whether I was using them to highlight the pleasure or blot out the pain, alcohol and other drugs automatically did for me what I could not do for myself: They gave me confidence, boosted my self-esteem, erased my shame, eased my despair.

Never mind that drinking too much gave me a thumping hangover and a baby beer gut or that cocaine burned out my mucous membranes until my nose bled suddenly and without warning. Or that when I took too much Valium (a fellow reporter gave me her extra pills), I wet the bed because I was too drugged to wake up. Or that I put my career and reputation on the line every time I drove drunk or carried illegal drugs on the job. The potential consequences didn't bother me because I figured I was too smart to get caught and the risk seemed a small price to pay for the glorious experience of getting high.

Getting high was also a way of numbing myself to the relentless stress of my job. I was making a name for myself, but I kept reminding myself that at my age, my father was the right-hand man to the president of the United States. I was a reporter for a good newspaper, but it wasn't the *New York Times* or the *Washington Post*, and I was far from the best reporter in the newsroom. Any success I achieved turned to failure in my mind because compared to my father's accomplishments, mine were puny. Once again, my dad tried to prop me up, sending me little notes of congratulations for my achievements.

"I am indeed proud of your efforts," he wrote in May 1984 after he read a front-page article I'd written.

> And not a little jealous. You have at twenty-three covered well bigger stories than I ever covered as a reporter. I wound up in government by a fluke, but you are a reporter by intuition, and while there is no way you could re-create my career—because what happens in politics is so happenstance—you can create for yourself a rewarding career and life in journalism, as long as you do not mistake notoriety for satisfaction.

But notoriety, which I equated with fame and recognition, was exactly what I wanted because that's what my dad had. I couldn't imagine being satisfied with anything less. When I'd get big scoops that resulted in page one headlines across the top of the massive *Sunday Times Herald*, I could barely look at the paper before fear and panic set in. Where was the next big story coming from and how long would it take me to get it? Even when I began to win awards for my work, it wasn't enough. Only a Pulitzer Prize would do because Dad didn't have one of those on his desk yet. (As it turns out, Dad did have a Pulitzer, or at least shared in a Pulitzer, which was awarded to *Newsday* when he was publisher.)

The reality of my life didn't match up with the expectations I had grown up with and the lofty benchmarks that I believed defined professional success. Constantly comparing myself to my father, I was doomed to fail no matter how hard I tried or how great my achievements. I tried to beat back the shame of my shortcomings by working harder and longer, fifteen-hour days six days a week (just like Dad), until it seemed that exhaustion defined my life. Restlessness, irritability, and discontent became a tight ball of raw emotions that festered inside. I needed relief, and I found it, as I had so often before, in marijuana, cocaine, and alcohol.

Like a mariner on the open sea in the time before weather radar or satellites kept watch from above, I had little warning and no understanding of the gale force winds bearing down on me. Whatever warnings I did receive, I ignored. No matter what concerns my father raised in his letters or how many times Mary broke down in tears and pleaded with me to believe in myself and to slow down, I was convinced I knew exactly what I was doing and that I could ride out any storm that came my way. I kept driving myself, lashing myself to the wheel, pushing hard to steer clear of the monster waves that threatened to engulf me.

Dad came for a visit in the spring of 1984. Mary and I were having problems, I was strung out from stress and too much cocaine, and my father's presence unnerved me. A week after his visit, he wrote me a letter expressing his concern about my state of mind and the priorities I had set for myself. As always, Dad delivered his concern in a thoughtful, beautifully written letter, but once again he did a delicate dance around the problem rather than stepping into the center of the ring and facing it head-on.

May 1, 1984

Dear Cope:

This is less father-to-son than man-to-man and friend-to-friend. I am concerned about your health. That you have recurring bouts of the debilitating malady is disturbing—almost as if nature is sending you an alert . . . the body saying SOS, stop hurting me. There may be something chemically wrong and you should put yourself in the hands of people who will try to find out if that's the case. However, I suspect the larger problem is your own self. Usually the body cries "ouch" when the self is hurting. And the self does that—unintentionally in a number of ways. Not managing stress well is one of them.

There is a lot of stress in journalism, and in the right proportion it can actually be a source of creativity. But too much poorly managed can cripple. I would urge you—strongly urge you—to get some help from an expert in the disciplining of stress. They have wonderful techniques of relaxing, of encouraging worthwhile distractions (one cannot always keep one's head in the world of work and the future), and of controlling the use of stress producing foods (for example, the worst thing for stress is coffee, which can stimulate an already excessive amount of stress). Your Uncle James got hooked at your age on too much coffee, and in time it wore down his nerves, his stomach, his system. There's plenty of evidence now, as with drugs, that coffee is bad for people like us, and I urge you to temper your intake.

Also, please come to terms with ambition and commitment. You are in this—life—for the distance, not the sprint—and things will come in season. Don't try to force them beyond giving of your best when necessary for the job. But give too, to your other needs: for recreation, entertainment, worship, civic opportunities, and above all to the one whom you have chosen to spend your life with. It isn't fair to her or you for the two of you to neglect the joys of life that are outside the marketplace. Don't worry about being famous yet—or ever. Remember that everyone has ups and downs. Try not to anticipate everything that's going to happen to you (that's impossible, a nuisance, and bothersome to your peace of mind). Be pleased with yourself—you're already a good journalist, a good husband, a good man. You have nothing to prove to anyone, and indeed I think you will find more of what you want in life by relaxing somewhat and, while still dedicated to the goals you have set for yourself, enjoying the day and the small opportunities each one brings.

You will say, justifiably: "He should talk! He's 50 and has made it." Yes, but when I was just a bit older than you—26— I came down with a dangerous ulcer from being just like you. Only your mother's care and my own realization that I had to stop being all things to all people pulled me through. That, and in time, the death of my brother, who smoked too much, consumed too much coffee, fretted over not being "successful" like his brother (and thus, by default, never realized how good he was in his own right), got hooked on all kinds of pills to do for him what he thought he couldn't do for himself, and became, in his early 30s, a driven, sad and unhappy man who always regretted that he never really found contentment with who he was and what he was.

I know you are eager to do well. I understand that. But there are many definitions of what that is—and you are doing well already as a young reporter, a loyal son, a dependable companion to your wife, and as a human being. Don't take chances with your health, or down the road you'll find your later years crippled by a bad stomach, shot nerves, or worse.

The word "malady" in the third line of my father's long and thoughtful letter is revealing. My father knew I was suffering and the word he chose to describe my condition spoke directly to the emotional and spiritual depths of my problem but also disclosed his ignorance about its real cause. He didn't know that I was snorting cocaine on a daily basis. He knew I drank alcohol regularly, but he had no idea how much and how often I drank. It really wasn't difficult to hide my excessive use from my parents—at that time I rarely if ever got drunk or out-of-control high in front of them—and, even more important, their denial was firmly in place. No parent wants to think of their child as a drug addict, no matter how obvious the signs, for most people (and my parents were no exception) believe that drug addiction is synonymous with weakness of character, a personality disorder, or a failure of willpower. While I had significant emotional problems, I wasn't an inherently lazy or weak person. I had a steady job, showed up for work on time, exercised regularly, went to church, owned a house (and paid the mortgage every month), and had a wife who loved me. I was never beaten, abused, or denied anything I needed or deserved—how could I possibly be a drug addict?

But there was no doubt I was in trouble physically, mentally, and spiritually—the problem was trying to figure out what exactly was causing my misery and despair. What was the nature of my wretchedness? While unaware of the true scope of my troubles, Dad suggested all sorts of possibilities. Maybe it was a chemical problem that a doctor could diagnose or a pill might relieve. Maybe my problem was working too hard. Maybe it was too much stress, too much ambition, or too much coffee. Maybe I just needed to learn how to relax and focus on the simple joys in life rather than always trying to race to the finish line.

Dad's reference to his older brother, James, who died at age thirty-nine when I was seven years old, caught my eye. I remembered Uncle James as a tall, stern man who wore big black-framed glasses just like my dad's. Like Dad, James worked in the White House for President Johnson—my dad, then press secretary for the president, got the job for his older brother. (I always thought it should have worked the other way around.) I also remembered that every time I visited my dad's parents in Marshall, Texas, my grandmother Mimi would tell me how much I reminded her of Uncle James. I always assumed she meant I had his temperament. "You're so energetic, Cope," she'd say, "just like your Uncle James."

I always thought Uncle James died of cancer, but in his letter Dad explicitly referred to his brother's drug use, something we had never discussed before, much less linked to his death. When Dad wrote that Uncle James smoked too much, consumed too much coffee, and got hooked on all kinds of pills "to do for him what he thought he couldn't do for himself," was he suggesting that Uncle James was a drug addict? The word "hooked" sure seemed to imply addiction. Was Dad suggesting that I might be addicted to drugs, too? Did he fear that I might end up with the same fate as Uncle James, who was also haunted, even tormented, by comparisons to his famous brother?

All those questions running around in my mind annoyed me. I was nothing like my Uncle James. I tossed Dad's letter into a cardboard shoebox. I kept all Dad's and Mom's letters, and a lot of other things I couldn't imagine throwing out, in shoeboxes and when the shoeboxes were full to the brim, I put them in an old camp trunk. That trunk was filled with shoeboxes.

A week later I received a different kind of letter from Dad.

May 9, 1984

Dear Cope:
I was cutting the hedge today and thinking of all the times I would look out my study door and see you doing the same with the grass. You are still around here, although you are gone.

You are one fine fellow. You are also an excellent journalist—a credit to this business. I am very proud of you. I am proud of you most of all because you are a decent human being in a world that rages with indecency. Hang in there. Life is not getting somewhere. It's traveling that matters.

I love you.
Dad

I appreciated the comment about decency but strongly disagreed with Dad's assessment about life. Life is all about getting somewhere, as his own life proved, and more than anything, I wanted to get somewhere, to be something, to achieve some kind of fame and recognition. Those were my goals in life and so the days and months passed, the coffee consumption increased, the stress intensified, my ambitions remained unsatisfied, and I drank more alcohol and snorted more cocaine than ever before.

A year later, after yet another visit, Dad wrote to express his growing concerns about my state of mind and the values I seemed to have left behind.

Dear Cope:

I was troubled in Dallas because you were troubled. It is prudent to think about the future and normal sometimes to be anxious about it, but there was in your distress a deep discontent that seemed to go beyond the usual concern over your career. I think you are a very conflicted man, so much so that you are being unfair to yourself (by judging yourself too harshly, or feeling pressured to choose a direction you fear incompatible), to Mary (who sometimes needs just the simple joy of your presence, without the distraction of the future), and to the only life you have to live, which is the life of this moment. No one can dwell constantly in the future without tormenting himself and those who desire his presence here and now.

However, I think it is not so much anxiety over the future as it is the struggle you are having to find your own identity, as you put it to me when we were driving back to the hotel. That means choosing the values that are most deeply significant to you. You cannot be comfortable in another man's suit—either your father's or some imaginary figure you might see yourself to be if you lived in a handsome mansion in North Dallas.

When you were a boy you loved the basic things. You loved the discovery that was the purpose of a metal detector;

the search thrilled you more than the find, or it was the imagination provoked by the find, and not its actual value, that you found most delightful. You loved searching the stars in your telescope. You loved reading. You loved feeding the birds and watching the squirrels. You loved being with people who loved you. You loved sharing yourself with them. You loved lots of talk. I don't recall ever hearing you mention owning a Jaguar or being a millionaire or wanting the world's approval. You just exulted in life.

I do not know the Cope who, somewhere along the way, got his thrill from drugs or alcohol (and once was almost ruined by it); I know the Cope who thrilled to the pursuit of the news. I do not know the Cope who sees himself a member of the Petroleum Club or the Highland Park country club; I know the Cope who felt most at home in the simple precincts of Wilmer, with Joe Davidson, who never belonged to a fancy club or drove a fancy car but served a simple church and a small community and cherished his family and died beloved by the people who knew him.

Because I know this Cope, I think you should do what gives each day the most meaning, according to a measure of self-knowledge which you can determine yourself; you're the only one who can hear the pitch of your personal tuning fork. Hear the inner man, and do what he says now; you will change by the time you are 30, and change again by 40; you can decide then what it is you are supposed to do at that time; for now, hear the only voice you can judge is true, the one within.

I am for whatever you choose to do. But I know which Cope I'm rooting for. I'm rooting for the real thing.

Love,
Dad

What was the "real thing"? Damned if I knew, and it irritated the hell out of me that Dad was trying to tell me what I should be. Dad was remembering the child Cope, the boy who felt at home in Wilmer in the company of his grandfather, the kid who looked at the stars every night, the teenager who loved to walk the cathedral grounds with a metal detector looking for rare coins. Well, Pa Pa Joe was dead, Wilmer was in a world I never visited anymore (even though it was just twenty miles from downtown Dallas), I didn't have time to stargaze, and my metal detector was stored in a closet gathering dust.

I wasn't a little boy anymore—I was a grown man. Sure, I wanted material possessions—who doesn't? There wasn't anything wrong with aspiring to own a fancy car or belong to an exclusive club, especially in a glitzy town like Dallas. Dad lived with Mom in a spacious, beautifully decorated apartment in an exclusive neighborhood overlooking Central Park. He was a successful journalist with a bunch of Emmy and Peabody awards, most of which they kept in a closet because there were too many to display at once. It only made sense that I wanted what my parents had.

I was infuriated with Dad after reading that letter because it seemed like he had set a double standard—he was telling me to listen to my inner voice, but that wasn't what he had done after being called to the ministry, moving on to public service in Washington, and then becoming a newspaper publisher, a broadcast journalist, and an author. More than once in the recent past, he admitted that he worked too much and didn't pay enough attention to his family. That, he said, was one of his greatest regrets.

Dad always liked to say that his counsel was forged from the mistakes of his own life, but it seemed like those very mistakes had paved the way for his present-day success. Any little missteps he had taken—forks in the road, he called them—helped to launch his career, but my errors and imperfections were like boomerangs that kept coming back to whack me on the head when I wasn't paying attention. I just wanted to be good at what I did. What was wrong with that? He'd gotten away with it and I would, too, if I just tried a little harder.

Like father, like son. Dad's success was a bright flame that blinded me because it was all I could see. I was the moth that was about to get torched, but was it the fault of the flame or did the moth fly into it?

In 1986, I left the *Dallas Times Herald* for a reporting job at *Newsday*, the Long Island daily newspaper that received two Pulitzer prizes and other prestigious awards during Dad's tenure there as publisher. Many of the editors and reporters there worked with my father back in the late 1960s, and when I arrived they regaled me with stories about how Bill Moyers had turned *Newsday* into a great newspaper. Delivery truck drivers, office staff, the folks who ran the presses, and janitors would stop me in the hallway or stop by my desk to tell me how much they loved working with my father.

"He knew everyone's name, even mine," a middle-aged woman who worked in the advertising department told me one day when I was rushing back to my office to meet a deadline. "No matter how low you were on the totem pole, he treated everyone like a member of the family. He was always stopping by our desks just to chat, or sitting down in the lunchroom to find out how things were going."

That was Dad, and as much as his fame taunted and goaded me, his simple human decency made me proud to be his son. Nobody ever called my father a bastard, a double-crosser, or a scoundrel, at least not to my face. He was a good man with a good soul, and I actually relished the stories people told me because Dad never talked about his successes. I don't know why. Maybe he felt guilty, thinking that he didn't deserve so much praise and adoration. Maybe he was trying to protect me, knowing that I would make the inevitable comparisons and come up short.

One day, not long after I started at *Newsday*, a fellow reporter stopped by my desk to ask a question.

"Aren't you the Moyers kid who got arrested for breaking and entering, or something like that?" he asked me.

The question stunned me because I was so unprepared for it. Six years had passed since the fish market incident, and I hardly ever thought about it anymore. I didn't think anyone else did, either. I could have laughed off the question with a "Yeah, that was me, pretty stupid prank for a drunk college student, huh?" but instead I lied in an attempt to hide my shame.

"That was my brother," I said. "He got in trouble once, but he's doing okay now."

That night I stayed late in the newsroom, waiting until most of the staff had left for the day. When the place was nearly empty, I walked into the newspaper's morgue, the library where old clips were stored. Under M for Moyers, I found a gigantic file on my dad and a smaller one on my mother, whose philanthropic and civic efforts on Long Island and in New York City made her newsworthy in her own right. Then I found what I was looking for: Moyers, William Cope.

"Son of Bill Moyers arrested for burglary" announced one headline on a long story on December 24, 1980. A shorter follow-up story in February 1981 gave the details of my plea to a misdemeanor and that was the extent of the file of my lifetime achievements as chronicled in *Newsday*. I tucked the folder under my shirt and left the building. In my car in the parking lot, I tore the clippings into tiny pieces and tossed them out the window as I drove down the street. Like the criminal record that had been expunged from the court files years before, my slate was clean again, and for a moment I felt relieved.

But driving home that night the truth hit me—once again I was a two-bit burglar, this time propelled back to the scene of the crime by the very shame I had tried to expunge like that old newspaper story. I could tear up the article but I could never erase the memory. Only after I stopped at a local bar and downed a couple of cold beers did I begin to feel better.

Of course there were reasons to feel good in those days, too. One warm spring day in 1988, I returned from my morning jog to hear people yelling down the hill from my house. Running down the hillside to the two-story apartment building on the street below, I saw smoke and flames pouring from the windows of a ground-floor unit.

"There are two people trapped inside," a woman in the parking lot screamed. Several firemen were outside the unit, struggling to reach through the broken window to the people trapped inside. I climbed onto the window ledge to get better leverage and reached inside. Broken shards of glass sliced open my arms and cut my face as we pulled out the dead body of an elderly man.

"This one's still alive!" one of the firemen yelled as we pulled out the second body. Saliva was frothing from the elderly woman's mouth when we laid her on the ground and an emergency medical technician immediately gave her CPR. I looked at my hands, then, in horror and disbelief, for my skin was coming off right before my eyes. I remember feeling amazed that there was so little pain, but then I realized that it was not my skin at all but the burned flesh of the two elderly people—their skin had come off in my hands. My face was badly cut and my lungs were filled with smoke, so paramedics rushed me to the local hospital where they stitched up my wounds and treated me for smoke inhalation, releasing me later that day. That night I was too tired to even have a drink.

Several days later I received a letter from Robert A. Howard, chief of police at the Northport Police Department.

May 16, 1988

Dear Mr. Moyers:

My officers and myself were indeed impressed by your actions last Friday at the scene of the tragic fire on Main Street. We want to let you know that your help was very much appreciated. Unfortunately, at the scene of the fire I did not have an opportunity to personally thank you for your help in extricating the fire victims from the apartment.

Your actions were obviously taken without concern for your own safety and were indicative of your consideration for the lives of others. Your willingness to get involved and to "do something," when it really counted, was evident.

I hope the injuries you received were not too serious.

Northport is fortunate to have residents such as yourself who are willing to take risks which help make our community a great place to live.

You have my appreciation and my respect.

Thank you.

Sincerely,
Robert A. Howard
Chief of Police

I held that letter in my hands and thought about the police chief typing away in his office, praising me for actions that made the community a great place to live. He should have busted me instead. How many times could his officers have arrested me in this town for buying and using cocaine or for driving under the influence? Hell, I'd take my dog for a walk to the park at night so I could snort cocaine where just a few hours earlier little kids were playing ball. Sometimes, early in the morning after an all-night binge, I'd go down to the waterfront and drink an entire bottle of white wine or a six-pack of beer. I'd sit in the lifeguard chair looking out over the sandy beach, dreading the sunrise, trying to stave off the depression and anxiety that overwhelmed me when I finally had to stop.

The day the police chief's letter arrived, I also received a letter from my mother.

May 15, 1988

Dear one,

It was Confirmation Sunday today and I thought of you throughout the service. It seems like such a short time ago that you were confirmed. Wow! How time flies. But I got rather sentimental thinking how proud of you I was that day. I remember what you said as you participated—I even remember what you wore! I began to feel a little sad and worried—worried that perhaps I began to relax my parenting responsibilities too soon. Did I? I reassured myself that, at least, I had not stopped being concerned for your spiritual well-being—not ever. But I wish I knew more about your spiritual journeys since your confirmation. SO much has transpired in your life since then. Sometime, if you feel like it, please tell me where you are spiritually. I remember several times in my life when I neglected my spiritual life—and felt the effects of it later. Without the spiritual side of me, I may as well be a monkey. I'm enclosing the part of the church bulletin the kids wrote to remind you of what it was like to be sixteen!

Our yard is a pink haze of blooms—so beautiful! You were very sweet to remember me at Mother's Day and on my 53rd birthday. I can't believe I am that old.

I love you very much. You are special and have a mission

on this earth, don't forget it or despair of it. Try to find a little time every day to feed your spiritual self. Don't count on anything or anybody to do that for you. It's between you and you. But you do have help available, if you will call on it.

Much love,
Mother

I put those two letters in the old camp trunk in the attic and shut it tight. I forgot about them until I opened that trunk many years later, hoping to understand how a life that was so broken apart could be made whole again.

6

On My Knees

I NEEDED A DRINK, and I needed it bad. The Long Island Expressway was bumper-to-bumper with rush hour traffic, and I was on edge
after a rough day at work pushing up against a deadline on a story
about a major murder mystery. A young boy at a yeshiva on Long Island had been murdered two years before but the murderer had never
been found. Now I had the scoop on a break in the case—some newly
discovered evidence and a possible motive—but I had to finish the
story before other reporters beat me to it.

Deadlines were like drugs. They energized and focused me, supplying stamina to reach the finish line where the payoff was often
exhilarating—especially if the story was good enough to appear on the
front page. But the rush of seeing my byline rarely lasted more than
a day. As soon as I started to come down from the high, I'd start chasing the buzz again. I lived from deadline to deadline, one story after

another, but whatever thrills they gave me, they took at least that much away.

Like most days, this one started with a hangover that I tried to relieve with a jog before breakfast, a few aspirin with my bowl of bran flakes, and, as the day wore on, a growing craving for a cold beer or two. For years I had been careful never to drink during the day, a self-imposed rule that I was starting to violate whenever I could slip by with one or two drinks at lunch or in the middle of the afternoon. Drinking during the day seemed like the only way to relieve the craving, which began soon after I woke up in the morning and intensified as the day dragged on. Some days, especially when I was working on a story at my desk in the newsroom, it was impossible to drink and I'd have to wait until after work to drive to the deli for a six-pack of Coors Light or to the bar for a few quick glasses of ale on tap.

Alcohol had become the foundation of my existence, but cocaine was the elevator that took me to the top floor. By the time I was twenty-nine years old in the summer of 1988, everything in my life included alcohol, marijuana, or cocaine, and when I wasn't getting high or drunk I was thinking about getting high or drunk. My life was a mess, but I didn't pause for even a second to worry about it—I just got high as often as I could. Hangovers and all-nighters, snorting cocaine in the newsroom in the middle of the night when no one else was there, embarrassing nosebleeds, chronic stomachaches that sometimes doubled me over in pain, the death of any real intimacy with my wife—it was all beginning to come apart.

I merged onto the Long Island Expressway. I hated rush hour. Weaving in and out of cars, drawing a chorus of honking horns and a few raised fingers, I kept thinking about the cold beer waiting for me at home. Tonight I'll go straight home, I thought. I'll just have a few beers, maybe some wine with dinner (Mary had promised me one of her healthy meals full of vegetables and grains), play with the dog, get to bed at a decent hour. No cocaine tonight, I promised myself. The nosebleeds were getting worse, and it would be good to take a break for a few days.

At the red light on Main Street in Northport, just four blocks from home, I impulsively turned left and drove two short blocks to Gunther's Tap Room, a neighborhood tavern that had become my home away from home. I ordered a beer at the bar and sat down at a table in the corner. As always, I was the only person there dressed in a shirt and tie. I liked the feeling of rubbing elbows with people who appeared to be a little worse off than me.

The first glass of cold beer out of the tap instantly cut through the tension of the day. I wasn't tired or hungry anymore. The deadline I'd been stressing about all day didn't seem so impossible after all. Thoughts of my wife and dog waiting at home faded away. The beer was working, even if my synapses kept telegraphing little reminders to go look for some cocaine. I tried to ignore them—tonight I'd get by with just a few beers.

I ordered another beer. For a couple of bucks, the buzz wasn't bad. I liked the way alcohol helped me relax and let down my guard—I didn't have to play the role I imagined people expected as a *Newsday* journalist or the son of Bill Moyers. In the past year Dad's career had really heated up with a new book, edited by Jacqueline Onassis, and his PBS interviews with Joseph Campbell, a professor at Sarah Lawrence College whose call to "Follow Your Bliss" had become a mantra for millions of people around the country. I smiled as I finished off another beer, thinking that my bliss had dragged me into blue-collar taverns where no one had ever heard of my father. Nobody in this bar knew or cared who I was, what I did, or where I came from, and that was just how I needed it to be.

I should go home, I thought. But what the hell, I'll have another beer or two. I looked at my watch; it was close to ten p.m. Mary was probably already in bed. Dallas would be asleep on the floor next to her, dinner would be in the refrigerator, the porch light would be on, and the rest of the house would be dark. Eventually I'd stumble in, take a quick shower to wash off the smell of the bar, crawl into the king-size bed, and fall asleep within minutes. I never knew what Mary thought or felt when I came home late, because I never asked and she never brought up the subject. We just didn't talk about it.

I think we never talked about it because I was full of excuses and Mary, a deeply spiritual person, put her faith and our future in God's hands. She knew I was, deep down, a good person, and she hoped and prayed that I would eventually work out my "issues," as we called them. I drank too much, that was obvious, but she believed my drinking was a symptom of deeper emotional problems rather than the primary source of those problems. In a letter she wrote to me many months later, she told me that during those days she always tried to visualize me as a whole and healthy person, knowing my potential and innate goodness. She chose to live her life to the fullest, hoping that by her example she would help me choose a healthier route. But I was too far gone to get the message.

So that night in Gunther's Tap Room I looked at my watch, assured myself that Mary was at home asleep, and decided to have a few more rounds. On one of my trips to the bathroom, I found myself standing at the urinal next to a guy with scraggly blond hair, a solid build, and glazed eyes. He sniffed and ran his hand across his nose.

Maybe he's got some cocaine, I thought.

"How you doing?" I asked, keeping it casual.

"Good," he said. "You?"

"I'm drunk." I laughed.

"You, too, huh?"

We both forced a laugh. In the world of drug taking and drug dealing, that kind of laugh is a secret sign that lets strangers communicate. I knew what the guy was thinking, and he knew what I wanted. We both understood the risks, but the potential payoff was worth it.

"I'm looking to score some coke tonight," I said.

He looked at me again, sizing me up.

"You a cop?" he asked.

"Yeah, and so are you." I laughed again. "That makes us both guilty."

"Sure," he said. "I've got some." He stepped over by the stalls, away from the door, and pulled a small plastic envelope out of his shirt pocket. I took a quick snort. It was real. It was good. I smiled.

"What's your name?" I asked.

His name was Jack. We shook hands and then we went back to the bar where we kept drinking, getting up every so often to go to the bathroom to share a few lines of coke.

"You ever smoke any of this stuff?" he asked during one of those bathroom trips.

"Not yet," I said. We finished our beers, I paid the tab, and we headed over to his apartment, a few blocks away. For a brief moment I thought about calling Mary. But then I thought, why bother? She'd be asleep and I'd use the same excuse I had been using for years now—a reporter's work is never done.

For just a moment I hesitated to walk into Jack's apartment. Here I was about to smoke cocaine for the first time with a person I'd just met in a tavern. I knew that crack cocaine was highly addictive, and I'd even written some stories about how the crack epidemic was killing people, ravaging neighborhoods, and fueling a crime wave from New York City to Los Angeles. And if the cocaine didn't screw me over, Jack might. Did I really want to do this? I didn't bother to answer the question. I just went in.

Jack drew slowly but steadily on the pipe and I watched, fascinated, as the solid rock turned first to a pasty liquid and then into a beautiful white fog that he pulled into his lungs. Then it was my turn. In seconds my brain exploded, and I fell to the floor on my knees. My heart felt as if it would explode with light, with love. Everything inside me became mixed up with everything around me, all fear disappeared, and only the rapture of light and love remained. Pure bliss. Ten orgasms packed into one.

"Oh God, oh-my-god," I whispered, not to the God of my upbringing, but to this new magical god that I loved with a passion that exceeded anything I had ever experienced. For a few minutes the rush held me captive, and when it released me, I wanted more, needed more, had to have more.

Whatever else happened that night is irrelevant. That first hit off the crack pipe marked the exact moment when I turned my back on marijuana, warm whiskey, cold beer, chilled vodka tonics, and powdered cocaine. Crack was everything I had ever wanted, and it gave me everything I had ever needed. Nothing else mattered except reaching that peak of rapture over and over again.

AS FAST AS I fell in love with crack cocaine, Jack and I became great friends. He was unemployed, a former U.S. Marine who was dishonorably discharged for drug possession and who moved from apartment to apartment, just one step ahead of landlords who were after him for back rent. He always smelled of yesterday's women and stale beer, and the only money he ever had was in his pocket, earned from a day job working for his parents at the family machine shop. But none of that mattered, because this was a relationship based on need and convenience—he had the street connections and I had the bank account. Addiction was our common denominator and everything else faded into insignificance.

Just a few weeks after we first met at Gunther's, we began making regular crack runs into New York City. There were as many crack deals made in the city as there were rats living in the sewers. Crack was everywhere—on street corners and in dark alleys, in walk-up tenements in Brooklyn and swanky high-rise apartments overlooking Central Park. I once bought crack from an editor at *Forbes* magazine. We made the deal in the lobby of the Forbes building where Malcolm S. Forbes's priceless collection of jeweled Fabergé eggs were on display.

But Harlem was the hot spot, and Jack knew exactly where to go. After work on Friday night I'd pick up Jack in a park-n-ride lot just off the Long Island Expressway. We'd each pop open a tall boy beer as we drove west across the Nassau County line into Queens, past the cookie-cutter row houses into Flushing Meadow, the site of the 1964 World's Fair, and Shea Stadium, where Dad and I had watched the Mets beat the Orioles in the World Series when I was ten years old. Then onto the Grand Central Parkway to LaGuardia Airport, the Triborough Bridge spanning the East River, and finally into the crowded neighborhoods and burned-out brownstones of Harlem.

We'd drive along the streets of the inner city to 104th Street where Central Park West runs into Harlem. I'd drop Jack off and drive around the block, parking on a side street. My parents lived in an exclusive fifth-floor apartment less than thirty blocks away, but they might as well have been on the other side of the world. I'd sit there, a white guy in a gray Honda in a black neighborhood, trying to look inconspicuous as I watched the homeless bums dig through the trash barrels for dinner, the old ladies dressed in their Sunday best struggling to cart their groceries home, the kids playing ball on the sidewalk, the drug dealers and prostitutes making their deals, and the cops slowly cruising by in squad cars. I never felt out of place there and, with all the activity going on nobody seemed to notice me.

Most of the time it took Jack just ten or fifteen minutes to score some crack. I'd see him coming around the corner and everything just felt so good, so right. On the way back to Long Island we'd stop just before we got to the toll booth at the bridge, and we'd smoke a rock or snort a line or two if he'd scored some powder cocaine to cook up later. From that point on, I could have driven to the moon on an empty gas tank. I always felt completely in control, even when we were stopped at a roadblock as police checked drivers for licenses and proof of insurance. Jack panicked—we had an eight-ball of cocaine and two open beers in the front seat, but I told him to keep cool, hide the beer, and let me take care of the rest. Pulling up next to the policeman, I played the part of a wayward driver from the quiet suburbs of Long Island.

"Excuse me, officer," I said, rolling down the window to make sure that he could see my starched shirt and tie. "We're trying to get to the Grand Central Parkway, but I think we're lost. Would you help us?"

The friendly officer stepped into the middle of the road, halted traffic both ways, and instructed us to do a U-turn. "You want to go back four blocks and turn left," he said, smiling and waving us on. "Have a good day and drive safe."

"I will, sir, thank you," I said, smiling and waving. "You have a good day, too."

Back on Long Island, the ritual rarely varied. At Jack's apartment, he'd get out a small pan and mix together the cocaine, baking soda, and water, a careful pinch of this, a bit of that, slowly turning up the heat, stirring, mixing, waiting. We were watching something being born, and I never failed to be amazed at the process of creation. I liked to think of the baking soda as the sperm and the cocaine as the egg—when they came together, they formed an entirely new creature that looked like a tiny asteroid, an imperfect marble, a chipped gumball.

Jack drained the rocks onto a paper towel, I gently patted them dry, and then we broke them into pieces, filled the pipe, flicked the lighter, and off we went. I always gave Jack an extra rock or two as a reward for his hard work. That made me feel good about myself, superior even, because without my seed money all his hard work would count for nothing.

Once in a while I brought Jack over to my house for dinner. Mary was happy to entertain him, thinking that I had finally found a friend. I liked to tell her stories about how Jack had been down and out until he met me and how giving him a hand made me feel good about myself. "I feel validated," I told her once, making it sound like I was helping the homeless at a Salvation Army shelter or something. It was pure bullshit, but she believed me.

Sometimes we'd play cards with his parents. They were impressed with the fact that Jack had a new friend who was a newspaper reporter, a married man, and the son of Bill Moyers. One night his father pulled me aside to thank me for helping Jack out.

"His whole life I've told Jack to stick with the winners," his father said, shaking my hand. "You're a winner, I'll tell you that."

Later that night, Jack and I drove into Harlem to score some crack.

Whenever we made a crack run, we'd stay up all night smoking, drinking beer, and playing round after round of backgammon. Cocaine wipes out your appetite, so we never ate. Time seemed to stand still, so we never watched the clock. Every thought seemed worthwhile, so we talked nonstop. There was no routine except going up, coming down, going up, coming down. Then the gray light of morning and the birds singing outside triggered the depression and despair that followed every binge.

I always hated leaving Jack's apartment and to help ease the transition, I'd stop at a convenience store and buy a sixteen-ounce beer. I'd stand in line with people who were buying milk for breakfast, the morning newspaper, or a cup of coffee, keeping my eyes on the floor and counting the seconds until I could pay for my beer and get out of there. For a few days I'd struggle to get my life back together, jogging every morning, working hard all day, spending my evenings at home with Mary and Dallas. Then I'd get the craving and the routine would start all over again with another run into Harlem followed by an all-nighter and the early-morning line at 7-Eleven, strung out, waiting to pay for my beer.

I don't know when I started getting paranoid, but at some point that summer it occurred to me that Jack was ripping me off. He was bringing back less cocaine for the same amount of money, disappearing too often into the bathroom during our smoke-a-thons, and fidgeting in his pockets when it was his turn to roll the dice during our backgammon games. Maybe his paranoia was contagious—he'd often tiptoe over to the door and peer through the crack at the bottom or sneak a look outside through the curtained windows. Sometimes he showed up for our crack runs already drunk. He was getting sloppy and weird on me, and I began to wonder if I needed him anymore. Maybe I should solo.

One night in January or February of 1989 I drove into Harlem alone and parked at my usual spot. I walked to the building where I had watched Jack disappear into the basement so many times, opened the outside door leading into a narrow hallway, and knocked on the door of one of the ground-floor apartments.

"What do you want?" The voice came from behind me. I turned around to see an old man standing in the hallway by a metal radiator. I'd seen him before, hanging around on the street outside the apartment.

"I'm a friend of Jack, the guy from Long Island," I said. "We've been here to score before. I'm on my own now."

"Man, what the hell are you doing?" he stepped farther back into the shadows. "Don't you know this place is hot? The cops are all over the neighborhood. Ain't nobody doing nothin' right now. Go away."

It suddenly dawned on me what he was talking about. Earlier that week two police officers had been gunned down in an undercover buy-and-bust about twenty blocks away from this crack house. The dragnet that followed flooded the streets with cops, and the dealers disappeared, waiting for things to cool down. Even the junkies, at least those with half a brain, knew that this wasn't the time to score. But here I was, trying to buy crack in the same neighborhood where two cops had been shot dead. I was suddenly scared to death. What the hell was I doing alone in a city swarming with uniformed and undercover policemen, walking into a crack house, knocking on a stranger's door, talking to an old man in a dark hallway?

I eventually did score some crack that day and for the next few hours used my car as a mobile crack house, parking on the street to light up, then driving around for a while, parking, lighting up, driving around, on and on until the crack was gone. Early the next morning I drove home feeling sick with shame, swearing to myself that this was the last time, I was done, it was over. Like most days, Mary would be sitting in the kitchen having a cup of tea or studying for one of the classes she was taking for her master's degree in social work. Like most days, I'd give Dallas a pat on the head and make up some story about an all-nighter at work. Deadlines, you know. More than once, when my nose wouldn't stop bleeding, I told Mary I'd been pistol-whipped in the city. She'd beg me to be more careful, and I'd reassure her that everything would be okay. Then I'd tell her that I needed to get some sleep. I'd crawl under the covers, sweating and shaking, my nose bleeding onto the sheets, listening to those damn birds singing, wanting to die.

Mary knew something was seriously wrong with me, but she didn't know what it was or what to do about it. Sometimes she blamed it on the fact that I was under a lot of stress at work; other times she tried to build up my self-esteem, hoping that my problems would gradually disappear if I could only feel better about myself. She knew I had an alcohol problem, but she was convinced that I drank too much because of some deeper, inner torment related to my issues with my father. Maybe she suspected the truth, but she just couldn't bring herself to say it out loud. Maybe she thought that if she put words to her fears, they might come true.

My parents were also deeply concerned about my erratic behavior and emotional instability. Just before Christmas, eight years to the day after my arrest at the fish market, my father wrote to congratulate me on an investigative series I had written in collaboration with two other *Newsday* reporters. As soon as I saw the letter, I knew something was up—we lived just an hour away from each other and he could have picked up the phone to offer his congratulations. But that was my dad's way—when emotions were strong, he wrote letters.

After two paragraphs of praise for my part in the *Newsday* series, Dad eased into his concerns about my emotional stability.

What I wish for you, whatever you do, is a life with a little greater measure of serenity and joy. I speak now not just as your father but as your friend. That is, I would be saying this even if you were not my son—I would say it to any soon-to-be-30-year-old with whom I shared values and counsel, the way real friends do. Time speeds by like a bullet, and I hope you make within it space for those pursuits that give you such inner satisfaction—feeding the birds, the walks with your wife and your dog, good movies, dinner with friends where no one has an agenda, the leaves in the fall, a fire in the hearth, a book that moves your soul, your church (I was deeply touched by your work last Saturday with delivering those packages to needy families), above all, the nurturing of your relationship with Mary. . . . I sense in you a yearning for a well-rounded life instead of always striving. One can succeed at work but fail as a man, and I sense your awareness of that possibility. While it appears of late that you have gained control over some of the pressures that were driving you earlier this year, you still seem under a strain. When I asked you on the phone Tuesday if you were in the office, you said, with a hard edge, "Unfortunately, I'm always in the office." And I could sense either resentment over being there or guilt over enjoying being there but afraid to admit it. During the Thanksgiving weekend you were very stressed (and again last weekend, although Mary's illness was certainly a cause for stress); you disappeared often during conversations and meals, you seemed unable to relax, you sometimes seemed "not there." I sensed a struggle and pain and wanted to reach out and say so, but—not ever wanting to intrude, or even being very good at intimacy (male intimacy) I held back. Sometimes I think you are fearful that I will take as a sign of weakness a confession of hurt, when in fact I think the ability to share what is happening inside is a measure of strength; it takes strength to admit a need for help. All of us need someone to confide in, and fathers in fact do not make very good confessors.

By now you must be saying, "Butt out!" And I will. I could be all wet, anyway. But I admire you, my friend, and I wish for you the life you want. Whatever that is—fame, fortune, *or* a contemplative, peaceful, circumscribed life on your own terms—go for it. Above all, seek peace within.

With love, always,

Dad

I was almost thirty years old, my marriage was falling apart, I didn't have children and would have made a mess of them if I did, my faith in God was dead, and every time I looked in the mirror I felt sick with shame. My father had good reason to be worried about me, but I bitterly resented his assessment of my life and wanted to laugh out loud at his solutions. He wanted me to feed the birds? Was he kidding? I couldn't remember the last time I put seed in the bird feeders. I used to love feeding birds, listening to birds, watching birds. Now I hated the sound of a singing bird, especially in the morning when I hadn't been to bed all night.

Why didn't he just leave me alone? What the hell did he mean by "peace from within"? Did he really think I was going to find peace now, with all the stress and responsibilities I had, when I'd been in conflict with him and with myself for my entire life? Did he ever consider that maybe I liked to drink and take drugs because that was the only way I could handle the stress?

I knew I should nurture my relationship with my wife, as Dad suggested, but the relationship was beyond repair. We didn't share our intimate thoughts, make love, laugh, eat dinner together, hold hands or go to the movies. We didn't have any friends anymore. We weren't friends anymore.

I wasn't even succeeding at work anymore because it was taking too much energy just to show up and act normal when I was coming down off a crack high. So I quit. "I had a good three-year run here," I told Tony Marro, the *Newsday* editor, "but it's time to move on." I was on the run. I couldn't sit still. Nothing satisfied me except getting high, and so it made perfect sense to accept an offer from my parents to work as an associate producer for their successful television production company right in the heart of the city, close to my drug dealers, making more money, and enjoying significantly more flexibility in my schedule.

Perfect sense? How could that decision have made sense unless I was completely out of my mind? How often had I complained about my father's "meddling" and my mother's "overprotectiveness," but now I was willing to go to work for them? I was addicted to cocaine and needed it to function, yet I took a job working for my parents, in the same building, with a cubicle just a few doors away from their offices. Did that make sense? It would be easy to conclude that I wanted to get caught, but I was terrified of anyone finding out the truth because I couldn't imagine getting out of bed or making it through the day without cocaine. Nothing I did made any sense because my addiction had short-circuited whatever parts of the brain made sense of the world and my place in it.

And yet, somehow, I still managed to show up at work and look normal enough to avoid detection. My first assignment was to prepare research material and organize the shoot for a PBS documentary on World War II veterans returning to visit the D day battlefields in France. After a weekend binge or a long sleepless night, I'd vow to myself that I wouldn't repeat the experience, but it wasn't long, maybe a day or two, before the craving returned in waves, one wave after another, and I broke down. I found myself leaving the office in the middle of the day not on research visits to the New York Public Library, as I claimed, but on taxi runs to Harlem to score rocks and smoke for a couple of hours in the alleyways. When I was hurting for cash, I'd ask Diana, the office manager, to advance me a hundred dollars from the petty cash drawer. I never brought back receipts. Sometimes at lunch I'd slip out to a bar for a few vodka tonics to calm my jittery nerves. Once I missed an important meeting with my dad and called him from a pay phone in Harlem with the excuse that I was at the doctor because I had discovered blood in my urine.

Even on the days when I put in a full eight hours of productive work, I'd start drinking as soon as I got on the train for home. Several times I passed out and missed my stop; someone would wake me up at the end of the line where I'd have to reboard a train going in the opposite direction. When I commuted into the city by car, I'd light up the crack pipe as soon as I got on the Long Island Expressway headed for home, steering with my knees.

My behavior became increasingly erratic. Sometimes I'd nod off at the table in the middle of dinner. I'd walk into a room and then immediately leave, unable to sit still. And then there was the "lobster incident," as my father still calls it. One evening in July I drove from the city, straight from a two-day cocaine binge, to the beach house my parents rented that summer. Mary, who thought I'd been working hard to meet another deadline, met me there. When I arrived, still flying high from the cocaine I'd smoked on the Long Island Expressway, everyone was sitting down for a big meal of steamed lobster with melted butter, coleslaw, potato salad, and fresh bread. Like a starving scavenger dog that came across a carcass in the wild, I ravaged the meal, tearing apart the lobster with my hands, slurping the juicy meat until it ran all over my shirt, the table and the floor, slobbering down the fixings, and playing with the empty shell of the poor dead lobster, trying to make everyone laugh. I didn't even notice that the looks on their faces had turned from revulsion to horror or, if I did, I just didn't care.

Several weeks before the scheduled D day trip, Dad asked me to meet him for lunch at a Holiday Inn on the Long Island Expressway. From the tone of his voice, I knew the charade was about to end. Something was coming down and there wasn't a damn thing I could do about it except show up. At the restaurant I wanted a beer more than anything, but I ordered a Coke and told Dad I wasn't hungry.

"Cope, I'm worried about you," Dad said. "What's going on?"

Dad was asking me to tell him the truth. He knew something was wrong, and he wanted me to confide in him so he could help me. I often wonder what would have happened if I'd told the truth that day or any other day when Dad or Mom expressed their concern about my behavior. "Mom, Dad, I'm a crack cocaine addict, and I'm spinning out of control." Why didn't I do that?

Because addicts don't tell the truth about their drug use. We lie repeatedly, and we are incredibly inventive with our deceptions and obfuscations, turning and twisting them to fit the situation. We lie not because we are inherently dishonest people but because the nature of addiction is such that we have to lie in order to keep using and we have to keep using because our bodies literally need the drug to function. That is the fundamental truth about addiction—when "want" becomes "need," truth, honor, integrity, and decency cease to matter. All that matters is the drug.

For years I had lied to my parents, my wife, my siblings, and my friends, and they all believed me because I was so convincing. They believed me because they had confidence in me, because they loved me, and because even in their wildest dreams they could not imagine that I was a drug addict. The lying was easy and the believing was a desperate grasp at hope.

"I'm having some personal problems," I said. "My marriage is bad. Real bad."

We talked about the possibility of marriage counseling for a few minutes.

"Is there anything else?" he asked. "Are you having any problems at the office?"

"No, everything's fine at the office," I said. "It's my marriage that's in trouble."

My father sat back in the booth and sighed deeply, his mind now at ease. "So," he said, "how do you think the Yankees will do in the playoffs this year?"

The next day, I drove into Harlem and asked my drug dealer if I could move in with him.

"Man, you're fucking crazy," he said, shaking his head. Like most successful drug dealers, he was happy to take my money and give me drugs but he didn't want me hanging around anywhere near him. At the same time, he didn't want to lose the steady business of a reliable customer, so he walked me up three flights of stairs and introduced me to Jeffrey.

"Let this guy in," he ordered the young black man who answered. The one-room apartment had a pullout bed, two chairs, a badly stained carpet, a walk-in kitchen filled with pizza boxes, and a sink stacked with dirty dishes. Jeffrey looked vaguely familiar—I'd probably seen him on the sidewalk outside the apartment building during my frequent drug runs. He didn't recognize me, though, and he looked spooked by the sudden appearance of a white guy wearing a Brooks Brothers blue blazer with a matching tie and carrying a leather briefcase. The briefcase was empty, but I carried it everywhere for insurance, figuring that any narcotics officers in the area would think I was a lawyer meeting a client, not a crack head looking for dope.

"Let's smoke," I said, handing Jeffrey a marble-sized rock of crack. That was my modus operandi—I disarmed junkies by proving I was one of them. It worked every time.

I stayed with Jeffrey for six days. It was blazing hot outside and Jeffrey had an air conditioner, a rare commodity in Harlem. The apartment was our cave, the place where we dreaded the dawn and avoided the day, looking forward with relief to the long shadows heralding the approaching night when we'd finally be able to venture onto the streets to restock the staples of our survival—malt liquor, Newport cigarettes, Bic lighters, and another eight-ball of crack cocaine. We never lingered out there because the crack epidemic was raging and cops and crack heads like us were playing a cat-and-mouse game. Thieves desperate for another hit stole from one another or robbed decent people trying to live in what had become an unlivable place. Prostitute junkies with no other assets except their worn-out bodies threw themselves at customers. Homeless mentally ill men and women lay on the sidewalks or hid themselves in the alcoves of buildings. Gangs of young thugs ruled the street corners. In that upside-down world, the streets were hell and the crack house was a haven.

I couldn't stop using, and I didn't even attempt to try. Desperation propelled me—not to avoid the inevitable, because I knew that I couldn't hang on much longer, but to try to avoid the pain as long as possible. Only when I took a hit of crack did I find a fleeting respite from the chaos. My life was compressed into the five or ten minutes of the high when the race to avoid the inevitable ended and, for a moment, time stood still. I felt like a man hanging from a crossbar after doing too many chin-ups. My muscles burned and my body ached, but smoking that last rock or swigging that final can of beer kept me hanging on, vainly trying to get high enough to get my chin over the bar.

Jeffrey and I played spades or backgammon between hits off the pipe. I don't remember anything about our conversations, except the time Jeffrey asked me if I had any family.

"Yeah," I said.

"You married?"

"Yeah," I said again.

He looked at me sideways for a minute. "Does your wife know you're here?" he asked me.

"She doesn't know I'm a junkie," I said. "She has no idea where I am."

"You have a wife and you left her alone? Man." Jeffrey didn't even try to hide the contempt in his voice. He lived alone. Nobody cared about him or wondered where he was, but I had a wife at home waiting for me, worrying about me. What the hell was I doing here with him?

"Man, you better go and call her," he said.

I finished my beer and walked down the three flights of stairs. It took a few minutes for my eyes to adjust to the early morning light. The corner newsstand was filled with people getting the *New York Post* or *Daily News*, and the deli down the street was overflowing with customers buying bagels and coffee. An old man swept the dirty sidewalk, making a neat pile of empty crack vials left over from the night before. Cabdrivers honked and gestured at people on the sidewalk, looking for a fare. A few people stared at me, then looked away. The city was waking up to another day. I hadn't slept or changed my clothes in six days.

There was a pay phone on the corner and after a few rings, Mary answered.

"It's me," I said. "I'm okay."

"Oh my God, Cope, where are you?" She was crying. "I've been worried sick, why didn't you call, what happened to you?"

"I'm okay," I repeated. My brain was fried. Simple sentences were all I could manage. "Don't worry. I'll be home."

Walking back to Jeffrey's place, I felt relieved. As irresponsible as I was, at least I had connected with Mary. At least she knew I was alive. A group of young children were playing in the street. Nearby a man with an aluminum cart and a multicolored umbrella was selling shaved ice with coconut, grape, or strawberry flavorings. I handed him ten bucks and bought all the kids a treat. They smiled and laughed and jumped up and down, and for a moment I felt good about myself in a way that I hadn't in a long time. I took one last look at them as they waited for their flavored ices and then I walked back up the steps and disappeared into the world of the crack den where I didn't need to feel or think about anything.

After I called Mary from the pay phone, she called my mother, who immediately contacted Bill Josephson, a lawyer and devoted friend whom Mom and Dad knew from the Peace Corps days. Bill, who had lost his arm due to a childhood illness, has contacts everywhere, and somehow, in just a few hours, he was able to contact all the police departments and hospitals in Manhattan and Brooklyn and confirm that I wasn't locked up in jail, lying in a morgue or unconscious in an intensive care unit.

Mom picked Bill up in Brooklyn—it was a Saturday morning on what would turn out to be a 104-degree day—and they drove to La-

Guardia Airport, searching through all the airport and motel parking lots for my Honda. They stopped at a service station on the parkway so that Mom could use the pay phone to call Mary. While Bill stood outside the car waiting, a young man pushed him aside and stole my mother's purse from the front seat of the car. A white-haired lady and a one-armed man distracted by fear and grief, driver and passenger doors wide open, a busy highway and no cops in sight—Mom and Bill Josephson were an easy target.

The phone company was able to trace the number to a four-block area in Harlem, and Mom and Bill drove around Harlem searching for the Honda. They found it on a side street, and Mom parked the station wagon right behind it, pulling up close enough to touch the bumper so I couldn't get out. Then they started looking for me. Mom searched the block where my car was parked and Bill ranged out farther. Every half hour or so they'd meet up. There were no bathrooms anywhere nearby, so Bill kept guard while Mom, dressed in a navy blue linen dress, relieved herself in an alley behind one of the apartment buildings.

Sometime that afternoon a woman emerged from one of the better-kept apartment buildings. She wore a dress and carried a shopping bag.

"I'm looking for my son," my mother said, ignoring the woman's efforts to step past her. "He's a really tall blond young man, and I have reason to believe he might be in this neighborhood. I'm really worried about him. Have you seen him?"

"Oh no, I haven't seen anyone like that," the woman said, hurrying away.

Mom was waiting when she returned with her groceries. "I'm still worried, I think he might be in this building, and if he doesn't come out soon, I'm going to call the police because he is sick, really sick." When the woman didn't respond, my mother repeated the threat. "I'm going to get the police."

High on crack, I was completely unaware of the scene that was unfolding outside. The frantic knocking on the door startled me; Jeffrey and I looked at each other, our eyes suddenly wide open, our hearts beating fast. We could hear people shouting at one another, arguing loudly. Jeffrey opened the door to see what was happening and a wide-eyed kid, sixteen or seventeen years old, came charging into the apartment, pointing his finger at me.

"There's an old white lady in a blue dress and a man with one arm in a fancy suit outside and they say they're looking for somebody like you," he said, his face twisted in anger and fear.

Jeffrey turned to look at me, his eyebrows raised. He didn't say anything, but I knew what he was thinking. Who the hell are you, anyway? What the hell are you doing bringing rich white people down here, messing things up?

I knew who it was—my mother and the only one-armed man I knew, Bill Josephson, our family's attorney. I couldn't run or hide, because they'd find me, and in the meantime I'd bring the heat down on Jeffrey and everyone else in the building.

"Stay here, don't move," I said. "I'll be back." Jeffrey sat down on the bed, paralyzed by fear. He was trapped in that room with no place to run, no place to hide. I could walk out the door, get in my car, go home, even go to treatment. I had options; he had nothing.

I walked down the stairs and stood on the front steps of the apartment building, struggling to force my eyes to adjust to the bright light of a fine summer day in Manhattan. I saw my mother and Bill standing on the corner, looking up at the building. Mom moved toward me at the same time I began to walk toward her. I sometimes wonder if her unconditional love for me and my need for that love were what brought us together that day, more than any relentless pursuit or methodical plan to find me.

We stood face-to-face on the sidewalk. "Son, I've been so worried about you, you're sick, please, let's go, come home with me," she pleaded, reaching for me but not threatening me in any way. Later she told me that my eyes were as yellow as a tiger's eyes, hostile, angry, and threatening. There wasn't one bit of blue left in them.

I didn't know how to respond. Even I knew that it would be insane to tell her not to worry.

"Mom, go home," I said, worried now that the standoff would create a scene and attract attention I couldn't control. As if I could control anything anymore. "I don't want to talk to you right now. I can't. Go away."

My mother has never been a quitter, especially when she knows what she wants—and she wanted me out of there, right now.

"You need to come home with me; you aren't well, we will get you help," she said, her voice firm. I didn't see any sympathy in her demeanor, nor did I hear any in her voice, and that confused and then angered me. Didn't she know I was a grown man who could make my own decisions?

"I'm okay, I'm with some friends. I'm having problems, but I'll be okay," I said, backing away from her. She followed me, and I stopped again to argue with her, but she was not going to debate me.

"You need to leave right now," she said, "and I'm taking you."

I appealed to Bill, who was standing a few steps behind my mother. I wanted to strike a bargain.

"Get her out of here," I told Bill. "I'll talk to you, but only if Mom goes away."

Did she back off or did I turn and walk away from her? Was she crying or were my eyes, dilated from cocaine, having difficulty with the bright sunlight? All I know for sure is that she stayed behind as Bill and I walked down the street and around the corner of 105th Street and sat on the stoop of a dilapidated brownstone.

"Cope, you're in trouble," Bill said.

"I know." I was scared and exhausted, but mostly I was angry. Furious. What was my mother doing chasing me down? What did she think she was doing here in Harlem? I ranted and raved. I told Bill how hard everything was, how my mother was always after me, never letting me alone, how my marriage was falling apart and I got no satisfaction out of Mary, how I'd blown my job at *Newsday* and once again disappointed my father. *Life is hard,* I kept repeating. *It's impossible. I can't do it anymore.* I didn't know what I was saying. I was trying to find something or someone else to blame, take the focus off me, get out of the spotlight, run, hide.

Bill just listened.

"Okay," he said, when I was done talking. "We have to deal with the facts. We need to get you out of here as soon as we can."

"I'll leave," I said. What else was I going to do? I didn't have any other contacts in Harlem. Jeffrey was my source, and now they knew where he lived.

We walked back around the block to the Honda and the station wagon snuggled up right behind it. Mom rolled down her window. "Son, you need to get in the car," she said. "Bill and I will drive you home."

"No, I'm not going to do that. I'll take care of myself. I have to go back in and tell my friends good-bye." I wasn't going to leave with my mother or Bill or anyone else. I'd do this under my own power, on my own terms. Even in those final desperate hours, when the inevitable end was obvious even to me, I was trying to hang on to some semblance of control. More than anything, I had to stave off the totality of my failure, the consummation of my shame.

"You have to promise me you're going home," my mother said.

"I promise."

Twenty minutes later I got in my car, feeling really annoyed that the station wagon was still parked behind me. My mother backed up so I could pull out, and she followed me for a few blocks until I lost her. I drove to Northport, smoking crack the whole way. A few blocks from home, I took one more hit. The pipe was clogged with cocaine and so hot I couldn't hold it any longer. I jammed it into a gardening glove and threw the glove in the trunk of the car.

When I walked into the house, Mary was talking on the phone in the kitchen. The lights were off, and the place was dead silent. Everything was so neat and tidy and it all symbolized the failure that had become my life. The neat rows of books on the shelves. The comfortable furniture and cozy easy chair that had been my favorite place to read books in that time so long ago when I used to read. The painting Mary gave me for a wedding present, a watercolor she had labored hours over, depicting the outdoor scenes that had been meaningful in our lives. The original *Harpers Weekly* illustration of the bombardment of Fort Sumter that started the Civil War. That was my wedding present to Mary, a symbol of my own victory because over and over again when we were dating I told her I'd bombard her into submission until she agreed to marry me. Dally, short for Dallas, who was always so excited to see me that it looked like her tail was going to fly right off. The spic-and-span kitchen with the little table against the wall where Mary and I often drank our coffee in the mornings while talking about a future that was over before it could ever begin.

This was my house, those were my things on the shelves and on the walls, that was my dog and my kitchen and my dreams, but they didn't belong to me anymore. I felt a sudden yearning for the crack house, an intense desire to run away. Mary looked at me, and walked down the hallway and up the stairs. I heard the bedroom door shut behind her.

In the kitchen she had left me a plate of food—cold lasagna, bread, salad, a carton of milk—and I gorged myself until I was sick. When I went to the bathroom, my urine had blood in it and my stool was as black as new tar on a roadway. I looked in the mirror for the first time in six days, and I didn't know who was staring back at me.

My skin was gray, my eyes no longer blue. I looked closer—all the color was washed out of them. My freckles had disappeared. Tiny burns, some calloused over, some new, covered my lips and chin.

I took a shower. The soap smelled good. I thought about shaving, but I needed both hands to hold on to the sink so I didn't collapse on the floor. Bracing myself against the wall, I walked down the hallway to the guest bedroom, crawled under the sheets, and instantly fell asleep.

The next morning I woke up to see the first light of dawn throwing shades of pink and rose and orange against the wall over the headboard. I heard a bird singing in the evergreen tree outside the window. It was going to be a beautiful day.

There was a flash, a fleeting instant of happiness, before I remembered.

7

Psych Ward

MARY DROVE WHILE I sat slumped over in the front seat of our Volvo station wagon. The ride from our home on Long Island to St. Vincent's Hospital in New York City took sixty minutes, but it was the longest hour of my life. My head ached and my gut felt twisted, but most of the pain wasn't physical. I wanted to cover myself in shame, to conceal my whole self, but how best to hide? I knew the answer to that question. A hit of crack would erase the emotional, deep nagging ache of my failures. A shot of whiskey or a can of cold beer would dull the agony of my helplessness. But those options were denied me, so I closed my eyes and tried to pray. *Help me, God. Help me get through this. Help me out of this mess. Help me find a way to ease the pain.*

I walked across Seventh Avenue to the front door of the hospital admitting office, following Mary, who was several steps ahead of me and moving fast, as if trying to hurry me into the hospital before I turned and ran away. It was a hot, sticky day, just like the day before—was it only yesterday?—when my mother and Bill Josephson found me at the crack house in Harlem. Ninety blocks and an entire world away.

I moved slowly but deliberately through the hospital's front door, pausing to hold it open for a man who was wrangling with a bouquet of colorful balloons that got stuck in the door frame. I looked back through the door at the world I was leaving, and for one fleeting moment, I felt paralyzed, unable to go back and terrified to move ahead. If only I could have one more hit off the pipe. Just one.

I waited in the reception area while the admissions counselor talked to Mary and filled out some forms.

A few minutes later I felt Mary's hand on my shoulder. "He wants to talk to you, Cope," she said.

I'm not sure I ever made eye contact with the man. He wanted to know my name, address, place and date of birth, insurance information, next of kin in case of an emergency.

I answered some questions with the truth and some with lies. I don't know why, maybe I was playing some sort of game with this stranger, holding something back so he didn't know every little detail of my life. I just felt so damned exposed. Maybe I was trying to protect Mary somehow. Or maybe I was so used to lying that I didn't know anymore what was real and what was fiction.

"William Cope," I said when he asked me my name. To this day I have no idea why I dropped my last name. Was that Mary's idea? Had we discussed it in the car before we arrived at the hospital, hoping that I could remain anonymous and avoid attracting attention with my famous last name? Or did I come up with that name at the last instant because I wanted to erase my life and start over again? It doesn't really matter because in that instant I took on a new identity, which I would spend the next several years building up and tearing down before I discovered who I really was.

"My address is 130 East Eighteenth Street," I said, watching him write the information on the paper attached to the clipboard. I hadn't lived at that address for seven years, but how would he know?

"Born May 27, 1959, Fort Worth Texas." That was the truth.

Insurance? "I don't have insurance," I lied. Whatever this was going to cost was coming out of my own pocket. I didn't want my insurance company to know that I was being admitted to the hospital after a six-day crack cocaine binge.

Emergency contact? "Call my wife in an emergency," I said. My secrets were safe with Mary.

"Why are you here, William?" It was just a standard hospital question and the standard answer should have been easy, something like "I have a 104-degree fever," or "I fell down the stairs and can't remember anything," or "I have chest pains." But I wasn't exactly sure why I was there and for some reason the question both irritated and amused me. What a ludicrous thing to ask, I thought. Why was I here? The events of that summer rushed at me in a kaleidoscope of images. Let's see—I've been holed up in a crack house in Harlem with an addict who let me hang out and smoke crack in his apartment in exchange for drugs. I abandoned my wife, my golden retriever, my house, my parents, my job, and all the responsibilities of everyday life without saying a word to anyone. I vanished and lived on crack for days on end. That was my fuel, it's what kept me going, hit after hit of crack, and when I was going up too fast or coming down too hard, I'd drink malt liquor to take the edge off, and when I was hungry I'd eat Twinkies or pizza, and when I was tired, I couldn't sleep, so I'd take another hit.

Why am I here? Because I'm sick, I need help, I'm not normal. Because something is wrong with me. Because I am rotten to the core.

"I have a long-term love affair with alcohol and cocaine," I said. It was a stark-naked answer because it was the truth, the only real truth I had spoken in a long time.

The man with the clipboard seemed startled and took a moment to collect himself as he shuffled through the paperwork. "That's not what your wife said. She thinks you have a 'short-term alcohol problem.' "

He stared into my eyes. Was he searching for a way to connect with me, or simply looking through me out into the hallway where Mary was waiting? "I think you'd better go out to the waiting room and tell her the truth," he said.

The truth. What would the truth do to the woman who loved a man whose entire life was a lie? Mary had no idea I used crack cocaine. She thought Jack was a nice guy, a little down on his luck, but a U.S. Marine for God's sake. She never doubted my stories about having to stay late at work to finish a story, and she never asked me why I had so much trouble sleeping or why my nose kept bleeding or why I couldn't get rid of my hacking cough. She thought I had a little drinking problem, a little too much white wine after those fifteen-hour days.

The waiting room was crowded and noisy, like a train station at rush hour. Doctors and nurses hurried by. A priest huddled with a family in a corner. Somewhere a baby cried. An old man in a wheelchair used one leg to pull himself down the hallway. I wondered what happened to his other leg. I felt like I was the only one in the room who was standing still. Then I saw Mary sitting off in the corner, and I walked slowly toward her.

The truth spilled out. I told Mary that the husband she had vowed to live with "till death do us part," the lifelong friend who knew her most intimate secrets, the companion who she believed in and supported and told a thousand times was worthy, the man she had trusted and loved with all her heart, was for almost the entire time she had known him a junkie and a drunk.

All these years later I can still see the look on her face—the blood vessels in her eyes, the way her lips twisted open and then closed, the sudden intake of breath and then the stillness, as if she had stopped breathing completely. A moment passed and then she stood up and walked away without a kiss or a hug or even a good-bye or good luck. Later on a hospital orderly told me that she nearly collapsed in the foyer and had to lean up against the wall to steady herself. Somebody helped her. She was crying, he said.

A nurse escorted me to the elevator and the fifth floor of the hospital. I don't remember anything about those first days on the psych ward, but my mother remembers virtually everything.

"When I came to visit that first day," Mom told me many years later, "I had no idea what I was going to find. On the phone you told me not to worry, you were fine, you weren't having the DTs or anything like that, but you needed water, lots of water, and salt. So I stopped at the corner store and bought several quarts of bottled water, peanuts, potato chips, and crackers. I had no idea you were on a locked ward. A psych ward! That almost did me in. I just couldn't believe it. They went through my purse and the grocery bag and wouldn't let me take any glass bottles into your room. Nobody said you were on suicide watch, but I could tell they were worried about you. You were in a room by yourself, which surprised me, and you were sitting in the corner in utter misery. You were in terrible shape."

My mother also gave me a three-subject Mead notebook. (Seventeen years later the $1.79 price tag is still attached to that notebook.) For days I stared at those blank pages, unable to form a coherent thought or hold a pen in my shaking hand, but on the fourth day I decided I'd had enough of the psych ward. I was sick and tired of lying in bed, attending meetings, and talking to the psychiatrist about my "issues." I felt fine physically, and mentally I was in far better shape than most of the other patients. They had misdiagnosed me, I was ready to leave, and there was no doubt in my mind that I knew more than all the counselors, the doctors, the nurses, and the social workers combined.

I drafted a letter signifying my intent to transfer out of St. Vincent's as soon as possible.

To Whom It May Concern:

My treatment at St. Vincent's Hospital has given me the opportunity to get back on my feet and on the road to recovery.

However, I believe it is necessary for me to transfer to another rehabilitation program to continue my recovery. I request such a transfer as soon as possible.

I have no regrets about my stay at St. Vincent's and only wish differences of opinion with members of the staff had not gotten in the way.

William Cope Moyers

I don't remember what the "differences of opinion" with the staff were, but I can clearly recall how I felt those first few days when I walked into the smoke-filled common room. An old woman sat on a wooden chair in the corner staring at the shadows on the wall, humming to herself in her own world somewhere far away. A group of five or six African American women, all in their teens or twenties, sat in a circle braiding one another's hair with the intensity and focus of a surgical team in the operating room. Two men standing by the far wall peppered each other in rapid-fire Spanish that I couldn't even pretend to understand. An attractive young woman with coffee-colored skin walked around the room, offering to sleep with anyone who would help her escape from the psych ward. An old man—or did he just look old?—occupied a worn leather couch. Everybody seemed to avoid him. He had an IV in his arm and in between drags on his Camels, he'd cough up phlegm. Somebody told me his name was Willy and he was dying of AIDS.

Flotsam and jetsam, that's what they seemed to me, the survivors of a sunken ship who had washed up on a deserted island with nothing in common but their sad and seemingly endless stories of the cruel storm that left them stranded. My story, I told myself, was different. I wasn't poor and toothless. I wasn't uneducated and unemployed. I had a college degree and an impressive résumé, although I guessed that most of the people in that room had never seen a résumé. I wasn't homeless, trapped in the inner city, doomed to stay there my whole life—I owned a two-story house in a secluded neighborhood with a wooded backyard on Long Island. A dozen European countries were stamped in my passport. Once upon a time I drank Cuban rum and smoked Cuban cigars with Cuban dictator Fidel Castro. CBS news correspondent Dan Rather was a close family friend. President Lyndon Baines Johnson ate dinner with my family, and afterward, while the grown-ups talked, I played hide-and-seek with the Secret Service agents. When I was in college, my family vacationed in Jamaica and I introduced myself to Paul McCartney and his wife Linda. One day we were having a drink at the open-air bar and I asked Paul if it was hard to write so many songs. "No," he said, "it's easy," and in two minutes he wrote a song on a paper napkin and gave it to me.

Grandiosity, it's called. In those first few days on the psych ward I held on to the only defense I had, which was convincing myself that I was better than—in this case, not as sick as—the other patients. They might be there for the same reason, but my situation wasn't nearly as serious as theirs. My problem was too much drugs and alcohol were messing up what was otherwise a good life, while their problem was their entire lives. I didn't want to believe that I was looking in the mirror when I looked at them.

In my first group therapy session I listened to the other patients introduce themselves.

"I'm Stacia, I'm an addict."

"My name is Luis, I got a drinking problem."

"Stephen, alcoholic."

"Debbie, a drunk and an addict."

"I'm Willy, and I'm a junkie."

Around the circle we went, and then it was my turn.

"My name is William. I think I'm probably an addict, an alcoholic, too."

"Think I'm probably." I wasn't willing to jump in there with the rest of them. I'd take part in the group, talk when it was my turn, but I wasn't really like these other people. I was different; their problems were much deeper than mine. My problem was just drugs. I couldn't control how much beer I drank or how much crack I smoked, at least I couldn't control it all the time. And when I got out of control, I did stupid, irrational, insane things. But I wasn't down on my luck like the rest of the group. My problems were nothing compared to theirs. Stacia was homeless, Willy had AIDS, Debbie was a prostitute, Stephen was unemployed. I didn't see a whole lot of hope for any of them, to tell the truth. But me? I just had a problem with drugs. Once I got that under control, I had a good life waiting for me.

Of course the psych ward was the great equalizer, the common denominator beyond the color of our skin or where we came from or whether we had a bank account or owned a car or liked sushi for lunch or believed in God. But I couldn't see it that way. Already I yearned for that veneer of superiority and self-importance that would put me at the front of the pack. I kept telling myself that all I had to do was be me and, almost by default, I'd become the leader of the group, who I really didn't see as equals anyway. What could they teach me that I didn't know already?

I hated being locked up in that place. The fluorescent lights were on all day and all night, the patients argued nonstop with one another or with the staff, nurses made the rounds in the middle of the day and night, the cold hot dogs, rubbery chicken, and tepid milk were all but inedible, I was ordered to attend group meetings where griping and criticism topped the agenda every single time, and our daily exercise routine consisted of a fifteen-minute walk around the perimeter of the hospital roof, around and around and around, looking at the surrounding buildings through the chain-link cage topped with razor wire.

Most of the patients stood in one place, smoking cigarettes, and watching the pigeons.

Even on the roof you couldn't get away from the cigarette smoke but at least you could breathe some fresh air for a few minutes. The smoke on the psych ward drove me crazy, hanging over everything like a solid layer of fog, settling into the fibers of my blue jeans and T-shirts. Smoking was allowed in the community room, and everyone, it seemed, was a chain smoker. My room was at the very end of the hall, as far away from the community room as you could get, but even the sheets on my bed smelled like smoke.

I smoked, too—I wasn't going to turn down the chance to get legally buzzed—but that didn't stop me from complaining. I felt closed in, choked up, suffocated, and there was nothing I could do to alleviate my misery. Helpless to change anything that was happening inside me, I focused my anger on the smoke (even as I smoked), the bad food (even as I ate everything on my plate), and the noise (even as I contributed to it). Not once did it occur to me that just a week or two earlier I could have cared less about an "unhealthy atmosphere" of smoke, bad food, noise, or keeping company with social outcasts. St. Vincent's was The Ritz compared to the Harlem crack house.

Other than my daily walks on the roof, the only way to escape the noise and the smoke was to retreat to my room and stare out the window, trying to ignore the black iron bars that kept people from escaping or jumping from the fifth story to their death. I'd pull the chair up to the window and stare out of my portal into a world that had changed in ways I did not and could not understand until I returned to it. Out there was freedom. My life. The future. My past was out there, too, because once I got out, all I had to do was catch a cab to Jeffrey's apartment in Harlem, ninety blocks away. A few days after I arrived at St. Vincent's, I actually called Jeffrey from the pay phone in the community room.

"Sorry I disappeared, man," I said, or something like that, "but

I'm locked up in a psych ward downtown. I'll see you in a couple of weeks when I get out."

I must have scared the shit out of him.

Day after day I sat in my room, stared out the window, and dreamed about what could have been and what might still be. One day I picked up the pen and started writing in my journal.

SUNDAY AUGUST 13

One week has passed since I crawled into this prison, one week filled with despair, frustration, anger, fear, uncertainty and a sense of having failed everyone I know, including myself. It wasn't easy coming here. It was even tougher admitting that my disease was drug addiction.

But a week later, I am still intact and alive. I am sober, and that is good. Physically my body is healing. I feel good.

My psyche is what hurts. For a week I've dwelled in the immediate realization that I'm an addict. That hasn't been easy, yet somehow I've come to accept that as fact. What I have barely considered to date is the fallout from this realization, and the damage I've wrecked on my family, my friends and coworkers and, most of all, my wife. In their eyes, I am no longer C. M. (Cope Moyers) the journalist, C. M. the jogger, C. M. the war buff, or C. M. the man who doesn't know what he wants to do. Forever, and through no fault of theirs, I'll be most easily identified by the black flag that is my illness. Even if I succeed in beating my addiction, I'll be known as the man who was victorious over drugs. Kind of a dubious distinction, huh?

One week out of the rest of my life has passed. That is terribly scary. It's not like a broken arm that needs healing. I almost wish I had cancer. Then I'd either beat it or die from it. But my disease, even if successfully treated, will never go away. And it might not kill me. But it will hang over me like the blade of a guillotine, more threatening inert than if the blade suddenly slips and mercifully turns out my lights. This is my war to end all wars.

Once I started writing, I couldn't stop, and the pages filled up with thoughts, emotions, ideas, and concepts that were new and unfamiliar to me. *I'm an addict,* I wrote. Did I really believe that? Had I willingly accepted my new identity as William the alcoholic and crack cocaine addict, finally shedding the illusion that I could "cope" with life? I thought I had come to the psych ward to interrupt the insanity of the crack house, but now everyone was telling me I had a disease that was permanent, progressive, and deadly if I didn't get my act together. A disease, in other words, that would never go away, a label that would define me for the rest of my life. I nodded my head, pretending to understand what words like "unmanageable" and "powerless" and "denial" meant, but all the while wondering how and when and where I was going to grab this disease by the throat and beat the living hell out of it.

This disease would kill me if I wasn't careful, but no matter how vigilant I was, it was incurable—I'd never get rid of it, it would always be with me, the label would always define me. Addict. Alcoholic. If those words defined me, then I deserved to be in this place because I was a weak-willed pathetic thirty-year-old man who couldn't control his own behavior (and whose parents would probably have to pay a significant portion of the hospital bill). I had every right to feel bad about myself. I deserved to be locked up because I lacked the willpower to stop doing something that was destroying my mind and my body and the lives of my wife, my parents, my sister, my brother, and everyone else who loved me. What I had done was crazy, impossible to understand or explain, no matter what the counselors said about addiction as a disease that I didn't cause and couldn't cure. What was wrong with me?

If only I had allowed those questions to take me deeper into my self, but as soon as I asked them, I shied away from looking inside. It was too awful, I was too worthless, I had failed once again. I couldn't face the truth of myself, so I hid from my shame and focused instead on my guilt. I had done something terribly wrong and I needed to make it right. If I accepted responsibility for my behavior didn't that somehow absolve me and free me to get on with the business of fixing what I had broken? If I mended my ways and worked hard to become a better person, couldn't I lick this problem once and for all? My guilt was intense, monstrous, and it fed my addiction in ways that I did not and could not understand. By focusing on my guilt—what I had done—I could avoid taking a good hard look at my shame—what I was. What I had done was unforgivable but—and here were the seeds of my downfall—I truly believed I could make up for everything by proving that I was stronger and more resilient now that I knew exactly what I was facing.

Do you see? I wasn't taking this disease into myself, absorbing it into my pores, accepting it as part of me—instead I was using guilt to fire up the cannons of my defense. Yes, absolutely, I acted selfishly with no thought for others—but now that I knew what I was facing, I could rise above it and move beyond it. I could exercise control, regain power over my decisions and choices, apologize sincerely to the people who had been hurt by my actions, make things right again, and put all of this behind me.

"To let it go, let it out." That's what my psychiatrist said, hoping to prepare me for the face-to-face encounter with Mary and my parents. "Tell your drug story from beginning to end, and don't leave anything out."

Okay, I thought, taking a deep breath. *I'm in control here. Nobody knows these facts like I do. And when it comes to drugs, nobody in my family can even begin to compete.* Those thoughts comforted me when I walked into Dr. Fabian's windowless office cluttered with books and paperwork and took my seat in the small imperfect circle formed by my father, who sat opposite me, my mother on my right, and Mary seated on my left. Dr. Fabian sat behind his desk, just outside the circle, pen in hand; every few minutes he'd scribble something on a yellow legal-sized pad of paper.

I started at the beginning, like I'd been instructed, and told them almost everything, leaving out only a few details that I would guard for the rest of my life. I talked about smoking marijuana in Aspen when I was fifteen and getting stoned in the garage on weekends after taking my high school girlfriend home from our dates. There were the stories about binge drinking in college and the first LSD trips in the spring of 1980 followed by dropping more acid during my trip to Europe the following summer. The car wreck my senior year in college when I was too drunk and stoned on quaaludes to follow the winding country road (and then blamed the accident on an imaginary farmer driving his imaginary tractor into my path in the middle of the night). The cocaine-fueled journalism career in Dallas and the insanity of walking into the police station and the district attorney's office under the influence. The hundreds of dollars I pinched from my mother's handbag and my father's dresser, the thousands of lies, the journeys into Harlem with Jack, and the trips back home, speeding at eighty miles per hour along the Long Island Expressway focused on lighting the crack pipe, not the traffic.

I told them just about everything, and it felt good to admit the truth and even, I had to admit to myself, to wear all those experiences as a perverse badge of honor. What I did was worse, I told them, than they could ever imagine.

How long did it take? Ten minutes? Half an hour? Two hours? I have no idea, but at the end, exhausted, I listened to the silence, the shifting and creaking of chairs, and the Kleenex being pulled out of the box. Mary was crying uncontrollably. My father looked bewildered. I was surprised to see tears in the corners of his eyes, but I was immediately suspicious that they were less about the story of my downhill slide and more about his failure to see it coming or to stop it from happening. Even my mother couldn't hide her pain. I saw it in the lines in her forehead, the way she pursed her lips, and the sudden twitches in her cheeks even as she immediately jumped to my rescue, just as she had done hundreds of times before.

"You are a good man, a fine human being," she said. "You have always been considerate and loving, even in the last few years when you were struggling with drugs. You've always been such a joy to us, son."

That was my mother, the eternal optimist, always striving to take care of me and make me feel better. But I didn't want or need her to defend me this time. I had dedicated my life to the god of cocaine and in the process used and abused everyone I had ever loved. After years of lying and deceit, I had spoken the truth, and I felt purged. That night I fell into a deep, dreamless sleep, and when I woke up the next morning that feeling of being washed clean was still with me. I walked into group therapy and in that circle of people who had been strangers just a few days before I felt an intimacy that had been missing my whole life. I did belong here. I was one of them.

"I'm William," I said, "and I'm an addict and an alcoholic."

William, addict and alcoholic. Not Cope, not Moyers—not resilient or perfect—but just plain old William, a thirty-year-old man with a new name and a new identity discovered in the harsh and unforgiving reality of addiction. It was all strangely comforting. That night I sat in my chair by the window and wrote about how good it felt to accept the truth.

It is a wonderful and somewhat scary feeling because I haven't felt this way in a long time. Already I'm starting to speculate on how my new identity (i.e., C. M. without drugs) will assist me on the outside. Is it possible a "clean me" will soar, take a renewed interest in old passions and discover a life that was shrouded in addiction? The potential is awesome!

I stared out the window for a while, thinking about all the possibilities, and then I listed the things I needed to do in the near future:

Heal—my body must live and grow without drugs
Choose another rehab vs. outpatient treatment
Find a job I do well and feel comfortable with
Renew my ties with my family
Decide who I love
Find my friends
Find my religion
Write all the time

I could fix this mess, I thought, looking at that list—there was still so much to look forward to! Locked up in a psych ward, separated from the people I loved, removed from the drugs I thought I needed to function, I was suddenly hopeful about my future. I was stronger than I thought, I told myself, more resilient than I imagined I could ever be. Everything was going to work out. I had faith.

One evening, after dinner, Mary came to visit. She sat in the chair in my room while I lay on the hospital bed, my hands propped behind my head. We both looked out the window while she did most of the talking. The light faded and the room grew dark. I could barely see her face, but neither of us wanted to turn on a light.

At one point she said she felt dishonored and violated by me. I didn't say anything because I wasn't exactly sure what she was talking about. Did she mean that she felt emotionally violated? Had I dishonored her, shamed her by my actions? Did she find me repulsive? Was she disgusted by the sight of me? I suddenly deeply regretted my confessions a few days earlier. Why did I tell the whole truth if the facts condemned me as a despicable human being? Why didn't I lie and deceive, if only to protect my relationship with the woman I loved?

"You're not the person I thought you were," I remember her saying. I had a "whole other life" that she didn't know about and if I had fooled her once, I could fool her again. How could she ever trust me after this? The person she loved the most had deceived her the most. She had invested so much in our life together, and now it was all lost, gone forever.

Mary began to sob. I stared out the window as I listened to her describe how she felt cheated and used by me. Her tone was bitter. All she ever wanted was to be close to me, to laugh and cry together, watch movies, ride horses, walk on the beach, watch the sunsets. But I was never home, I always had an excuse to be somewhere else, living with me was like living with a missing person. I lied to her and deceived her and because she had believed in me and been fooled by me, she felt scared and vulnerable. Her world no longer felt safe.

I sat there, numb, not knowing what I was supposed to feel or think or say. I had poisoned myself with crack cocaine, I realized that now, but apparently I had sickened her, too. We would both live through this, but the more she talked, the more I realized that whatever we had between us was dying, maybe even had died. Self-pity washed over me. In that moment and in so many moments, days, weeks, and years of my life, I couldn't see beyond my own problems. I couldn't understand the pain I was causing Mary or anyone else who loved me because all I knew was what I felt and all I felt was my own agony. As I was to learn many years later, what I was feeling was a classic symptom of addiction—an overwhelming sense that I had been unfairly wronged and that my problems were everyone else's fault.

Wallowing in my resentment and anger, I began to wonder if things had ever been right between us. Maybe the love between us was gone; the sense of unity that joined us together had been broken by my addictions. Maybe I should just accept the fact that nothing I could say or do would change the past or alter Mary's opinion of me. For now I was one of "them," one of those nameless faceless addicts who lack morals and willpower and who can't ever be trusted.

After Mary left I continued to stare out the window at the dark buildings and the lights turning on all over the city. People lived in those lighted rooms, watching television with their families, or playing cards, or talking on the phone, laughing, sharing the news about the day, getting ready for bed, making love. Had Mary and I ever lived a "normal" life, like the kind I imagined took place behind the window blinds? When we were dating after college, I was an alcoholic pothead. When we were engaged and living in New York City, I started adding cocaine to the mix. When we were married and moved to Texas, I was driving myself crazy trying to match my father's success and using drugs to take the edge off the insanity. When we moved to Long Island, I spent long days at work, lying to Mary about the evenings I spent in the bars, snorting (and later smoking) cocaine when I took Dallas for a walk in the evenings, pretending all the while to listen and care about Mary's life but having no emotional connection to her at all. I spent more time tossing a ball for my dog than I did talking to my wife.

Lights were going out as people went to bed, but still I sat at the window. Had I ever really loved her? The question haunted me. I must have loved her. I fell in love with her for the first time in seventh grade. I secretly loved her all through high school, even though we were both with other people. We didn't see each other for almost two years after graduation, not until she had a car accident in college and I brought her flowers. A year later, after my arrest at the fish market, she stopped by to tell me she would always believe in me. Another year passed before we ran into each other again, almost as if we were meant to be together. Isn't that how it works? Wasn't she the love of my life?

She must be—I married her. But was I really capable of loving anyone else? If I doubted my love for Mary, how could I believe that I was capable of committing myself to any relationship? Had drugs turned me so inside out that nothing mattered to me but getting high? Any emotion I felt could not compare to the rapture of lighting the match, putting it to the pipe, taking in the smoke, lifting off, floating, soaring, being taken over for a moment that seemed to last for an eternity. Had my love for crack cocaine come to surpass and subsequently replace any love I could ever feel for a human being?

I didn't know the answers to these questions, but just thinking about crack made me feel dizzy, lightheaded. I didn't feel that way when I thought about Mary—my heart didn't speed up, my jaw didn't tense, my hands didn't clench and unclench when I imagined being with her. I didn't want her, need her, yearn for her like I wanted, needed, and yearned for crack. Nothing Mary could do or say would ever give me the pleasure I got from cocaine.

That night I faced my addiction and, for a brief moment, realized the truth—cocaine owned me, body and soul. I had lived my entire adult life under the influence of mood and mind-altering substances. It wasn't that I was high on drugs every minute of every day—I was sometimes clean for several days at a time—but my obsession with drugs altered my perspective and my feelings about everything else, including my love for Mary, my relationship with my parents and siblings, my job, my soul, even my God. I hadn't just become addicted— addiction had become *me,* and everything about me was about living a way of life that wasn't real. Fact was fiction, and fiction was my whole life. Even today, looking back from a vantage point of seventeen years, there is still so much about my past that I can't cleanly separate into piles of real or imagined, because lies and untruths were so deeply woven into the fabric of my everyday life. I wish I could keep what's good and true and throw away all the lies and deceit, but the lies ate their way through the truth as acid eats through enamel, leaving only damage behind.

The next day I called Mary on the pay phone in the common

room, praying that she would feel better about our relationship after getting some rest. I just needed to give her time, I reminded myself; we both needed time to heal.

"I don't want you back in the house," Mary said. Her voice was cold. "I had the locks changed."

"Why would you do that?" I asked, trying to remain calm.

"I don't want your drug dealers to come here," she said. "Maybe they know I'm alone now. It just doesn't feel safe."

"I understand why you might be scared, Mary, and I don't blame you," I said, desperately searching for a way to reach her, "but I didn't know many drug dealers and the ones I knew don't know my name or where I live."

"What about Jack? Wasn't Jack a drug dealer? He ate dinner with us, Cope. He knows where we live."

"Jack is an addict but he's not a drug dealer," I lied. Then I told the truth. "And besides, I haven't seen or heard from Jack in months."

"I just don't feel safe," she repeated. "I've made up my mind. I'll let you know when and if you can come home."

I hung up the phone and leaned against the wall. My wife had locked me out of my own house. What could I do? Where could I turn? Should I pray? I hadn't exactly given up on God, but I was pretty sure He couldn't help me out of this mess. I liked the way John Lennon put it—*God is just a concept by which we measure our pain.* And, like Lennon, I didn't believe in magic or Jesus or the Bible—I believed in me. What could God do for me? That's what I wanted to know. I had no answer to those questions, except to get angry. How dare Mary cast me as the villain? I was sick but I was getting better and from now on our lives would get better, too. I wouldn't allow any drugs in the house or drug dealers hanging around, and there would be no more late nights or unexplained absences. It would work out, everything would be all right. I desperately wanted her to believe that in order to believe it myself.

Only much later would I grasp the depth of Mary's despair and fear. The person she thought she had married was not what he turned out to be. Now that she had been exposed to the truth of my life as a crack addict, I became a demon dressed in a Halloween costume designed to make me look like a loving, honest, good man. The horror was too much for her to bear. All she could do was change the locks to try to keep me and the evil I personified from ever again violating her world.

Back in my room I picked up my journal and started writing.

AUGUST 16, 9:13 P.M.
I am despairing tonight, feeling like a rowboat in the middle of a gale with land in sight but powerless to get to shore. I'm alone in N.Y. I'm thirty years old (a man), and I'm confined to a psychiatric room with a damn payphone my only outlet to the real world. Mary seems to be more vengeful, angry is a better word, I guess, and less sorrowful and sympathetic. Tonight she told me she doesn't want me back in the house until further notice. And she's had the locks changed, she claims, because she fears nonexistent drug dealers. I don't blame her, but it's doubly frustrating since there's nothing I can do to affect the situation.

Now I cannot even pretend anymore that the past is over and things are getting better—with Mary, my parents, life on the outside, inside of myself even. I try to pretend that I'm on top of my recovery. My body is healthy and, more amazingly, my brain is showing marked signs of a rebirth. My short-term memory and ability to reason are much improved, something I am quite proud of.

What I am is what I am. A prisoner sentenced to a different kind of life because of this disease. I have utterly failed as a man, at least when it comes to women.

Strangely, I'm not as sad as I thought I'd be. Sure the rest of the patients have been so concerned about my new-found depression that one was assigned to discuss it with me. But I haven't cried and really don't feel sorry for myself. Why should I? Nothing would change because I can't do anything right now. And that acceptance is reason for optimism because I'm more aware of my emotions. I'm free from society's poisons.

Call me a bullshitter. Call me in denial. Call me the eternal optimist, the depressed patient, the resentful husband, or the good son—the fact is, I was all those things, and I was all those things because I was suddenly feeling emotions that I hadn't felt with any sort of purity for my entire adult life. They were all pouring out of me, a thick sludge of emotional gunk. I didn't know what I was feeling because I was feeling everything, and I couldn't separate the guilt from the shame, the grief from the fear, or the anger from the despair. I knew one thing, though—I was desperate to ease the pain. I had been taking drugs for years to avoid my feelings, but now I was in the psych ward, almost two weeks sober, and I was feeling what any human being would feel in such a situation. My life was broken into bits and pieces, and I couldn't handle that reality. How could I handle it? For a decade I'd been taking drugs to handle life. How do you do this thing called life? How do you do this thing called feelings? I didn't have a clue. If I knew how to do life or how to do feelings, I wouldn't have started taking drugs in the first place.

That's when I began to withdraw from everyone and everything at St. Vincent's. I refused to talk in the AA meetings. I told everyone I needed time to "think," and I'd silently brood in the corner of the common room, feeling sorry for myself, or I'd retreat to my room and stare out the window as dusk turned to dark, wanting to jump out that window and run down the street, fix everything in my life that was broken, make everything good again. I thought about getting high. I dreamed about getting high. I no longer felt safe in the psych ward because I couldn't control what was happening. But I stuffed those feelings. I told myself I wasn't sad. I didn't feel sorry for myself. What good would that do? Nothing would change. I told myself I had to accept what was happening and go forward. It's better that things are over with Mary, I told myself, because I can't worry about what other people are feeling, I have to concentrate on myself. If other people don't like what I'm doing, fuck 'em. I have this illness, it's mine, nobody else has it, nobody else can really understand. So fuck 'em all. Yeah, it hurts. Yeah, I'm frustrated. But that's life, after all. My life.

ONE DAY I WAS leafing through magazines as part of my occupational therapy group. I picked up an old *Newsweek* magazine, its cover torn and coming loose from the staples, and began to leaf through the pages searching for photos or graphics that I could paste on a piece of poster paper titled HOW ARE YOU FEELING TODAY?

I turned the page and there was a picture of my father smiling out at me. I stared at it, horrified—here he was again, reminding me what a mess I had made of my life. Even in a psych ward I couldn't escape his success. I looked around at the piles of magazines and wondered how many times my father's name or picture appeared in them. I watched Willy pour Elmer's glue on the back of a page ripped out of a *National Geographic* magazine and thought about the AA meeting where he'd told us his story of IV drug use, ending with the promise that he was going to defeat his addiction before he died of AIDS. After hearing his story, I wrote in my journal about how lucky I was, because unlike Willy, I was young, smart, talented, filled with dreams, surrounded by love, physically healthy, getting better every day. I wouldn't allow myself to see how alike we really were.

Yet there I was, thirty years old, a self-proclaimed drug addict, who was locked up in a psych ward, cutting pictures out of a magazine like I was in kindergarten again. And there I was, ten, fifteen, even twenty years ago, promising myself that by the time I was thirty, I, too, would be on the cover of a national magazine. I, too, would make a ton of money and people would treat me with respect, talk about how much I had done to make the world a better place, call me a hero, and give me standing ovations. I'd be just as famous as—if not more famous than—my father. Time went by, the years passed, and I became more frantic as my dreams seemed to slip ever further away. The ticking clock in my head told me that I'd better get moving, that time was running out. I drank to ease the pain of failure. I used cocaine to keep moving toward the finish line. Drugs fueled my passion and grandiosity, and then they stopped working and the only way I could keep going, keep dreaming, was to use more and more and more until I had to drop out of the race altogether.

Thirty years old, two months past my self-imposed deadline, I sat with scissors in my hand looking at my father's picture, a smiling head shot of success that threatened to reach out and grab me by the throat. I wanted to take the scissors and cut off his head, but I controlled myself. It was all about control, wasn't it? I carefully cut around the edges of the photograph and stuck my father's head on the poster.

It's funny, in a human kind of way, how we can convince ourselves that we're in control at the very point when we are beginning to lose it. My resentments were seething inside, a potent stew of shame and fury, yet on the surface there was barely a ripple. I was only dimly aware of these deeper feelings, for I had finished the assignment and I was feeling very proud of myself for facing the "issue" in such a calm, clear-headed way. That night I wrote in my journal:

> I didn't suffer a deflation of confidence and I didn't roll my eyes and tense my jaw or stomach in frustration. Instead, I concentrated on my own strengths as a person and went on with the day's assignment.

I love my dad. I respect him and his work. He makes me proud to be his son. But if I am to overcome my disease, I must, along with other things, revel in my own abilities and stop comparing myself to him. We are totally different men.

Around that same time, I wrote my father a letter.

"If you're going to stay sober, you have to come to terms with your inner conflicts with your father," the staff psychiatrist at St. Vincent's kept telling me. He encouraged me to write down my thoughts and feelings about my relationship with my father so I could better understand them.

I started the letter.

Dear Dad:

I love you. Not just as a son loves his father but as a man loves another man he has grown up with and comes to respect.

Frustrated, I put down the pen. The truth was strong and so were my feelings, yet I could not attach the right words to them. I scratched out what I'd written and started over again.

Dear Dad:

At age thirty you were on the cover of major magazines, a highly respected member of government, and a man whose ideals were never compromised by the temptations of your achievements.

At age thirty you were the father of three small children. As the oldest, I was vaguely aware that you were not just any old father. Famous people came to the house for dinner. We got to fly around the country on fancy air force jets. Everywhere you took the family, people gawked and sometimes pointed. It was a lot of fun.

Although I was a bit young to appreciate all the attention, my memories of you as my father are concrete. You were always there to celebrate my birthdays. Rarely did you miss the Little League games, even when I didn't play. Amidst the whirlwind of your job, you never failed to listen when I spoke or talk when I needed your advice. You weren't afraid to hug me. And when I deserved a spanking, you were careful that the bark was meaner than the bite. Sometimes I thought it hurt you more than me.

At age thirty you were a perfect father, at least in the eyes of a son who looked up to you and loved his father. When I grew up, I vowed, I was going to be just like you.

Well, here I am. Thirty years old and chemically dependent. A cocaine addict and alcoholic who is trying to get better, one day at a time. A man who, until he sought treatment, considered himself a failure to himself, his wife, and you.

I didn't plan it this way. In fact, I tried to imitate your success. For the last ten years I pushed and punished myself in the quest. I was good, but not good enough for me. I got promotions and substantial raises, but I wasn't satisfied. As I raced closer to the imaginary finish line on my thirtieth birthday, I began spinning my wheels, no longer moving forward but sitting in place and burning out. I couldn't accept that I wouldn't be just like you at thirty. Shame and guilt grew. My self-esteem disappeared. Cocaine and beer tempered these emotions. I began feeling shame. I had no self-esteem. I wasn't like you. I didn't feel worthy of your love. I turned to the only help I thought there was—beer and cocaine.

What has happened to me isn't your or anyone's fault. But as my mind clears and I grow stronger emotionally and physically, I've now realized that your desire for me to do better than I could was a demand I couldn't attain. You were never pleased with C's and the occasional B's in school. You urged me to play an instrument, join the Boy Scouts and work at certain summer jobs. What father wouldn't want his son to be the best he could be? But those were things I didn't excel in, and thus did only to please you, not me. Later in life I strove to achieve what was impossible for me. I tried to be just like you.

Right now I know my failures must be easy for you and those that love me to spot. My marriage is in shambles. I don't want to go back to the career I've spent the past eight years building. I'm vulnerable to relapse. I've spent thousands of dollars on drugs and thousands more on getting better. Most of all, I've sown a lot of pain among friends and family.

But I still want you to see the great possibilities that have emerged. I am alive and in treatment; I could be dead or still out on the street using. For the first time I know who I am. I'm trying no longer to be what I can't. I'm not ashamed to cry. And it's easier to laugh. I've come to realize my disease, and me, are to blame. At last I'm beginning to have pride in myself and my accomplishments.

Finally, I pray you'll accept me for who I am and what I am, a recovering alcoholic and addict. Don't judge your ability as a father on what I've done, but on what I'll be.

Love,

William Cope

I read the letter several times. It was filled with scratched-out words and edited sentences, but I was happy with it. It felt good to get everything out. In my journal I wrote, "I may even share it with him someday."

I never did.

ON A GLORIOUS August day I walked out the front door of St. Vincent's, my day pass in the back pocket of my jeans. For the first time in seventeen days I was free to walk the streets of New York City, and for the first time in years I walked those streets drug-free, taking in the sounds and the sights as a sober man. The staff at St. Vincent's trusted me to go out into the world and then return to the locked ward; empowered by that trust, knowing that I would meet my obligations and return to the hospital at the appointed time, I felt a sense of liberation that I had never known before. Walking down the streets of Manhattan that afternoon, feeling the sun on my skin and sensing a whisper of fall in the air, I felt a new kind of euphoria, a calmer, steadier sense of joy in the sights and sounds of the real world. I walked fast, feeling the muscles in my legs stretching to their limits, noting the sweat on my brow, listening to the horns honking and the wail of the ambulance sirens, watching the pigeons fight the starlings for scraps from an overflowing garbage pail.

I met my parents for lunch at a neighborhood bistro. We talked about everything and nothing and I felt like I was a normal man again, a good son, a flawed but fine human being. My parents seemed happy and relieved, and after lunch we strolled along Madison Avenue in no hurry for the afternoon to end. It was the strangest feeling in the world—I wasn't hiding and they weren't searching for me anymore.

At the corner of Madison Avenue I hugged my parents, thanked them for lunch, and walked down East Twenty-ninth Street to The Little Church Around the Corner. It was 2:50 p.m. and the AA meeting was scheduled to start at three p.m. I stood outside the gate for a few minutes, looking at the flowers in the English garden in front of the chapel, and stretching my neck to look up at the Empire State

Building five blocks away. I looked at my watch—ten minutes to spare. Ten minutes. I couldn't waste a minute of this rare afternoon—what could I do with those ten minutes? Should I walk around the block a few times? It was such a beautiful day, and I was free. I could get to Harlem in ten minutes if I took a cab.

"For the first time, you alone are in control of your life." I heard my father's voice inside my head. Those were the words he said at the bistro when we were eating our thick deli sandwiches. Standing by the church gate, I realized that I really was in control of my destiny. No one else was pulling the strings. It was up to me whether I walked through that gate or kept on going up the block, destination unknown.

I walked into the church, found the meeting room, sat down, and waited patiently while others walked in for the meeting. I took control. Dad was right—only I could control my life, and I had just proved to myself that I could make the right choices and be trusted on the outside. I can make it, I thought, if I just put my mind to it. All I have to do is put my mind to it.

In my final days at St. Vincent's, I kept thinking about that word *control.* Maybe I was an addict, but that didn't mean I was powerless. I didn't have to let this disease control my life. "This is my war to end all wars," I wrote in my journal just one week after I arrived at St. Vincent's. Two weeks later, full of confidence, I was prepared to fight this disease with all my strength and courage and win.

I had no idea, not even a clue, that before I could defeat my addiction I would have to destroy myself.

8

Hazelden

The beverage cart was coming down the narrow aisle aimed right at me. Suddenly I was breathing in short, quick gasps, and I swear the hairs on the back of my neck were sticking straight out. Was it fear or anticipation?

Northwest Flight 105 was cruising at thirty thousand feet heading due west to a place I'd never been and never even considered visiting—Minnesota. My parents had made all the arrangements (since Mary, I thought bitterly, wanted nothing to do with me, my addiction, or my treatment). I was going to one of the best treatment centers in the world, Mom told me halfway through my stay at St. Vincent's, a place that focuses on the physical, mental, and spiritual aspects of this disease. It didn't really matter to me where the place was or whether it was spiritual or not as long as it wasn't where I'd been, as I wrote in my journal just a few days before I left the psych ward.

AUGUST 23, 1989

Addicts are constantly reminded not to look beyond now, that "One Day at a Time" is more important than a date book. Nevertheless, I'm excited about the next month of my life. Yesterday I officially learned I'll be going to the Hazeldon Clinic in Minnesota, one of the top rehabs in the country.

Although I've actually come to enjoy my time at St. Vincent's, I'm glad to be leaving for Minnesota. I need some physical activity, more open space, better food, and a group much like me. That sounds elitist; it's not. St. Vincent's was the perfect place for me. But I'm much better now, and eager to take the next step back into the kind of world I'll live and work in. That's why Hazeldon is for me. It isn't St. Vincent's, and it isn't open society. It's in-between, I hope.

Reading that journal entry today, I can't help smiling to myself. *Hazeldon*—I didn't even know how to spell the name of the place that would not only change my life but, so many years later, literally become my life. Nor did I know that this next stop, which I imagined was my final destination, was only the beginning of this journey called recovery. And when I wrote that I longed for "a group much like me," I didn't know yet that every alcoholic and addict is, in the most important sense, just like me.

The young flight attendant's smile never left her face as she moved down the aisle, popping beer cans, handing out Bloody Mary mix and vodka bottles, collecting cash for wine, vodka, gin, and whiskey. The person in the aisle a few rows ahead ordered a Budweiser, and the woman next to him ordered white wine. Chardonnay, I guessed from previous experience with the beverage cart. My favorite. Back in Northport, I always kept several bottles in the refrigerator, immediately replacing the empties.

When the metal cart finally stopped at row thirteen, the flight attendant hit the brake and disappeared up the aisle to retrieve more napkins and ice. Staring at the cart, just inches away, it occurred to me that this was my Berlin Wall, the obstacle standing between me and the freedom to get where I was supposed to go. The metal drawers, I knew, were filled with perspiring cans of ice-cold Budweiser beer and miniature bottles of booze.

I wanted a drink. Just thinking about sucking down one of those bottles warmed my throat, burned my belly, and sparked a chain reaction of intense craving. Then I remembered the nightmares at St. Vincent's when I woke up drenched in sweat, dreaming I had relapsed, terrified of throwing everything away. Threat and release all wrapped up into that metal wall just inches from my face. Nobody would know—the airplane was filled with strangers who were clueless that the thirty-year-old man sitting in the aisle seat of row thirteen, dressed in jeans and a light blue Polo shirt, was an alcoholic and crack cocaine addict who was released that morning from a hospital psych ward and put on this plane to go to rehab in the middle-of-nowhere Minnesota. I hadn't had a drink in three weeks and one day. Twenty-two days.

Just one, maybe even a sip, enough to take the edge off. The taste is all I want, I just want to know one more time what it's like to savor one last drink before I give it up altogether. Just one drink, that's all. What harm could there be in one beer, just to take the edge off my nervousness, just this one last time? After all, alcohol wasn't my primary problem, not anymore. It was crack that did me in. I only used malt liquor or cheap wine to help me come down off the cocaine high, to mellow the crash.

The flight attendant smiled pleasantly at me. "What would you like today?" she asked.

Today, tomorrow, every day. I'd like to get high, be high, stay high.

"I'll have a Diet Sprite." I don't know where the words came from or how my head somehow overruled my gut in that moment. Maybe it had something to do with pride: I wanted to walk in the front door of this treatment center wearing my twenty-two days of sobriety like a badge of honor that would set me apart from all those other poor souls who probably would show up still drunk or high or otherwise out of it. My clean time would set me apart, get me noticed, give me an advantage, and earn me the attention I needed, craved, deserved. "He's got it; he's serious about his treatment," I wanted the counselors, nurses, and other patients to say. I needed them to see me as the best patient ever to arrive at Hazelden's front door. Every second that passed, every mile that separated me from New York and Mary, filled me with fear that I had lost it all. Hazelden represented my last, best opportunity to prove that I wasn't a failure after all.

Just a few hours before, at gate ten in LaGuardia Airport, I had twisted off my wedding ring and handed it to my mother.

"I won't need this anymore," I said, not even trying to hide the bitterness in my voice. Where was Mary? Why wasn't she seeing me off at the airport? I had no idea what was ahead, but I knew exactly what I was leaving behind—my marriage, my dog, my reputation, and my self-respect. In giving up that platinum band that had once been Pa Pa Joe's, I was admitting defeat and surrendering to the fact that life as I knew it was over. At least that's what I told myself. I'd soon discover that I had a lot to learn about the meaning of the word *surrender.*

My mother took the ring and closed her hand around it. "I'll keep it safe, son," she promised me as I boarded the plane for the face-off with the beverage cart somewhere in the skies over middle America.

"HELLO, YOU MUST BE William, glad you're here." My pupils weren't dilated and I didn't smell like a drunk, but it was obvious to the man who greeted me that I was like the countless others whose rendezvous with Hazelden starts at carousel thirteen at the Minneapolis/St. Paul International Airport. Why else would I be standing there looking lost and not exactly eager to be found? Patient confidentiality prevented him from holding up a HAZELDEN sign. Shame kept me from asking him if he was there to pick up an alcoholic and a drug addict. Yet the drivers for Hazelden know their passengers. Some of them had once stood there, too, waiting to be picked up. Once our eyes met we both knew each other, and in a few minutes I was in the passenger seat of the Hazelden station wagon heading north up Interstate 35.

Cornfields stretched out to the horizon on both sides of the highway and every few minutes we'd drive past one of those ten thousand lakes. Everything looked so different, so clean and open and, well, healthy. Nobody tailgated us or flipped us off and the farther we drove, the less traffic we encountered. *This is all right,* I thought. *I might like this.* I felt free, unencumbered. The psych ward and the crack house were part of my past, I told myself. Now I could start all over again in this new place. Looking out the station wagon window at the serene, barely inhabited landscape, seeing it all for the first time, I had no way of knowing how familiar and well-traveled that road to Hazelden would become.

Nervous and excited, suddenly filled with hope, I started asking questions.

"How much farther?" I said, sounding like a five-year-old kid.

"Twenty minutes, more or less," he said.

"I hear your winters are pretty long here," I said. "When does it start snowing?"

"Any day now." He laughed.

I wanted to know all about Hazelden and every time he answered a question, I had another one for him. What time do the patients wake up? Is the food good? Do people swim in the lake? When do patients have to go to bed? How many patients are there? Would I get my own room?

We turned off the highway onto Pleasant Valley Road—I liked the sound of that—and the rolling cornfields turned into acres upon acres of prairie grass and rows of neatly planted pines with an occasional oak or maple. He wasn't kidding about the snow, I realized; the leaves on the trees were already turning color.

"This is the private road into Hazelden," he said.

All I saw were trees and a long straight road stretched out before us. "How big is this place?" I asked. I suddenly felt like I was on a great adventure, the same kind of feeling I used to get when my parents drove me to Camp Hawthorne in Maine back when I was ten or eleven years old.

"Five hundred acres," he said. I let out a nearly breathless "Wow," watching the trees go by, and then I saw the end of the road with the lake sparkling in the distance and the one-story brick buildings spread out over a campus-like area filled with walking trails, a small pond, and rolling green lawns. I was not prepared for the serenity of the place. There were no gates, no potholes in the road, no peeling paint on the buildings. The grass was mowed, the gardens were tended, the walkways were smooth and even. People walked freely in and out of the buildings, smiling, friendly, relaxed.

Somewhere inside I felt a deep tension give way, like a sigh, and I knew everything was going to be okay. I understood, even though I couldn't articulate that understanding, that I was going to be treated well here. At St. Vincent's with its locked doors and barred windows, I felt abnormal, weak, even pathetic, a gross, unlovable man who deserved whatever punishment he received. The staff and other patients treated me with respect, and no one purposely made me feel inferior, but from the moment I arrived I was filled with a sense of hopelessness. I remembered the look of anguish on Mary's face, the man struggling with the balloons, the old man in the wheelchair staring out the window, the dimly lit hallways, the crush of people coming and going or just milling around waiting their turn for help, the dirty, gritty feel of the place, my sense of complete bewilderment as the elevator doors closed, leaving everything behind, and the razor wire strung around the perimeter of the hospital roof where we took our daily exercise.

From the moment I arrived at Hazelden, I felt different—peaceful, accepted, understood, even loved. Maybe this sense of belonging and acceptance, of fitting in and feeling at home, is what my mother meant by the word "spiritual." My father mentioned something about that, too. Before I left St. Vincent's, Dad told me that he had a conversation with Dr. Sherbert Fraser, an addiction medicine specialist, who told him that recovery was essentially a spiritual journey. "Take away drugs," Dr. Fraser said, "and that's good, but something—God or a new belief system—must take their place." Would I find God at Hazelden? Would God find me?

I began to believe He might. Everything was so beautiful. The grass was green, sailboats crossed the sparkling lake, and fish surfaced in a small pond on the corner of the property. Patients and staff strolled on pathways between the campus-like buildings. When I walked into the admissions office, I noticed that the floor was carpeted. A lamp threw soft light against the red-brick walls. An oil painting of a horse under a tree by a barn filled up much of one wall. People spoke in low voices, even in whispers.

I didn't realize then how incredibly fortunate I was to be in such a place. I probably thought, even though it seems ludicrous now, that any alcoholic, crack addict, or heroin junkie who wanted or needed help would be able to come to a place like Hazelden, maybe not in a peaceful corner of Minnesota but somewhere in the country. I had no idea that the county detox is often the only "treatment center" people can afford, nor did I know how few people make it even that far.

The receptionist in the admissions office gave me a big smile, welcoming me with what appeared to be genuine warmth. I signed a few papers—it was so quiet, I could hear the scratch of the pen on the paper—and a nurse escorted me down the hallway to the hospital unit.

"Do all patients go to the hospital unit?" I asked. I wanted to tell her that I was twenty-two days sober—that was what I had to hang on to—and so I wasn't like most of the people coming in here. I had a drug problem, no doubt about that, but I'd already come a long way.

I'm not as bad as the rest of these people, I wanted to tell her. *I'm ahead of the game. I'm different.*

"All new admissions to Hazelden are required to spend one or two days in Ignatia, the hospital unit," she said. "The length of stay depends on the withdrawal syndrome as well as any biochemical and mental health challenges that might present themselves."

I didn't quite understand what she meant by "biochemical challenges," but it didn't apply to me, anyway. Shoot, I had my three weeks and one day of sobriety, and even though smoking crack nonstop and drinking malt liquor all summer had been followed by forced exile in a locked psych ward, I was in pretty good shape, all things considered. She must have been talking about the really sick ones who come to Hazelden, not me.

"In your case," she added, leading me around the nurse's station that occupied the center of the hospital unit and into my room, "it's just a precaution." She put the blood pressure cuff on my upper arm, took my pulse, made some notations on my chart, and told me to relax and unpack. "We'll take good care of you, William," she said.

Once again, I felt that deep sigh, a feeling of release, a letting go of tension and fear. I was safe. They would take care of me here.

The next day I moved from Ignatia to Tiebout (pronounced teebow), the residential unit that would be my home for the next month. At the time Hazelden had six units (there are eight today), each housing approximately twenty patients; new admissions are randomly assigned to units depending on where there is an open bed. Almost every room has four beds, four desks, four chairs, and one bathroom. My roommates were Tom, an alcoholic in his late twenties from St. Paul; Christopher, a thirty-six-year-old alcoholic and prescription drug addict; and Jason, whose love affair with cocaine turned his mucous membranes to mush. After one sleepless night in that room listening to Jason blare like a foghorn in the dark of night, I bought my first pair of earplugs at the Serenity Corner Bookstore on campus. Some old habits never die, because I still wear earplugs to this day.

That first day on Tiebout I began to understand a little bit about the concept of tolerance. The cofounder of Alcoholics Anonymous, Bill Wilson, summed up the first inklings I had of this spiritual concept in this statement: "The way our 'worthy' alcoholics have sometimes tried to judge the 'less worthy' is, as we look back on it, rather comical. Imagine, if you can, one alcoholic judging another."

Talking to my roommates that first day, I realized we had little in common except for this one big thing—our addiction. Our common bond was our love affair with alcohol and other drugs and the fact that our lives were destroyed, to one extent or another, by this unquenchable obsession. We didn't share any strengths, really, but we sure shared weaknesses. If I had met these men on the outside, I would not have gone out of my way to get to know them, but here, at Hazelden, we immediately discovered common ground—we were all flawed, imperfect, hurting, ashamed, and scared. We struggled with the same basic demons, the same fundamental fears and sorrows, and we were all trying to do the best we could. When we told one another our stories, the others would listen and sigh, tears of compassion and empathy would flow, and laughter, too—a deep belly laugh that recognized and acknowledged that it was easier to laugh at ourselves than fight ourselves.

That night I went to my first medallion ceremony on the Tiebout unit. When you complete your treatment at Hazelden, you receive a medallion as part of the send-off from the staff and your peers on the unit. The medallion is about the size of a half-dollar coin but isn't round—a piece is missing, symbolizing the reality that recovery isn't perfect and is never complete. The Hazelden logo is stamped on one side of the medallion and the Serenity Prayer is imprinted on the other.

"If and when the temptation to drink or take drugs returns," a staff member explained that night, "grab hold of that coin as a reminder of what's at stake and how far you've come."

I was impressed by the guy who was graduating—his name was David—and I wanted to tell him that and also let other people know that I was really serious about my own recovery. So I stood up and gave a little speech, telling David that though I had only known him for a short time (less than one day to be exact), I was impressed by how seriously he took the program.

"You really know what you need to do to stay sober when you get home, so I think you're going to be okay," I said. "Thanks for being an inspiration to all of us."

That night I described the medallion ceremony in my journal. "I'm starting to fit in pretty well with the guys on the unit," I wrote. "I'm not so bad after all."

Like everyone else, I jumped right into the routine at Hazelden, learning about the "program" not from books or lectures but by doing it day in and day out. In treatment there's no real beginning or ending point; you just walk in the front door that first day and find yourself on a treadmill that's moving along at a steady speed, with people stepping on and off every day. As new people arrive and others depart, the process keeps right on going with only minor variations in routine. I became part of a group that existed before I arrived and would continue after I left, changing its shape but not its essential character. In those first few days at Hazelden I was absorbed into the process and the daily routine soon became familiar, even though every day brought new insights and experiences.

On the psych ward it was easy to distance myself from the rest of the patients because most of them were so physically sick and mentally ill. I could hide out in my private room, look through the bars of my little window at the same buildings day after day, get pissed off by all the smoke, the lousy food, and the razor wire topping the chain-link cage that kept the patients from jumping off the top of the building, and generally let the place feed the self-loathing and misery that reminded me of how deserving I was to be confined.

But everything about Hazelden was different. There were no locks on the doors or bars on the window. The only barbed wire I saw was around the farmer's dairy cow pasture next door. I had three roommates and no privacy. The food was so good I gained five pounds in the first week. And like my roommates, just about everyone else I saw looked and talked and acted a lot like me. I was part of a community of strangers who knew intimately why each of us was there, and so we all felt as one.

This wasn't a course of self study, I quickly learned, for the emphasis was never on "I" or "mine" but always on "we" and "ours." "We admitted we were powerless over alcohol and that our lives had become unmanageable" reads the first step of Alcoholics Anonymous. It would take me a long time to realize how critically important that word *we* is to life-long recovery—and how a self-centered focus on *I* can literally be life-threatening—but even in those first days at Hazelden I began to glimpse the reality that recovery happens within a community and not in isolation.

What I didn't understand and could not accept was that recovery had to involve surrender. That just didn't make sense, because I had always viewed surrender as quitting when things got difficult, weakness instead of strength, failure rather than success, and loss of control in the place of self-discipline. That's what alcohol and crack cocaine did to me—they made me weak and took away my self-control. Now that I was clean and sober I should be ready to fight, not surrender. I didn't come to Hazelden just to give up, did I? The whole idea that I had to surrender in order to get well seemed ridiculous. Maybe in those early days at St. Vincent's that formula applied because I was locked up and imprisoned like a criminal. I had to surrender because I had no choice. But at Hazelden I was free, regaining my senses, feeling stronger every day. Now wasn't the time or place to quit or surrender; now was the time to prove that I could defeat this enemy called addiction and recapture what I had lost.

My journals at Hazelden are filled with my struggle to understand and internalize the concept of surrender, especially as it concerned my marriage.

SEPTEMBER 1

Even though I told myself I wouldn't, I called my wife. She sounded better, and I did a better job explaining the healing process and my progress. However, near the end of the conversation, when I asked her to come to family weekend, she said no. Instead of trying to convince her, I backed away for now. I'm slowly coming to the realization that I cannot and should not try and do everything. I will concentrate on myself during this time and allow the counselors to talk to her. In other words, I'm going to allow my higher power, whatever that is, to call the shots and influence the total healing process.

SEPTEMBER 2

While I'm unsure what "surrender" means, or who my "higher authority" is, I decided to surrender to the higher authority on issues surrounding my marriage. To do so isn't easy for me, since I'm used to hands-on control of everything, and I'm not ready to give up on my marriage. But I realize I'm powerless right now to influence my wife's thinking. What I'm uncertain about is whether this surrender is comparable to admitting I'm powerless over alcohol.

SEPTEMBER 3

If I'm to enjoy the future, one day at a time, I must let go of the past, good and bad. Is that easy to do? I'm unsure. I'm not certain how to let go of everything.

Although I was willing to admit I couldn't control some things at some points in time, I was nowhere near willing to let go of the desire to be in control—not just of the matter at hand (Mary's refusal to attend the family program, for example) but of literally anything. I clung to the illusion of control and focused on that central phrase in the Serenity Prayer—*the courage to change the things I can*—all the while ignoring the fact that serenity comes from accepting the things one cannot change. When I felt truly powerless, I turned to God for help—God, I assured myself, would answer my prayers and give me what I needed.

"God isn't going to make my life easy or perfect," I wrote in my journal. "I know that now. But He is always there to comfort me when darkness covers my horizon. He will lessen my pain. He will strengthen me when I feel weak. This I know because I have surrendered."

On my fourth day in treatment, I sat down with my Significant Event sheets—a mustard-colored, lined, double-sided piece of paper on which I was supposed to record my thoughts and emotions on a daily basis—and tried to figure out what I was feeling. My emotions had run the gamut from the euphoria of realizing that life could be full of joy and wonder if I stayed sober to the despair involved in the understanding that even when I was sober I would experience waves of emptiness, loneliness, anger, and frustration. Trying to pin down those emotions and understand them a little better, I made a list of my most intense feelings.

1) The craving—until yesterday I had no craving for alcohol or drugs. But I realized just how vulnerable I am when

I read the chapters on freebasing in a book about cocaine. A brief but sudden and intense urge to pick up the pipe, coupled with the fear of my addiction, caused me to put the book down and catch my breath. It was scary! Merely looking at a glass stem or glass bowl, just looking at the words associated with drugs, brings back "fond" memories and sets off a reaction in my brain that tells me to do some coke, even though I know I shouldn't. Thank God I recognize the danger. Thank God I'm here.

2) The helplessness—Right now there is nothing I can do to make Mary feel better, get her to understand that I'm better, or convince her that I'm sorry. In fact, I can do nothing to help her understand my disease. This I learned, or continue to learn whenever I pick up the phone and call her. The result is I'm angry, frustrated and somewhat hurt that she listens but doesn't seem to hear. Links to the outside world, especially the damn phone, are dangerous to my rehabilitation. I first recognized that in St. Vincent's. It's ever more apparent now, since I'm getting stronger and in more control of my emotions each day I'm sober. Even last night, talking to my mom, I became upset when she began describing the success of the D day documentary they're shooting. There isn't a thing I can do for others right now, but I want to and that hurts. I'm going to stay away from the phone for a while, I think.

3) Sobriety—Life is meant to be lived to its fullest, meaning that drugs and alcohol have no place in life for me. I can live drunk and drugged, but I cannot experience life under the influence. God has given me so much—why should I numb myself to all that surrounds me? For now, at least, I want to stay sober not so I can live, but so I can live a full, healthy and exciting life on God's earth.

The next day I shared that journal entry in a one-on-one session with my counselor. Keith Jensen was twenty-eight years old—two years younger than me—and at six feet five inches tall stood two inches taller than me. He was wiser than me, too, which pissed me off, even though I tried not to show it. He had two pierced ears and black, prematurely thinning hair (that made me feel a little better about him).

I always felt comfortable in his office, which was about the size of a walk-in closet, even if the conversations were sometimes painful. Across from his desk I had a choice of three vinyl chairs, all different colors—one blue, one orange, and one yellow. Behind me was a bricks-and-boards bookshelf that held a boom box, a bunch of AA books, and probably a dozen coffee mugs. The walls were covered with rock band posters (the Sex Pistols and the Kinks, if I remember correctly). The only window in his office looked out on a giant dirt patch, the site of the original Hazelden farmhouse, where, starting in 1949, so many "hopeless" drunks got sober. The building had been torn down just the year before I arrived at Hazelden because it couldn't be brought up to code. Thousands of people still mourn that old building and consider the space it occupied, now the site of a meditation center, "hallowed ground."

"You're sugarcoating your feelings," Keith said, the Significant Event sheet on the desk in front of him. "Go deeper. Stop pretending. Stop feeling sorry for yourself and do the work."

I was shocked, at first, and my feelings were hurt. Nobody on Tiebout had worked harder than me on the daily assignments; I'd participated in every group and tried to be honest with Keith, my peers, and myself—especially myself. My journal entries were thorough and articulate. I had written about the agony of my failed marriage, the pain of the consequences of my drinking and drugging, my concern for my peers, the joys of experiencing nature during my morning jogs and evening walks, regrets of the past, and my hopes and dreams for the future. Hell, I even did my cleaning chores without once shirking my responsibility or complaining.

Pretending? Sugarcoating? Feeling sorry for myself? Was he suggesting that I was a bullshitter, a fraud, a baby? Well, he was dead wrong. Now I was really angry. *You don't know me, Keith,* I wanted to yell at him. *You may be a counselor but when it comes to counseling me, you've blown it this time. You have no right to tell me these things because you are wrong, off the mark, unfair. Aren't you supposed to be my friend in here, the one person I can confide in, trust no matter what, laugh with and even cry in front of without embarrassment? Why don't you just focus on helping me with my alcoholism and my drug use, and stop trying to tell me what and how to feel. Man, I'm trying as hard as I fucking can! I want to do this right, I don't want to fail. I can't fail.*

The anger and hurt gradually morphed into an overwhelming sense of shame. I wanted to crawl into a closet where nobody could see me, cover myself up, hide until they all went away. *What if Keith is right?* I whispered to myself in the darkness. Maybe he's seen something that I can't see, no matter how hard I look. Am I really failing when I thought I was doing so well? That would make sense, wouldn't it, since my whole life has been about trying to do better than last time, better than before, better than anyone else?

I couldn't stand to read Keith's comments, or to hear him repeat them in the days that followed, because I knew he was right. What I was doing wasn't working, it wasn't good enough, and I was falling short of what was necessary for me to cut it at Hazelden. With or without the drugs, no matter how hard I tried or how deep I was willing to go, I would always be trapped in that tar pit of my failure.

"Just getting sober isn't going to make everything all right again," Keith said several days later. "The work you have to do now is all about you, finding out who you are and what you are feeling on the inside."

The problem was that I was getting tired of "working" on my issues. I was running out of energy trying to keep up the good front. And somewhere, lingering in the back of my mind, was this fleeting thought that maybe, just maybe, one day I'd learn how to get high and do it right, avoiding the consequences. I wasn't going to confess that to Keith—I couldn't even consciously admit it to myself—and so I focused instead on doing my time at Hazelden. The daily routine grounded me: getting up at the same time every day, making my bed, cleaning my room, doing my assigned chores (cleaning bathrooms, vacuuming, raking leaves), eating three meals a day, meditating, exercising, participating in step groups where we learned about the Twelve Steps of Alcoholics Anonymous, going to outside AA meetings, attending evening lectures.

I was like a sponge, soaking up all the "gottas"—you gotta pray, you gotta eat, you gotta go to group, you gotta meet with your counselor, you gotta be honest, you gotta be able to take criticism, you gotta get and give feedback, you gotta show up, and you gotta be willing to look at the fact that the drinking and drugging are just symptoms of a deeper disease—an inability to accept life as it is. Until I learned how to accept the terms of my life—my flaws and imperfections, as well as my strengths, be grateful for what I had, forgive others for their weaknesses and limitations, give up my resentments, and "practice openness, honesty, and willingness in all my affairs," as *Alcoholics Anonymous* ("the Big Book") put it—I would never be released from my disease.

I understood all that in my head. I sure did, and I could list all the "gottas" like the A+ student I tried so hard to be. But those damn emotions kept tripping me up. Real life kept intruding on the serenity of Hazelden.

I just wanted to fix it, control it, and start over again. I wanted to screw in the hinges on the broken shutters, replace the shattered glass, caulk the holes in the wall, and call it a done deal. I was frustrated. I felt like I was living in two worlds, the new world of recovery and the old world of addiction. I was feeling better, life *was* better. I had this disease but I had it under control, so why wasn't everything falling into place? I stopped using—wasn't that what it was all about?

I kept looking for someone to blame, and Mary was the perfect scapegoat.

"I've been sober more than a month and still she refuses to consider a reconciliation," I said. "Why is she being so stubborn? Why won't she give me a chance?"

"You always want everything to happen on your time line, William," Keith said one day. "It's going to happen when it happens, if it happens at all."

"I know," I said, still trying to look like the cooperative patient. But underneath the surface I was starting to seethe. Why shouldn't things happen on my time line? Whose time line should they be on? Shit. If I waited for things to unfold at their own pace, I'd never get anywhere. This was going to take forever, and I didn't have that much time.

The next day George Weller, the head counselor on Tiebout, confronted me in group after I'd been complaining again about Mary's refusal to attend family week. An overweight, suspender-wearing old-timer who looked like they'd dragged him off a combine in one of Minnesota's cornfields, George was a man of few words. He waited until I was finished with my harangue and then he said what he always said.

"Get out of the way, Moyers, and let it happen." Good old George and his "get out of the way" wisdom. If only George was still alive today so I could go back and tell him the whole story about what happened after I left Hazelden. He'd look me in the eye and he'd say the same thing. "Moyers, you still need to get out of the way and let it happen." He'd be right about that, too.

"But she should come to family, shouldn't she?" I said, pounding the armrest of my chair in frustration. "She should learn about this disease, shouldn't she, just like everybody else? She should at least have an open mind and a willingness to change along with me. Why can't she just let go of the past?"

George waited patiently, his head tilted, and I can still see that wise smile and the gleam in his eye. He nodded his head, a gesture that said, "You done yet?" I nodded back, knowing what I was going to hear next.

"Should Shit," he said. "You gotta stop the Should Shit, Moyers." Every time I started with the Should Shit, George pointed to a poster on the wall showing a patient making a list that was so long it wrapped around the chair several times. "I will not should on myself today," the poster said.

Life happens as it happens, George was trying to tell me, and rarely if ever does it go how or where or when we want it to. Accept it. Get over it. Snap out of it.

But I didn't want to snap out of it. I was feeling sorry for myself and damn it, sometimes that felt really good. But whenever my self-pity became too obvious, George blasted me with another classic line.

"Oh, poor me, Moyers, poor me. Pour me another."

Halfway through my stay at Hazelden, Keith dropped the bombshell, and my carefully laid plans for rebuilding my life fell apart. It happened so fast. I had no idea what was coming.

"Have a seat, William," Keith said when I walked into his office. I sat down.

"The staff's recommendation," he said, not wasting one second on small talk, "is that after your twenty-eight days here at Hazelden you will move on to a halfway house."

I didn't know what to say. I must have asked him questions, maybe even argued with him, not in an unreasonable way—it was important to me to stay in control—but instead to use logic and try to outmaneuver him. It didn't work.

It didn't work because Keith, like most of the counselors, had anticipated my reaction. He knew from experience with lots of other patients that I was either going to fight the recommendation or avoid talking about it in hopes that one way or the other, I'd find some way to get out of it. So he employed one of the classic tactics of treatment—peer pressure.

I had to share with the other men on the unit my feelings about going to Fellowship Club. Like a bunch of ants on a sugar cube, they swarmed all over me. "You better go," they said. "Don't try to take control and do it yourself." "If Keith thinks you need a halfway house, then you need a halfway house." "Your way won't work." "You're lucky to have an option." Their advice was relentless, their sentiments undivided, and eventually I realized I simply had no choice, because I hated to think that my peers and the Hazelden staff might not like or respect me if I didn't go to Fellowship Club.

But I wasn't happy about it, and over the next several days I described my feelings of helplessness and powerlessness in my journal.

An overwhelming feeling of despair, the complete obliteration of the future, a deep sense of helplessness and genuine tears of sadness buried me this afternoon. I learned I will be going to a half-way house in Saint Paul after I leave the serenity of Camp Hazelden. Nobody can force me to go, of course, but I want to follow the recommendation for a simple reason—I want to get better. *I never want to relapse.*

But that cannot lessen at all the sadness I have. Is there nothing worse than a man who feels he has no control, no hope over his destiny? A man who is not only powerless over his career and his schedule, but a man who must stand by without the ability to stop his marriage from unraveling. Even if my marriage is to fail, I would have at least liked to try to patch it up first.

I am also powerless over my disease, something I realize

for the first time. I thought I was getting better. I thought I could measure my progress day by day. Self-confidence was surging through me, faster and stronger each day. Slowly I was coming to grips with my addiction, its implications and the emotional fallout. In one moment, the bull roared through the china shop. A gust of wind uprooted my newly planted tree.

I must somehow start again. Wasn't St. Vincent's supposed to be the first and last stop? I thought four weeks at Hazelten [*sic*] was my stepping stone to reality.

Now I'm not even sure what my reality is, or will be. I can't see four months down the road. I really can't even climb high enough to see beyond my immediate emotions.

No words can describe my anguish over the staff's recommendation that I go to a half-way house. While I somewhat expected it, it still was a blow to my hopes of making a steady recovery and return to the outside world. I guess I'm not getting better as fast as I thought. In fact, I'm starting to question if I'll ever get better. Like AA says, "once an addict, always an addict." Perhaps that's my destiny.

There's no doubt I'll benefit from a stay at a halfway house. It's logical that the longer I stay away from people, places and things, the better the chance I'll remain sober. But the four months in Minnesota are the death knell for my marriage and my career. I expect Mary will be relieved I'm not going home; that makes her life easier and probably will give her the final push she needs to divorce me. Should I blame her? Who knows!?

From a career standpoint, any hopes of returning to television production are dead. I had actually started to consider returning to my company in some capacity. Now I know that's impossible due to my extended absence. And how am I going to explain a six month gap in my résumé to companies that might consider hiring me?

I will go to this halfway house, not because I want to or think it's the best idea, but only because I have no other option. I have no control over my destiny anymore, except to stay sober. What kind of life can I ever hope to have? Sobriety doesn't guarantee happiness or success, does it?

These journal entries are still painful for me to read. I'd been in treatment for five weeks and I was as willful and self-pitying as ever, moaning about the "death knell" of my marriage and my career and railing against the unfairness of my "destiny." I wish I could step back in time and knock some sense into that slow-witted, self-centered brain of mine. I want to take myself by the shoulders and say, loudly, clearly, *Think about this, William. Imagine if you had a chronic, progressive disease such as cancer, diabetes, or heart disease and you've been told you need more intensive, longer-term treatment. Would you not give anything for that opportunity? Would you argue with the experts? But here you are, worried about a six-month gap in your résumé, blaming Hazelden for destroying your marriage, ranting and raving against anyone and everyone for presenting you with this terrible destiny. What destiny? Who guaranteed you happiness or success? You sound like Ahab hanging on to the harpoon and going under with the whale.*

I want to say those things and save myself from what was to come, but I was so filled with denial that no one's advice, not even words shouted down from the heavens, would have gotten through to me. Years later I'd find a perfect description of denial in a book titled *The Spirituality of Imperfection*.

Denial is self-deception. The alcoholic who swears "I am not an alcoholic" is really convinced that he is not one, and so this first level of denial involves being cut off from the wholeness of one's self. But denying one's own identity—as "alcoholic" or as anything else—means also deceiving oneself about the steps needed to regain that wholeness, to become whole again. This second level of denial involves holding back—hiding—the denied area, refusing to make it available for healing.

That's the most terrible truth about denial: You don't even know you're mired in it because the self-deception is so complete. Whenever Keith would accuse me of being in denial, the word went in one ear and right out the other because it made absolutely no sense to me. Denial? How could I deny that I was in a treatment center for a cocaine addiction, that my marriage was over, that I had caused unimaginable anguish to the people I loved best in the world? How could I deny those facts? They were undeniable and so I insisted I could not be in denial.

What I did not understand was that there was a deeper level of denial which entailed self-deception. I could not accept the identity that was so clearly mine to claim: addict. Hiding from that terrible, repugnant truth, I tried to pry out those parts of myself that were sick and putrid. If I could only separate myself from my flaws and imperfections—if I could only be perfect—I would be able to leave this addiction behind and get on with my life.

LIFE THROWS US opportunities in all kinds of disguises, but how often do we let those moments pass, unable to recognize the gift being offered? I'm reminded of the preacher in the flood who waits for God to save him. As the waters rise, a neighbor stops by to offer him a ride to safety. "God will save me!" he calls out. Hours later a boat passes by and again he refuses help, calling out, "God will save me!" Finally a helicopter lands on the church roof and helping hands reach out to the preacher, but again he insists that God will save him. But the waters keep rising, and the preacher drowns.

"Why didn't you save me?" the preacher asks God when he arrives in heaven.

"I tried, believe me!" God answers. "I sent you a car, a boat, and a helicopter—three times I offered to save you, and three times you refused!"

At Hazelden I was presented with hundreds of "teachable moments" from the stories other patients told about their lives—stories that were, in truth, mirror images of my own—to the insights offered by counselors and the sense of awe and wonder I experienced every time I paused to look at the beauty and magnificence of the world around me. But I kept waiting for something bigger, something more profound, something that I could hitch myself to and be carried away once and for all to the heaven-on-earth that I deserved. I kept struggling for control, which was really a demand for everything I wanted—peace, happiness, love, perfection—all at once, right now, and for all time. I wanted life to be perfect, always. And when it wasn't, which was most of the time, I got really anxious, and when I got anxious, I started thinking about how good it would feel to get high again.

I KNEW THE MOMENT I saw him that Eric was drunk. He appeared without warning from a path leading from the woods, dressed in running shorts, a T-shirt, and sneakers. But he wasn't running or walking off a tough workout or stretching his muscles. He staggered, struggling to keep his balance on the path coming up the hill. He wavered, righted himself, started up the path again, only to lurch to a standstill. Then he'd start again, and stop, pause long enough to try to collect himself, finally repeating the futility of his mission.

"Eric, what's the matter? Are you okay?" I asked, knowing the answer but finding it impossible to believe that he was drunk. Eric was my role model on the unit. He was the first one up in the morning, did his chores without complaint, read the Big Book every day, never argued with anyone, and always seemed to be the calm in the midst of the personal storms that are so much a part of the treatment experience. Eric was the epitome of serenity.

He looked right at me through his thick glasses, seemingly unable to hear, his ruddy face a deeper shade of red, sweat pouring from his forehead and down his cheeks. Were tears mixed in there, too? He was in distress, I knew that. He seemed utterly lost, even while he fought to resume his derailed journey back to the unit.

Then I could smell him, too. It was the first time I had experienced the tempting odor of alcohol, even if it was mixed with his sweat, since my encounter with the metal cart on the airplane. This time I recoiled. The scent scared me, reminding me of a dead animal half-buried somewhere nearby. I was afraid to touch him: What if the alcohol rubbed off on me and the counselors thought I was drinking? He needed help, but I backed away. A staff member appeared from one of the units, and Eric was led slowly back to the hospital unit.

Later that night our unit had an emergency meeting to discuss what had happened. That's when we learned that Eric had been jogging through the woods, along the lake shoreline, and into nearby Lindstrom several times a week to pick up a pint of liquor. He always managed to finish it before jogging back to Hazelden, but eventually the subterfuge and denial lost the race. The disease won. The disease, it seemed, always won.

I never spoke to Eric again. Given the option of returning to Tiebout for another thirty days of treatment, Eric opted to go home instead, where he likely faced a prison sentence for the drunk driving arrest that had landed him at Hazelden in the first place. Had he successfully completed his stay at Hazelden, he could have avoided incarceration. As a high-powered government official, the stakes were high, and Eric decided to go it alone.

Like many of my peers, I was deeply shaken by what happened to Eric, and all these years later I vividly recall that warm fall evening when the "senior peer" of the unit with an entire month of sobriety, a learned and respected politician, a witty guy whose thick accent made his jokes even funnier, a man who seemed so serious about his recovery, staggered back to the safety of Hazelden, a drunk all over again. Most frightening of all, I saw myself in Eric. If he couldn't do it, how could I?

That night, filled with confusion and despair, I wrote about Eric's demise, as I called it, in my journal.

As I saw Eric staggering along the path, futilely struggling for control, I saw myself. Not just walking a short path, but walking through life with an addiction I am powerless against.

Where was God when Eric needed him? Why couldn't Eric surrender? Is it that difficult? And whose definition should I use to describe surrender?

For the first time I feel hopeless and helpless. Why must my life be ruled by an incurable disease that is as dangerous today as it will be tomorrow, next week and, if I live that long, next century? I am a car out of control on ice on a dark winter night. I'm sliding into a darkness fraught with obstacles, yet I don't know when or what I'll crash into. I'm struggling with the wheel, reaching for some assurance of control, but no matter how much I try, I cannot do it. I am condemned to fight this spinning battle the rest of my life. Have I been sentenced to life imprisonment? Would it be better to have been sentenced to die?

Despair, not resolve, now mark my personal life. My

marriage, or lack of one, is getting the best of me. How can I surrender something I really don't want to let go of—a woman I love more than I realized? How can I be fair and good to myself when my disease isn't fair to me? Low self-esteem doesn't breed discontent. This disease does. I cannot be at peace with myself because I have a disease that thrives on fighting me "one day at a time." God, I hate that saying, not because it sounds trivial, but because it's true. I'm having trouble with getting through today. How can I look for hope in tomorrow?

I had no idea how much danger I was in. I had pitted myself against my disease, which I hated with all my being. I hated its power over me. I hated the way it controlled me, fought me, beat me down. What was this thing called addiction? A disease, they said, of body, mind, and spirit, a progressive, chronic, inevitably fatal disease. What did those terms mean, what were these impenetrable concepts that fell so easily from the lips of the all-wise and all-knowing counselors? I didn't really want to know, for just the words themselves seemed to set a trap, and I could almost hear the gates clang shut and the doors bolted from the outside. I'd been sentenced and condemned to life imprisonment with no chance of parole.

"I CAN'T DEAL with this anymore." I hardly recognized my wife's voice. "I want you to stop calling me. Stop writing me."

I hung up the phone and let the anger take over. For weeks I had stuffed it, trying to be conciliatory, hoping she would eventually give in and agree to come for family week. But she had made up her mind. She wasn't coming to family week, she didn't want me to call her anymore, and she asked me to stop sending her "love letters." What did she mean by that? I thought I was opening up my heart to her, trying to express the truth of my feelings for her, feelings that had been suppressed all these years by my addictions.

I'll give her time, I thought, *let her chart her own course. Maybe she'll forget me, or maybe,* and the thought gave me significant pleasure, *she'll drift aimlessly in the fog and later regret not seeing the strength and hope in me. She'll be lost while I move on, leaving her behind.*

I was suddenly sick and tired of it all. Did Mary think I wanted to be addicted? Was she so self-centered that she couldn't look beyond her own feelings of betrayal to think about how this disease had betrayed us both? Every time I remembered the way she looked at me at St. Vincent's, her mouth twisted in revulsion and disgust, or thought about her changing the locks on the doors in my own house, literally shutting out her own husband, I wanted to strike back somehow. *I'll file for divorce and get my house and my paycheck back,* I thought—*or at least half of it. I deserve half of what I own, don't I?*

Then I'd feel guilty and ashamed, knowing how deeply I had wounded her, thinking about her alone in the house with only Dallas to keep her company, and I'd pray, asking God for help, forgiveness, patience, relief. "Save this marriage, please," I prayed, "just help Mary see what she's doing to me and to us. Help me put my life back together."

It was all in God's hands now.

"SON, DO YOU remember the day last summer on the Long Island Expressway when we met at the hotel?"

Dad and Mom and I were in my room on Tiebout, relaxing after an emotional week in Hazelden's family program. This is the time when moms and dads, spouses and siblings, children and grandparents come to the same place at the same time for the same purpose—to learn about addiction. In group meetings, lectures, meditation sessions, reading assignments, individual counseling, and solitary walks along the lake, every moment is designed to help family members sort through their pain, confusion, shame, and guilt. In the process they learn that the disease is not their fault. "Hate the disease, not the person" is the constant refrain. More than anything, the program emphasizes that family members must take care of themselves, no matter what happens to the addicted person.

I'd last seen my parents at St. Vincent's in August, two months before, which now seemed like two years. I was so happy to see them when they arrived at Hazelden but the long days in the family program were very difficult as I became fully aware how painful my spiral downward had been for all of us. Feelings of anger, sadness, fear, and resentment came sharply into focus during the individual and group sessions. Healing is hard work, and we were exhausted.

Dad lay on my bed and Mom sat in the cushioned chair next to my desk. I was stretched out on the floor, feeling good that we'd come through this week together and trying my best to look confident, healthy, and in control of my emotions in order to ease their fears about my future. More than anything, I didn't want them to worry about me anymore. I was going to make it. They could be proud of me.

"You weren't in your right mind that day," Dad continued, "and neither was I. I should have known what was happening to you, but I didn't. All I knew was that I was starting not to like you back then."

Dad's eyes filled with tears, and I watched, stunned by the sudden display of emotion. I hadn't seen him this vulnerable for almost two decades. When I was nine or ten years old, I walked out of the kitchen and past the den one evening. The door to the den was closed but I could hear loud sobs coming from inside. I opened the door to see Dad on the couch crying uncontrollably, saying something about his dead brother James, while my mother rubbed his back. I was terrified. I had never heard such sounds coming from a man, and this was my father who was always so strong and unemotional.

Now he was crying for me. He was scared for me, scared for my mother, scared for himself. Was he thinking about his brother? Watching my father cry, all I wanted to do was lie on the bed and hold him tight. But he was a man, I was a man, and men don't do that. Somehow I had to be the strong one. I had to show him that I was going to be okay, that this was going to work out, and that what happened wasn't his or my mother's fault.

I reached over and grabbed Dad's hand. I reached over to my mother, too. "I'm sorry," I said.

That night, I wrote these words in my journal.

What I witnessed and heard from him was one of the most touching moments for me since I began rehab. It showed me how much I've hurt my father, and how much he hurts for me. At times in the past I often wondered why he seemed so emotionless. A void had developed through the years between father and son because I only saw one side of him—an incredibly successful journalist and father whose poker face made me think everything was perfect, or should be.

His tears seem to have opened a new avenue between us, channeling fresh emotions of love and support mixed with the pain and confusion of my disease. It hurt seeing him cry. And there's a lot of healing to go. But the message is clear. My parents love me as much as I love them. Finally we can share everything we feel, not just the good. We don't have to pretend we're perfect.

That night I had a vivid using dream. I was standing on a street corner with faceless strangers, waiting to buy drugs. It took forever to get the drugs and I began to feel apprehensive about the quality and quantity they would give me. When I held the crack in my hand, I felt angry because I'd been ripped off and hadn't received my fair share. Waiting to light up and take that first hit, I was flooded with guilt and

Time magazine, 1965.

The president and first lady,
Dad, and me, 1964.

My parents and me, 1960.

PaPa Joe (Henry Joseph Davidson,
my grandfather), 1959.

PaPa Henry (John Henry Moyers) and Mimi (Ruby Jewell Moyers), my grandparents, on their fiftieth wedding anniversary, 1976.

Nana (Eula "Judy" Davidson), my grandmother, 1982.

Dad and me, 1960.

Under my favorite tree in Wilmer, 1970.

College daze, 1979.

Pricella Mitchell, 1978.

Allison and I are married, 1992.

Dad, Henry, and me, 1993.

Home from Ridgeview, with Henry and Thomas, 1995.

Mom and me, 1997.

My family, 2005.

Nancy and me, 2005.

Author's collection

Photo by Allison Moyers

shame and yet I also felt resigned to the fact that my sobriety was ending. I asked one of the dealers for help and he used a hot metal rod to ignite the crack.

When I woke up, it took a few moments to orient myself in time and space. The dream was so real, so vivid, that I wasn't sure it hadn't really happened. *Oh God, please help me,* I thought, because that dream reignited the craving that seemed to heat up the very furnace of my being. Where did the cravings come from? How could I stop them? I knew the basic facts about craving—how drugs physically change the brain, altering the molecules and the chemicals, even modifying the basic structure and shape of the nerve cells. I knew that craving isn't a mental "want" but a true physical "need" that arises from deep within the network of cells that have been permanently changed by drugs. And I knew that the really dangerous moments come when your defenses are down and the world looks bleak. That's when the addicted brain fires up these euphoric memories that whisper to you in the night or in the morning when you are taking a shower or in the late afternoons when the day is coming to an end: *Remember how good it felt? If you just go back there, you'll feel good again.*

Maybe that's where the "spiritual" part of the program comes in, I thought. When your own brain conspires against you, maybe the only way to fight back is to dig deep inside yourself and find the spiritual courage to hold on and stay the course. If craving comes from the furnace of the addicted brain, then the fire in the soul has to burn that much hotter.

The thought comforted me, and later that day, taking my last walk by the lake, I noticed the leaves changing color and watched the wind move through the tall grass at the lake's edge. A flock of geese flew noisily overhead, and the bottoms of the clouds were crimson from the setting sun.

It was all so perfect, right then, so full of promise and possibility.

9

Fellowship Club

WEDNESDAY, SEPTEMBER 27, 1989

At the bottom again.

The true sense of overwhelming power this disease of addiction has over me is awesome. As I sit on the side porch of this giant house tonight, I should be feeling content. The sun has just set, a mild wind is blowing, and I have my feet up on the railing, looking at a real "Working Class" neighborhood for the first time in months. And I'm sober.

Yet that feeling of emptiness, mixed with loneliness and despair, has returned. I felt it at St. Vincent's, then again at Hazelden. It tells me that this disease never goes away, that I'm powerless over it. I'm always going to have to fight a lonely battle against it. There will be other days of loneliness and helplessness. I'll be in treatment each day of my life, one day at a time.

I WAS SOBER and back in the "real world." Across the street four boys played touch football, an elderly man raked leaves into a big pile by the curb, and somewhere out of sight a dog barked. The days stretched out before me, an endless procession of twenty-four hour blocks, with lonely, helpless, and powerless stamped all over them. This damn disease, I realized, was never going to go away, and there was nothing I could do about that fact. It was part of me, like my liver, my left thumb, or my seventh vertebrae, and there was no way I could shake it off or leave it behind.

A bus roared by on Seventh Street, car doors slammed, airplanes trailed white plumes in the sky. I realized suddenly that I had two diseases—the disease of addiction and the disease of Too Many Options. I'd been in treatment for fifty-one days and so far the choices had been easy because they were so obvious. After bingeing for six days in that Harlem crack house, I was out of my mind, and by society's logic, people who are crazy-out-of-control get locked up in psych wards. When the staff at St. Vincent's figured out that my problem was drug addiction rather than mental illness, arrangements were made to send me to a chemical dependency center. I don't remember being given a choice about where to go—my mother in her ever-efficient way researched the options and presented me with the top choice—but I was more than happy to give up the locked doors and barred windows at St. Vincent's for a five-hundred-acre inpatient treatment center that resembled a resort set on a lake in the middle of nowhere.

When the Hazelden staff told me that I needed to spend several months in a halfway house in St. Paul and live in a structured environment with other recovering alcoholics and addicts ("These four months will help you transition gradually back into society," they explained), I felt trapped with no way out. I didn't want to spend another four months in treatment, but how could I argue with the experts? I'd learned enough about the disease to realize that even after seven weeks I wasn't ready to go back to the my old life and the temptations I'd left behind. So even though I was anxious to get back to New York and try to patch my life back together again, I accepted the staff recommendation and went to Fellowship Club.

But now, sitting on the porch of this grand old house, watching the sunset and the lights go on inside the houses across the street, I realized that having too many choices in life could be much worse than having only a few. What if I made the wrong choice? At any moment I could step off that porch, walk down the street or hop on a bus, and head for the nearest tavern. Or I could get a cab and go to the airport, write a check, and get on the next flight back to New York. I wasn't going to do any of those things, I told myself, but that didn't lessen the fear of making the wrong choice and proving to everyone that I was the imperfect, flawed person I knew myself to be. I had always been afraid to make choices. I'd look at the two forks in the road and stand there for the longest time, worrying that one or both would lead me down the wrong path. Alcohol and cocaine helped me overcome the anxiety of indecision and the courage to move forward, even if it meant rushing headlong down a crooked path and right over a cliff.

Drugs eased my loneliness, too. I was never lonely when I was using, even when I was separated from the people I loved most in the world, because my best friends were always with me. Cocaine was my running buddy, my soul mate, my faithful lover, my reliable colleague, my fun-loving playmate who tagged along everywhere I went. Alcohol and cocaine were always there for me, they never let me down. I missed them, with a deep, aching longing that I hadn't felt in weeks. Would I ever get to see them again? Would I ever be able to experience the release they gave me?

Crack and alcohol weren't a crutch—they were my feet. For more than a decade they had carried me through my life and now, after seven weeks of separation, I felt like an amputee. How was I going to hobble around in the real world? This damn disease was never going to go away, and I was doomed to fight a lonely battle against it. Lonely.

That was my destiny. Just that morning at Hazelden I was at the top of the pecking order, a "senior peer" who had his own room and who got a lot of pleasure (and pride) out of taking "newbies" under his wing. Now I was at the bottom rung again, back in a room with four beds and three strangers, eating meals in a big dining room filled with fifty people who all seemed to know one another, scheduled to meet with a counselor whom I didn't know, stuck in an old house on a busy street with a working brewery next door.

"This is never gonna end," I thought.

LESS THAN FORTY-EIGHT HOURS later I was feeling much better: I had a job. According to "house expectations," every resident is required to find a job within two weeks of arrival at Fellowship Club and, as usual, I was on the fast track to success. On my third day at Fellowship Club I started working forty hours a week at Reclaim Center Incorporated (RCI). The "Reclaim" name comes from the reprocessing of sugar and flour. The owner of RCI, Jim Burt, is a recovering alcoholic who to this day hires people from Fellowship Club and Twin Town Treatment Center (his alma mater) to work at his warehouse, recycling canned and packaged goods that have been damaged in fires or other natural disasters. A few months after I started work at RCI we got a huge shipment in after the earthquake in San Francisco.

My favorite job at RCI was unloading the huge pallets of canned goods from trucks that arrived from Kansas, Texas, Maine—wherever there had been a fire, flood, tornado, or some other disaster. I'd wipe down the cans, hundreds maybe thousands of them a day, and reload them on the pallets and back into the trucks where they'd be taken to wholesale distributors all over the country. I liked the work, believe it or not, because it was such hard physical labor, and even that very first day on the job I felt like I was getting in good shape, trimming down, and developing some muscles. Feeling good about my body was a new sensation.

The worst job of all at the warehouse, which was unheated even in the dead of Minnesota winters, was sugar duty. I always groaned out loud when the foreman gave me that assignment. It wasn't hard, but it was gross. I stood on a platform in front of a big round sifter, something like the pan that's used in gold mining, and emptied damaged five- or ten-pound bags of sugar onto the wire mesh screen. The sugar filtered down to a container while the impurities collected in the sifter.

"Do we really eat this shit?" I must have said that a hundred times as I looked at the junk left behind in the sifter—whole bugs, pieces of bugs, and little chunks and bits of god-knows-what. To liven things up I'd try to guess how many insect parts would be left in the screen after the sugar passed through. Sometimes it was a dozen. That didn't bother me because I wasn't going to see that sugar again—it wasn't going to end up in any cake I ate.

Those ripped, soiled, or crushed sugar bags kept coming. I couldn't believe people ate that much sugar, and these were just the damaged bags. After we sifted out the bugs, we'd repackage the sugar in plain brown wrappers and send those suckers on their way to the wholesale distributors and the unknowing consumers who would buy them hoping to save a few bucks. At the end of the day, I'd take off my high-tops and dump half a cup of sugar out of each shoe. Sugar granules would still be stuck in my sweaty socks, and I'd sit on the bus on the way home to Fellowship Club (or stand if the bus was full, which it often was) and think about how good it was going to feel to take a shower and get that sticky shit off my feet.

I worked eight-and-a-half-hour days with thirty minutes off for lunch. Lunch hour was always great fun, talking and laughing with Stan, a two-time relapser of alcohol, and Charlie, a native of the

Caribbean who was addicted to heroin. Jim Burt, the owner, often joined us for lunch in the vacant storage room upstairs. We'd all stretch out on the dirty floor, eat the bag lunches we threw together that morning at Fellowship Club, and in thirty minutes, no more, no less, get back to work. Most of the time we'd swap stories about women we knew or wanted to know, our favorite sports teams, or what we planned to do when it was time to leave Fellowship Club. Thoughts of the future always brought us around to stories of the past. I'll always remember eating those tuna fish or peanut-butter-and-jelly sandwiches and going around the circle telling stories that were all different in the particulars but in the most important sense all the same.

I was a happy man on Friday afternoons when I walked out of the warehouse with my paycheck and a whole weekend ahead of me to relax. Two hundred dollars! And I earned every cent of it! What a feeling to know that every dollar was hard-earned. Back in the old days, the using days, my daily wages at RCI would have barely covered the cocaine I needed to get the day started. I spent hundreds of dollars a day, thousands of dollars a month on cocaine, and I never even thought about it, because that money meant nothing to me, it just went into my checking account and right back out into my dealer's hands. Mary sometimes wondered where all our money went and why we couldn't save anything, but she always believed me when I lied about how my paychecks were eaten up by normal household expenses. What she imagined as a slow leak was more like an out-of-control hemorrhage.

But now I had plenty of money to buy myself a CD or an ice cream cone and still put some away in a savings account.

Sorting sugar and wiping soot off cans of beans and corn gave me a sense of dignity and respect that I never had when I was making six or seven times that much at *Newsday* or working on documentaries for my parents' public broadcasting company. And you know what? I

deserved every penny I earned. In every other job I had, even in seventh grade when I worked at the Garden City store bundling the Sunday *New York Times,* I always felt that I had the unfair advantage of
being Bill Moyers's son. I was always willing to work hard and I had
definite skills and talents, but it was usually my father's name that got
my foot in the door.

At RCI, in that unheated warehouse with the soot-covered cans,
the wood pallets, and the sugar sifter, nobody knew my father and
"Moyers" was just another last name, no different or more important
than "Smith" or "Jones." I was my own man for the first time in my
life, earning my own money, opening a savings account, and starting
to feel really, really good about myself.

A letter from my father made me feel even better.

October 15, 1989

Dear Cope:

I think of you every morning when I wake up, not only for
reasons of love and hope but because the Serenity Prayer,
which I learned at Hazelden, connects me to you in a different way. As I go over the lines, trying to apply them to my
own day and to specific changes I need to make or accept, I
can envision you doing the same thing for your own reasons
and goals. I learned so much at Hazelden that I am overflowing with insights I have not yet been able to assimilate, but
one of the most specific boons was the prayer. I have come, for
example, to accept the limits of my ability to "fix" your recovery. Once upon a time I would have thought that part of a father's job description. No more. It was a hard lesson but I
learned it: no one can get well for someone else, not even a
beloved son. On my goal sheet at Hazelden I wrote down

as my goal for the week: "To understand the limits of my ability ..." By week's end I had crossed out the ~~understand~~ and written in *to accept*. That was a big step for me, and I couldn't have made it without our honest conversations. Our relationship *is* different, isn't it? And I like it. As I told John this weekend, the oldest son has come home ... and it's *really* him. There's no mask over the eyes now, no attempt to hide the disease or to engage in the deception that grows from fear. From my end, it's a wonderful return of the son I love. But you are a child no more, and I welcome the man you have become.

Incidentally, at a friend's house this weekend it turned out that just about everyone there has or has had a similar experience with a close member of the family. This disease is a great equalizer; no one's immune.

More later. Take care of yourself each moment and the second and third and other moments will take care of themselves (I learned *that* at Hazelden, too).

Love,
Dad

No mask, no hiding, no lies—this was recovery, I realized, this coming home to truth and joy and love, and everyone shares in it just as everyone shared in the shame and misery of addiction. After reading Dad's letter, I reached for my journal, feeling the need to chronicle exactly how drugs had taken over my life.

1. I became married to the drug—'til death do us part.
2. It was my life—nothing else mattered.
3. It was my companion and good friend—we went everywhere together.

4. It was my lover—I couldn't make love to the drug but it made love to me.
5. It was my work—I worked to get high every day. My career was a distraction from this work.
6. It was my recreation—I couldn't have fun without it.

Looking at that list, I realized that my addiction had controlled my life. I thought I was making all the decisions, but I was really just a puppet and the addiction was holding the strings. My life had become unmanageable, just like it said in Step One: "We admitted we were powerless over drugs and alcohol—that our lives had become unmanageable." I thought a lot about that word *powerless* in those first weeks at Fellowship Club, and I was more than willing to admit that I was powerless over drugs because despite my best efforts, they had nearly killed me—driving drunk, steering the car with my knees so I could light up the crack pipe, hanging out in crack houses where guns were hidden under the sofa cushions, snorting another line of cocaine through the blood streaming from my nose, taking another hit when my heart felt like it was pounding out of my chest. I just didn't understand how the concept applied to everything else in my life. Powerless over my marriage? Powerless to control what other people thought about me? Powerless over my own fear, self-loathing, loss of faith? Those were the things I should have power, control, and influence over—right?

I made another list. If I was going to stay sober, I had to stay away from the "people, places, and things" that almost destroyed me in the first place.

Who are the people? Former users, some of whom I love very deeply.
Where are the places?

1. The bars
2. Rock concerts
3. The street corners

Where are the things?

1. Obvious—the drugs
2. The paraphernalia
3. I love to get high
4. I love trying to figure out how to get control

Reading that list today those last two points jump right off the page at me. *I love to get high. I love trying to figure out how to get control.* I wonder why I didn't notice, or why I wasn't worried about the fact, that I put those sentences in the present tense?

WORK WAS AN important part of the daily routine at Fellowship Club, but the days were filled with other activities as well. Every morning we were expected to make our beds, clean our rooms, and complete our chores. The chores changed every week and ranged from cutting up vegetables for meals to raking leaves in the yard to scrubbing down the bathrooms. We usually ate breakfast on the run, grabbing a bowl of cereal, a banana, and a glass of juice and running out the door to catch the bus to go to work. During the day every resident was expected to be out of the house and at work or looking for a job. Only newcomers and those who were too sick to work had an excuse to stay behind.

The bus ride to and from RCI took an hour, so I didn't usually get back until an hour or so before dinner. That's when the house began to buzz and come alive again as we all returned from our jobs and shared the experiences of another sober day outside in the real world.

There was a real sense of camaraderie and even relief at being back in familiar surroundings. Gathering in the dining room for the evening meal offered a potent reminder that we all needed and depended on one another, for what brought us together under this roof was one basic problem—the need to focus on ourselves some more before we faced what was waiting for us in the real world. We ate at round tables, usually six to eight people at a table, and afterward everyone had a duty like cleaning dishes, wiping tables, sweeping floors, or stacking chairs.

Evenings were reserved for recovery discussions in small groups, community meetings, lectures, or AA meetings. We were required to attend at least two outside AA meetings every week. Most of us walked five blocks to the "West End" AA meeting, held on the ground floor of a two-story building with apartments on the top floor. A few doors away there was a local bar and across the street was Schmidt's Brewery, which at that time was still pumping out beer. Back then the Wednesday night meeting was a "topic meeting," and the topic could be anything from gratitude to resentment to sponsorship to powerlessness. The meetings always lasted exactly an hour, but a lot of us stayed afterward to talk around the coffeepot.

Smoke stains covered the walls and the smell of burned coffee permeated the room, but it felt like home there, and even all these years later, it still does. Two or three times a year I go to the West End meeting and every time I walk in the door, I am reminded of those days at Fellowship Club. Smelling the coffee, noticing the smoke-stained walls, I always whisper the same words. "Wow—what a ride."

Fellowship Club was a microcosm of the real world with all the little cliques that exist everywhere. All of us were oddballs and eccentric in one way or another, I suppose. But even among us, there were standouts. "R2D2" for one, a funny-looking guy in his midtwenties who spoke in an electronic-sounding monotone, moved his arms and legs in a herky-jerky way, and wore a perpetual grimace. Maybe the weirdest thing about R2D2 was how much he loved his nickname. There was "Blind Randy," a big bear of a man about my age from northern Minnesota or maybe somewhere in the Dakotas—the only person I ever heard of who was legally blind and charged with drunk driving. "It was all a misunderstanding," he told me in a running joke. "The cops said I was in a blackout, but that's impossible because I'm always in a blackout!" After Blind Randy graduated from Fellowship Club, I ran into him in downtown Minneapolis where he was running a concession stand.

Lisa, an attractive, confident, fast-talking New Yorker, had us all fooled. We elected her president of Fellowship Club just a few weeks before a staff member found her smoking crack in her room. She was immediately removed from the halfway house and went back through the twenty-eight-day program at Hazelden. I heard later that she relapsed and went to treatment again, a pattern that repeated itself for several years until she finally got sober, moved to San Diego, and set up a successful business, married, and had three kids.

And then there was Allison, a shy, beautiful brunette from Bermuda with big brown eyes, a huge smile, and an accent that made me want to be around her all the time, just to hear her talk. We were assigned to the same therapy group, and I always looked forward to those evening meetings just so I could be near her. One chilly October day when we were sitting out on the porch bundled up in our winter coats, she told me her story.

"I started drinking when I was fourteen," she said. "I was at a Christmas party, and I was so shy. I got really drunk. In high school and college I did the usual drinking, mostly at parties, but whenever I drank, I always got really drunk. Back in Bermuda after college my drinking career really took off. It really was the way of life down there, to go to parties and bars and drink—it didn't seem abnormal at all. I hopped from job to job, usually quitting because I wanted to party without having to go to work. Work really got in the way of drinking."

From that point on her story wasn't all that much different from mine. Drunk driving, blackouts, cocaine, crack, shame, depression, loss of control, self-hatred, and more shame.

"I hated myself and what I was doing to my life, but I couldn't stop," she said. "The shame was the worst part. I remember feeling so different from everybody—so empty and hollow and worthless. And I felt so lonely—whether I was alone or in a crowd. I couldn't have a meaningful relationship with anyone. I knew I was losing myself— that's what got me into treatment, really, was that sense of losing myself."

We were alike in so many ways. Allison was thirty-one when she went to Hazelden; I was thirty. Like me, she thought she'd only go to treatment for a month and then everything would be "good" again ("although I can't remember it ever being all that good"). In treatment she felt different from the other patients because she hadn't gone so far down "the dark hole," as she called it. Drugs, she said, made her feel like a "normal" person ("whatever that is," she laughed), but mostly she started drinking, she said, to *feel*.

I'd never had a female friend before, someone I loved to be with for no other reason than to listen, talk, laugh, or cry, and I always tried to sit near her at AA meetings or when the group would go out for pizza or to a movie. When I found out she was scheduled to graduate from Fellowship Club at the end of October, I was devastated. That was one of the worst things about both inpatient treatment and the halfway house—as soon as I got close to people, they left, and most of the time I knew we'd never see one another again. Just a few weeks before her graduation day, Allison told me she had decided to stay at Fellowship Club for an extra month because she wasn't ready to go home yet and she was scared that if she did, she might use again. Her decision would change both our lives.

Fellowship Club became my home, a place where I felt like I fit and belonged just the way I was. Other residents considered me a leader and they even elected me president of the house. I found it amazing that anyone would put me in a leadership position, but then again, I told myself, maybe I had earned it—like a career military man who had progressed up the ranks to a position of authority and respect, I had earned my scars and my promotions on the battlefield of life.

Those were the kinds of things I was writing in my journal on the weekends when I had time to relax a little. I loved being able to sleep in on the weekends, take a long run, round up some friends for a game of touch football, go to church, or just sit on the porch and talk to Allison. Once I settled into the routine at Fellowship Club, I spent a lot of time thinking about God and where He fit into my life. In my teens and twenties, especially as my cocaine addiction progressed, I usually prayed to God for something—I wanted Him to give me freedom from my cravings, help me be successful in my career, make Mary love me, erase my doubts and fears. That's what God does, I figured—you ask Him for things and either He gives them to you or He doesn't, for whatever reason. But at Fellowship Club I started thinking about God in a different way. I wasn't so much asking Him for things as thanking Him for things. When I was using, I was blind to the everyday wonders of the natural world—I did not see the beauty in sunsets or full moons, in the waves crashing on the shore, or the mountains rising into the clouds. I didn't notice the wind in the grass or the changing color of the leaves. The only joy I knew was the rapture of the smoke entering my lungs and, with my eyes closed, the feelings inside me. That was all I cared about, all I loved, all I could see.

But now, clean and sober, my eyes were open to the world around me and I felt a profound gratitude for the gifts that had been given to me, free of charge, no questions asked. I had to think, too, that God had something to do with my sobriety. I wasn't sure what role He played, but I knew it was significant. I'd sit on the porch at night and, when no one was listening, talk to Him. "Where are you?" I'd ask, and I really wanted to know the answer. Where was He? Where had He gone for all those years of my life? Had I abandoned Him or had He abandoned me?

I wasn't desperate for God—I was just really curious about how and where He fit in my life and how and when and where I would be able to recapture what I had lost so long ago in that New Mexico light-ning storm. I never doubted He was there, I just wasn't sure what I was supposed to do with Him or what He wanted from me. He wasn't going to make my life easy or perfect, I knew that much, but I trusted that He would be there to comfort me when I was alone and despairing, lessen my pain when it became unbearable, and give me strength when I felt weak and powerless.

But I was afraid, too, because I knew how easy it was to lose faith when bad things happen. If my parents died in a plane crash, if my house burned down, if my brother or sister got sick with cancer, would I still be able to love and trust God? Those questions haunted me, be-cause I wasn't sure how to answer them. When everything was going well, I felt God near me. When life hurt too much, I couldn't find Him anywhere. What kind of faith was that? What kind of spirituality could I claim if my belief in God depended on my mood at the moment?

Three months sober and almost halfway through my stay at Fel-lowship Club, I spent an hour writing in my journal about all the joys and triumphs of my recovery.

SATURDAY, NOVEMBER 4
My life is full of meaning, exciting and full of new discoveries. I'm so busy, so utterly satisfied with life experiences, that each evening brings complete but welcomed exhaustion.

In recent weeks my life has included:

1) A growing sense of myself, and a commitment to my sobriety. I am breaking free from a decade spent in a cave,

where I hid from responsibility, emotions, and a loss of identity. I am a leader here at Fellowship Club. I speak the truth from my heart. People look to me for some guidance, some sense of what sobriety is about. All I know is what I feel. It amazes me that others see me as a leader, though I too feel that my ability as a speaker, my genuine sensitivity to others, and my honesty are invaluable and worth sharing. . . . I respect the feelings of others because I have been through the same thing. I have the same problems. But I'm in touch with many of my issues because I'm willing to share with others. And I am willing to deal with them myself. I have as many pains and shame as anyone here. By the grace of God, I seem for the first time in my life willing and capable of dealing with them. No longer do I rush to a half-hearted conclusion, a quick fix. Some days I wish for a resolution to my problems, especially my marriage. At times I wish the future is now. But I am learning to pace myself, to seek good in everything I do daily. I don't procrastinate. My steps are a baby's, not those of a giant. It may take me longer to reach my destination, but I get there eventually. And finally, when I arrive, I seem more content with my travels, more firm in my belief in myself.

2) A using dream. Fear, shame and guilt were real emotions in an unreal world of my dream of getting high. I didn't really use. Still, I felt like I had.

3) Don (my counselor) validates my decision to use my first name instead of Cope. What an important affirmation for me. Using Cope always made me feel somehow inadequate. Instead of focusing on me initially, people who met me as Cope got caught up in my name and its origin. I'm tired of the jokes, the confusion. Besides, I couldn't cope with life as an addict. I often felt shame being called that. William is my real name. It is manlier. Sounds more confident.

In early recovery there is no greater truth than this: *This too shall pass.* At Hazelden and then at Fellowship Club, I learned that when I was feeling good, difficult days were sure to follow, and when I was feeling bad, something was sure to happen to make me feel better. But as the weeks passed—and especially as Allison prepared to leave Fellowship Club just before Christmas—I began to feel restless and irritable. All those messes I had left behind were piling up, waiting for me to deal with them. I'd been isolated and insulated for the past four months at St. Vincent's, Hazelden, and now at Fellowship Club, but the time was coming when I was going to have to face my deeply wounded wife, figure out how to pay back the loans my parents had given me, get a job, explain to my neighbors and friends where I'd been and what had happened to me, on and on and on. I had quickly reassembled my life in treatment and that life didn't include any of those problems. I began to feel scared about it all. And, of course, there in one corner of this huge mess of my life lurked a restive, scary creature—my addiction.

Thank God for my counselor, Don Hewlett, who was always available to give me good advice. A former Capuchin-Franciscan monk (or maybe he was a Jesuit, I wasn't sure), Don had an earring and long black hair that hung to his shoulders. I loved spending time in his windowless office with the fish tank gurgling and the lamps throwing soft light on the bookshelves filled with books about spirituality, religion, and philosophy. Not once did I see Don angry, combative, or even frustrated, and he was so soft-spoken that I sometimes had trouble hearing him above the noise of the fish tank.

One evening after dinner I talked to Don about a gnawing sense of self-pity that seemed to well up in me even when I was feeling happy and secure in my recovery.

"I think I'm learning how to live with this whole thing," I said. "I don't walk around depressed or anything, and I definitely don't hate myself anymore. But I do seem to take a certain amount of comfort in wallowing in the mire, dumping mud on myself—you know, feeling sorry for myself because I have this 'affliction.' "

"You know, William, you don't have to put yourself down when you call yourself an addict," Don said. "Accepting the truth of yourself and the reality of your disease doesn't have to be accompanied by self-pity and self-doubt."

I understood those words in an intellectual way, but I found them as hard to accept as Mary's constant reminders over the years that I was a "good man." When you're feeling bad about yourself, it's hard to feel good about anything else. A few days later I went back to Don's office because I was afraid things might be "too good." I'd heard about that "pink cloud" that recovering people discover in early recovery. Was it all going to come crashing down?

"Don't worry about why life is working so well right now," Don said. "Accept it as a miracle, which it is. William, learn how to let the emotions come—don't fight them. Let them roll out and then deal with them as they come. You can do this. It's not easy, but you can do it."

Don was repeating the same basic truth that George Weller kept trying to hammer into my stubborn brain back at Hazelden: "Get out of the way, Moyers, and let it happen." And the truth that so many of us repeat, over and over again, day after day: *Accept life on life's terms.*

Those words sounded reassuring in the moment, and I understood them, I really did, but I just couldn't help thinking that recovery wasn't all it was cracked up to be. Today when I speak to patients, I offer another nugget of wisdom that's been passed down through the ages: "The only thing more difficult than living life sober is living life drunk." But in my last two months at Fellowship Club, I kept thinking that maybe the equation should be reversed. As difficult as it was back when I was using, as bad as I felt sometimes, at least I didn't have to deal with all these unpredictable emotions. I was tired of hearing that even in recovery life is hard. I wanted life to not hurt so much, and I was trying to figure out how to manipulate and control my life so that I could avoid pain. I still looked good on the outside, and I felt good on the inside, most of the time. But I was getting anxious, afraid that I would lose momentum as I approached the finish line. I needed to keep moving forward because if I stumbled or took a step backward, I felt like a failure. It had always been that way with me—any setback I had ever encountered in life, no matter how trivial, convinced me that I wasn't good enough.

Right about that time I started having using dreams.

"I had another dream last night," I told Don, "and this one was similar to the others in that I felt the guilt and shame and the pain of using. However, what was remarkably different this time around is that I never actually used in the dream. Instead, my guilt and shame came from my decision to use. I scored rocks, which I carried around with me in my mouth as I looked for a pipe, and the entire time I was in such mental pain because I knew that as soon as I found the means, I would get high. In the dream I resigned myself to this decision. And as I searched for the tools, the means, the pipe—that search seemed to go on forever in the dream—I began to accept my fate. Thank God I woke up."

Just talking about the dream brought all the emotions back—the guilt and shame, the resignation, the desire, the need, the craving. "What does that dream mean?" I asked Don. "Am I going to relapse?"

"Using dreams are a natural part of recovery," Don reassured me, explaining how cocaine and other drugs physically change the brain and rewire the way the nerve cells communicate with each other. These alterations are permanent—the brain cells actually adapt their structure and their functioning—so that when an addicted person feels anxious, nervous, angry, or afraid, the brain sends out a little messenger that says, "Hey, remember how good it was when you used cocaine, let's do that again!"

Talking to Don made me feel better, but deep down I didn't really believe him, because these dreams seemed to come not from my brain but from my gut, my very soul. If the dreams were confined to my brain, I could say, "Okay, come on William, you almost destroyed your life with cocaine, knock it off! Get your act together!" I'd be able to talk myself out of the thoughts and emotions that ride right along-side the images in the dream. But I couldn't do that because while the demon of craving might originate in my drug-deranged brain, I was convinced those dreams were cooked up deep down in my soul, under my rib cage, in the very center of my being. Those dreams scared the shit out of me, but there was something else about them, too—they in-trigued me. I kind of liked them. And that made me feel ashamed, be-cause I saw my weakness and I knew that if I had the drugs and the tools, I would use again.

The holidays came and went. Allison moved into an apartment in St. Paul, and several times a week we'd meet for dinner or a movie. I thought I might be falling in love with her, but I knew I had to get back to New York to see what I could salvage of my old life. I had no idea what I would do for a job. Mary had kept her distance for four months, and we'd stopped writing and calling each other. The mar-riage was dead, I was almost sure of that, but still I'd have to go back and figure out a divorce settlement, say good-bye to Dallas, meet with my lawyer, and try to figure out my finances. But how was I going to handle all the pressures and old memories, all the people, places, and things that would remind me of my drug-using days?

One of those questions was answered just a few days before I graduated from Fellowship Club when I opened an eleven-page handwritten letter from Mary. From the very first sentence I knew there was no hope for us. The envelope was postmarked CENTER CITY, MINNESOTA, where Mary was attending family week. I was angry enough about the fact that she didn't attend family week four months earlier when I was a patient at Hazelden, but the letter, obviously written as part of an assignment ("I am to write this letter to you from my heart"), infuriated me.

I am ashamed to say that I read that letter, written with such openness and honesty by a woman I once loved with all my heart, with bitter resentment. I didn't feel her pain, because all I could think about, all I could feel, was my own anguish. She doesn't understand, I kept thinking; she won't give me a chance. For God's sake, why can't she get over this? Then, suddenly, I felt sorry for her. I was going to move on, create a new life, leave the past behind. But Mary? Poor Mary. I didn't see any hope for her.

Today I read that letter and every word fills me with deep sorrow. More than once I wished that I had torn it up and thrown it away, because every time I read it, I find something more to regret about the depth and the breadth of the suffering I caused her. "My heart is broken," read the first sentence. "I remember when my heart used to feel joy, and I don't know how I'll ever get back there again."

I had always told her I would protect her, she wrote, but I had endangered her and hurt her more than she had ever been hurt before. The person she had trusted and believed the most had deceived her the most. The person she had let into her heart had broken her heart in two, and it was all too much for her, too much for too long, with all the losses, disappointments, and broken dreams all piled up on top of the shattered trust. She was suffering physically and mentally from the strain, experiencing memory lapses, disorientation, fears for her safety, anxiety attacks, and depression. She hoped these symptoms would resolve in time, as the counselors at Hazelden assured her they would.

"I still have trouble believing what's happened," she wrote. "I have trouble believing that you are not the Cope I thought you were, that you had this whole other side to you because you kept so much of it from me. It scares me that you've been my husband for all these years and I didn't know so much. My naïveté scares me. I know that I'm smart, that I knew so much of what you were dealing with, and I cannot believe that you were addicted and I didn't know."

At the end of her long letter, Mary wrote: "My main feeling with you is 'don't hurt me, just don't hurt me'—don't come too close and don't hurt me. I don't want to hurt anymore."

God forgive me, but when I put Mary's letter back in its envelope, I didn't feel anything but a strange sort of release. It was over. Time to move on.

10

Secrets

ALCOHOLICS AND ADDICTS in early recovery are like used cars. Even after years of neglect and a lack of routine maintenance, if you take away the alcohol and other drugs, the obvious wear and tear vanishes and we hit the road again looking almost new. But what really matters is what's under the hood, and without continued attention to routine maintenance and repairs, it isn't long before the same old engine spoils the new ride.

In early 1990, after five months of overhaul, I looked a lot better than I ran. I had barely driven off the lot before the engine conked out, and I began to coast faster and faster, eventually running smack into a brick wall at the bottom of a very steep hill. I never once thought to heed Hazelden counselor George Weller's famous warning: "If you're coasting in recovery, you're going downhill."

From the early days at Saint Vincent's to the tentative experiences of a life rediscovered at Hazelden and Fellowship Club, my daily journal entries capture a unique period in my life: For the first time I was able to experience life in all its emotional complexity without the numbing, warping effects of alcohol and other drugs. After fifteen years of being driven by drugs, all the while pretending I was in control, I was back in the driver's seat. Everything seemed to be on the move and the speed of change was exhilarating, even though my hands were clenched tight on the steering wheel and I was so intent on keeping my eyes on the road ahead that I avoided looking in the rearview mirror.

At the end of every day I couldn't wait to record everything in my journal, chronicling the extraordinary journey I was taking through uncharted territory. And yet, looking back today with all the benefit of hindsight, I shudder at what those words convey about my state of mind and my willingness to invest in my recovery. I spent page after page in those journals talking about surrender, the very essence of recovery, but even after several months in treatment, I couldn't grasp the deeper meaning of the word. I wanted God to help me, but I wasn't even sure I believed in God and when I asked for help, it was more a command than a plea. I felt sorry for myself and my self-pity sent me spinning out of control into the potholes of bitterness and resentment.

"I want it when I want it and I want it now!" I wrote in the margins of a meditation book I'd been given at Hazelden. I didn't want drugs, necessarily—I just wanted things to be settled, orderly, predictable, and predictably good. What I really wanted was to be normal, because in my mind normal was perfection, perfection was order, order was predictability, and predictability was serenity. I wanted it all—perfection, order, predictability, serenity—and I wanted it now. When it eluded me, I started to think about the fastest, surest route to get it.

Things were wearing down inside, but I didn't dare let anyone look under the hood.

MOST PEOPLE early in recovery and, even later, after many years of being clean and sober, imagine getting high again. For many of us, the craving floats to the surface of our consciousness in vivid dreams and sweat-drenched nightmares. I'm convinced that's one way to separate "normal" drinkers or drug users from addicts and alcoholics. Only those of us who are addicted have nightmares about getting high again. And when we do, we wake up terrified that we have broken all our promises and used again.

"I dreamed about freebasing," I wrote in my journal at Hazelden on September 23, 1989. "I remember my shame as the freebase became heated, and then I woke up. I was so shaken by the experience that I laid in bed for several minutes."

Years later, I still have those dreams. I know there's a scientific explanation related to drug-damaged nerve cells gone permanently haywire, but for me those dreams have more to do with the soul than the brain. They illuminate the yearning for wholeness, for perfection, for making everything feel good and right again. They're about the deepest human hunger and thirst to experience rapture, joy, heaven. Dreaming, I want it all to be good again. I want to be back in Wilmer, free, unencumbered, at peace with myself. And if those longings were all neatly packaged and tied up in my brain with no leakage into my heart or soul, I'd be able to talk myself out of them. "Come on, William," I'd say to myself, "that's ridiculous, you know what it's like in those crack houses, you don't want to go back there." So while these dreams may originate in my drug-deranged brain, they are fixed and fired in the furnace of my soul, way under my rib cage, in a place where CAT scans and PET scans can't penetrate.

Those using dreams reveal the very essence of my illness and the reason why it is so different from other diseases. Addiction is at the core of my being, and I cannot escape its terrible truth, its eternal flame at the center of everything that I am and ever will be. I can no more leave it behind than I could remove my lungs and still breathe or cut my vocal cords and continue to talk. My disease is less about the drugs I took than the reason I took them—to blot out pain, to alter reality, to change perception, to numb my fear—because the deepest truth of my illness is my inability to live with what is right here, right in front of me. Accepting life on life's terms—that's the challenge. Even as I stay sober my dreams remind me of my relentless yearning to go back to the myth of what once was or to reach out for some imaginary heaven that lies just in front of me, out of my reach.

Backward or forward, it doesn't matter as long as I don't have to live in the pain of this moment. But when you're trying to escape pain, there's only one thing more difficult than living life drunk, and that's living life sober.

ON JANUARY 20, 1990—five months and fourteen days clean—I packed my few possessions into a small suitcase and four Dole food boxes that we used at the warehouse to pack salvaged grocery items. My time at Fellowship Club was over, and I was moving to a small two-bedroom apartment on the twenty-fifth floor of a building in downtown Saint Paul. Moving in with me were two good friends I met at Fellowship Club—Jim, a crack addict from Kentucky, and Allison.

I was in love with Allison. I loved her Bermuda accent, her big brown eyes, her unchecked smile, the fact that she loved to play Trivial Pursuit, and the kindness she showed to the people at the homeless shelter where we both volunteered. She was my best friend. Just walking down the street with her was exciting because we were sober and we were seeing the world for the first time. During our months together at Fellowship Club we discovered an intimacy that went beyond anything either of us had ever known because with each other we could talk openly and honestly about our hopes, dreams, and fears of a future that didn't include what our lives had been about for so long—getting high.

When the counselors at Fellowship Club noticed us spending so much time together, they strongly urged us to use caution. They knew what was happening before we did.

"If the relationship is worth it, then you can wait a year and it will last a lifetime," Don advised. Everyone else seemed to agree. Go slow, they said. Avoid major decisions. Concentrate on yourself this first year. Allison and I both knew the advice was solid, but we couldn't slow down because we were in love and it felt so damn good to *feel* again—not just to feel normal, not even to feel good, but just to *feel*.

As I was packing up to leave Fellowship Club on that frigid January day, Mary dropped by for a visit. I was expecting her—after spending a week at Hazelden's family program, she asked if she could stop by on her way back to the airport. I hadn't seen her since she dropped me off at St. Vincent's five months earlier, and I wasn't prepared for my feelings as I watched her walking up to the front entrance of the halfway house. I felt sad—she looked older and smaller. Had she lost weight? I felt angry—from the moment I saw her I felt her presence as an intrusion in my new, sober world. After so many months of ignoring my phone calls and spurning my pleas for reconciliation, after reminding me over and over again what a mess I'd left behind in New York, after refusing to go to the family session while I was there and we could have worked out our problems together, here she was getting in the way of my new relationship, reminding me of the person I used to be and wanted to leave behind. She was like a billboard advertising the chaos and confusion of my life, and I wanted to tear the whole thing down, bulldoze it over, walk away, and never look back.

But here she was in Don's office, and here we were holding hands, trying to find a way to close the awkward distance between us. Her hand felt cold and stiff in mine—how many times in the last ten years had we held hands? It had always felt so right, as if we were extensions of each other, but now I felt as if I were holding a stranger's hand. Sitting with her, trying so hard to bring back part of what we had lost, I felt like a soldier who has been away at war and returns home to a world where he no longer fits in. I looked in Mary's eyes, and I didn't know her anymore.

We talked about Hazelden and what she had learned in the family program. My disease was beginning to make more sense to her, she told me, but that didn't take the pain and grief away. She felt tired and worn out, she said. She needed to think about herself now.

Mary sighed and squeezed my hand as she talked about how she wanted the sadness and grief to wash away so she could be healthy again. The past several years had taken so much out of her, she said, and she still couldn't believe what had happened to me, to her, to us. But the pain was still far too real. Squeezing my hand once more, she told me she wished things could have been different but it was time for her to let go so she could heal. "I need to take care of myself," she said, and she advised me to let go of her, too, and use all my energy to stay sober and heal myself.

We both knew it was the end, but admitting it to each other was the hard part. We talked for a few more minutes, and she asked if I wanted to go to dinner or maybe a movie; her flight didn't leave until later that evening. I could show her around Fellowship Club, she suggested, or maybe we could visit the cathedral in St. Paul. She was so beautiful, so gentle, so sweet and kind, and for a moment I thought maybe we could try, maybe we could make our marriage work. But it hurt me just to look at her and to know what I had done to her. Pain filled the chasm separating us, and I just couldn't imagine how we would ever bridge the divide.

"This is a challenging day for me, Mary," I said, as gently as I could. "It's my last day at Fellowship Club and I have to pack up and say goodbye to people who have been a part of my recovery."

I didn't mention Allison, but I think she knew. We hugged, and then she was gone.

THAT NIGHT ALLISON and I moved into our new apartment and celebrated the beginning of our new life together. It was a good life. We had close friends who were clean and sober, a "home" AA group that we loved, a church where we felt we fit in and belonged, and, when Jim moved out a few months later, an apartment all to ourselves.

I was such a "good" recovering person. I said and did all the right things, but I never told anybody, including Allison, that I wanted to get high. How could I confess that secret, which was more burning need than a desire now. I was hungry, thirsty, starving for cocaine. I craved that feeling of numbness and fullness. I needed to reach the pinnacle, to feed that insatiable appetite, to blot out the pain, to experience the rapture once more, just one more time.

I didn't tell anyone about my cravings because I didn't want them to see the weakness inside me. Why would I admit to being less than I looked or show more to others than I wanted them to see? I had the crazy idea that if I didn't say anything about the craving, maybe it would eventually go away, and I also had my reputation to protect. I prided myself on being the model of how recovery works, quickly rebounding from a crack cocaine binge that would have killed a weaker, less resilient person, rebuilding my life from square one all by myself, talking the talk better than anyone, always willing to lend a helping hand.

Of course it was all about me. I was special, unique, and no matter what I said at meetings or in private sessions with my counselor, I still didn't really believe that I was like all the other addicts. Bill Wilson, the cofounder of AA, summed up my attitude pretty well in a 1959 article he wrote for the *AA Grapevine*:

> The skid-rower said he was different. Even more loudly, the socialite (or Park Avenue stumblebum) said the same. So did the artists and the professional people, the rich, the poor, the religious, the agnostic, the Indians and the Eskimos, the veterans and the prisoners. But nowadays all of these, and legions more, soberly talk about how very much alike all of us alcoholics are when we admit that the chips are finally down.

People in AA were a fine bunch of folks, but they weren't me. I had too much going for me, and I figured my life experience was enough to pull me along without too much help from people who weren't really anything like me. Raised to be independent and self-sufficient, I was determined to be a stellar example of a recovering drug addict, an inspiration to others, proving myself worthy of their admiration. If I told the truth about my craving for cocaine, the facade would peel away to expose the deceit, obliterating the myth that I had worked so hard to create. I had to keep the secret, even while I despised myself for my weakness and hated my disease for sticking to me like a blood-sucking leech.

It wasn't hard to play the part of the solid, sincere recovering alcoholic in public. Four or five meetings a week, dinner parties with newly sober friends, a men's Big Book study group, and regular meetings with my sponsors Bob B. and Paul L. Every newcomer in AA is told to get a sponsor, somebody who has been sober and in the program for an extended period of time. A sponsor is really a teacher who has "been there and done that" and who is willing to share his or her experience with others. When I met Bob and Paul, I liked both of them so much that I asked if they would both be willing to help me through sponsorship. (They are still my sponsors today.)

So I had two sponsors whom I met every week for a cup of coffee, I went to meetings, I socialized with other people in recovery, and I studied AA's Big Book—I had it all down until even I was convinced that I was okay. I was doing so well, in fact, that I thought I could handle a return to my old stomping grounds and the "people, places, and things" connected with my drug-using past. When Allison booked a flight to Bermuda to finalize her own divorce and sort out her finances, I decided to return to New York at the same time. We'd clean up the wreckage of our past to clear the way for our new life together.

I had a lot to think about on the trip back to New York, but I didn't spend one minute going over the details of my upcoming divorce, the mess of my finances, or the long list of amends I needed to make to my family and friends. I thought about one thing and one thing only— the old gardening glove with the crack pipe inside it that I threw into the trunk of the Honda.

Six months had passed, I was on my way back to Northport, clean and sober, and all I could think about was that damn glove. Did Mary find it? Did she throw it out?

When I showed up at the house, Mary met me at the door, warily sizing me up before letting me in. I felt like a door-to-door salesman standing on the front step of my own house, waiting to get permission to walk in my own front door. It was the worst feeling in the world because I felt humiliated and helpless to remove myself from the source of my shame. We talked in the living room while I sorted through six months of bank statements and unopened mail. That night I slept in the guest bedroom, and for hours I listened to Mary sobbing upstairs in the bed we once shared. I wanted to run up the stairs and hold her, comfort her, but I just lay there listening to her crying. Eventually the house was quiet and I fell asleep, exhausted.

In the morning Mary told me she wouldn't be spending any more nights in the house alone with me. I scared her, she said. She gave me two days to pack my things and leave.

Just before Mary left the house that morning, I casually asked her what she had done with all the stuff she had found when she cleaned out my Honda after I went to treatment.

"I put everything in two big garbage bags," she said. I think she knew what I was up to, but she didn't care anymore. "They're out in the garage."

I couldn't wait for her to leave.

Crumpled empty cans of Coors "Silver Bullet" beer, a pizza box and Hostess Twinkies wrappers, a faded *New York Times*, a pair of running shoes, a silk tie with a burn hole in the front, and a Marine Corps hat that belonged to Jack spilled out of the bags when I ripped into them like a kid tearing into presents on Christmas morning. I tossed them all aside, searching for the prize, and there it was near the bottom of the bag. The glove. Inside the glove was the crack pipe, still packed solid with the vestiges of that last binge. The thing was loaded, cocked, and ready to blow my brains out. I couldn't wait to pull the trigger.

The flame curled into the end of the pipe, and the mesmerizing sizzle of a solid turning into a liquid drowned out all sound as the smoky gas filled my lungs, lifting me up, propelling me once again into space, all the way to the dark side of the moon. I wasn't sure whether to hold on or let go, to cry out in despair or shout in ecstasy. This was better than ever before, and worse than I could ever have imagined. All my shame vanished, for maybe two minutes, three, four, and then it came roaring back at me. I could feel it coming, but I couldn't get out of the way, and it knocked me down to my knees. In the flick of a lighter I had thrown away six months of sobriety. I had failed. I was a failure. In my shame I swore that I would never tell another soul what I had done.

I was scared to death because I knew that I was powerless to stop what I had just set in motion. I threw the pipe as far as I could into the woods behind the house and then I got in my car and drove as fast as I could, trying to run away. I drove to my parents' house in Garden City, hoping to escape, but I was being pursued and there was no getting away from it. The floodgates were open, and I was swept away.

The next evening I drove across the railroad tracks to the town of Hempstead. It wasn't Harlem but it wasn't prim and proper Garden City, either. I slowly cruised the streets bordering the public housing project, watching the people milling about, feeling oddly at home again. I knew exactly what to look for, and I found her on a street corner, dressed in high heels and a tight, short dress with a plastic purple windbreaker draped over her shoulders.

She spotted me, too—a well-dressed white guy driving around the projects at night in a nice car—and I knew what she was thinking. I liked having the upper hand.

"Hey baby, what do you want? You want me?" she asked, letting the windbreaker fall off her shoulders. "Tell me what you want, and I'll tell you how much it will cost."

"I'm looking for some crack," I said. "I'll give you fifty bucks if you can take me to a dealer."

She pulled her head back, turtlelike, and looked me over.

"Look, I don't want sex," I said, feeling confident, in control. "All I want is drugs. I'll give you fifty bucks if you just show me where I can buy some crack."

Looking past the shaved and showered exterior, right through the dry-cleaned shirt and new blue jeans, she saw the addict desperate for dope, and for some reason that made her smile.

"Okay, sugar," she said. "Just don't do anything stupid."

We drove three blocks to a two-story house next door to a small machine repair shop in a neighborhood where single family homes had become hybrid dorms for people trying to eke out a living in one of the most expensive areas in the country. Someone lived upstairs, but the only person I was interested in was the drug dealer who lived in the basement.

He looked like a Masai warrior I'd once seen in a *National Geographic* magazine, skin the color and texture of dark-roast coffee beans, long, straight nose, high cheekbones, silver bracelets lining his forearms. The bracelets jangled every time he moved.

"Ben, this guy wants to get high," my companion said.

"I've got plenty of money," I said. That was the way I disarmed drug dealers—money was power. I didn't have to steal or lie or sell my body to get what I wanted. I had money for drugs and extra money to pay people for their efforts to get the drugs. There wasn't anybody on the streets like me. Or so I liked to think.

He paused, looking me up and down, and then he turned and walked back into the dark cave of the basement. "Come with me," he said.

Ben's basement was cleaner than any crack house I'd ever seen. Safer, too, because he refused to keep guns in the house. I didn't really care what the place looked like, though, because I figured I'd only stay long enough to get high and buy some dope to take with me—but I came back every day for two weeks. Most of the time it was just the two of us in the basement, smoking crack, listening to jazz, watching the NCAA basketball playoffs on a black-and-white television, and playing game after game of backgammon. Once or twice a day we were interrupted by women willing to trade Ben their bodies for drugs and I'd either leave the basement to go to the convenience store a block away to buy more malt liquor and Bic lighters or I'd sit in a back room until they were done. Sometimes Ben would disappear upstairs to spend time with his wife and twin baby boys but most of the time he stayed in the basement with me. I didn't think much about his family upstairs. I didn't think much about Allison, either. I only thought about getting high.

When we ran out of drugs, I'd walk to an ATM and withdraw two hundred dollars in cash. ATMs made my life as a crack addict so much easier. I'd give Ben the cash and watch him from the basement window as he walked across the Long Island Railroad tracks and disappeared. Then I'd wait. That was the hardest part, waiting for him to return. I'd sit on the sofa, stand up, pace the room, sit down, stand up, pace, all the while listening for the soft clanking of his bracelets, a sound that always made my heart beat a little faster in anticipation.

Ben would walk in the door, lock it behind him, and take his place in a high-backed chair that he called "the Throne." I sat on the sofa, leaning over the coffee table, watching. Out came the glass test tube where Ben mixed the powdered cocaine, some baking soda, and just the right amount of water. He'd swirl the tube over a candle flame and we'd watch the mixture crystallizing inside the glass. As the cocaine began to rock up, Ben waited until just the right moment before he gently drained the water and dropped that baby out of the womb and onto a paper towel to dry. We'd look at it lying there, big and beautiful, not quite white, but milky and translucent like the moon with its craters and pockmarks, and we'd keep watch over it. We loved it. It was the most important thing in the whole world, the only thing that really mattered until the moment when we cut it in two and set it on fire, a ritual sacrifice that we repeated over and over and over again.

The days passed and then, just like that, it was over and I was at the end of the run. I looked at my shaking hands, feeling the nausea rising up inside me. I needed sleep. I needed food.

I drove home to the house in Garden City. My mother was waiting for me in the kitchen.

"Are you using, son?" my mother asked, moving closer to look in my eyes. Could she see through my eyes and into my soul? I walked over to the refrigerator and pretended to look for something to eat.

"You smell like you've been drinking. Where have you been?" She was relentless. I felt caged, trapped, but I forced myself to turn around and face her. I took the offensive, always a good strategy when you're backed into a corner.

"I haven't been drinking, and I resent what you're saying to me," I said. "You don't know how hard this is. I'm spending time with some new friends who are like me, who can relate to what I'm going through."

She didn't say a word. I kept talking. "My life is wrecked, something you and Dad wouldn't know about, would you? Look at your lives, then look at mine. All I've got now is back in Minnesota, and I'm going back there as soon as I can. All I ask is that you trust me."

The next morning I found a handwritten letter from my mother under my bedroom door.

Dear Son:
I talked to Pricella after you left the house last week only because she came into the den where I was sitting and sat down. She said (after five minutes of chat) that she thought you were 'making it' in spite of the fact it was hard. I did not quiz her for a minute—everything she said, she volunteered. Most of her concern had to do with your staying out late. I did not ask her what time she meant by that, I just listened. So I felt she needed me to listen. I did not expect anything different from what she always has as her bottom line regarding you or your brother and sister: She loves you unequivocally and is always concerned about you like a grandmother would be—about the same love and about the same kind of gaps in understanding of current conditions. I ended the conversation this way: "Pricella, all we can do for him is listen to him and encourage him to continue to make progress. He's come a long way, but this is a very difficult time for him." She had tears in her eyes when she said, "I'm going to get the Bible out for him." I told her you do some Bible reading and she talked about some pas-

sages she likes in troubled times. Then she went into the kitchen and hummed old black songs (what I call "slave songs")—laments and praises. Wish I had it on tape. Over these 23 years together I have heard this on many important occasions in our house—sad *and* glad.

Later that day I found Pricella's Bible on my bed, opened to the Twenty-third Psalm—her favorite prayer. I struggled to read the page through my tears.

> *The LORD is my shepherd; I shall not want.*
> *He maketh me to lie down in green pastures: he leadeth me beside*
> *   the still waters.*
> *He restoreth my soul: he leadeth me in the paths of righteousness*
> *   for his name's sake.*
> *Yea, though I walk through the valley of the shadow of death, I*
> *   will fear no evil: for thou art with me; thy rod and thy staff*
> *   they comfort me.*
> *Thou preparest a table before me in the presence of mine enemies:*
> *   thou anointest my head with oil; my cup runneth over.*
> *Surely goodness and mercy shall follow me all the days of my life*
> *   and I will dwell in the house of the Lord for ever.*

The next morning I packed the Honda and left town. I knew I had to get out of New York or I'd end up back in treatment or dead. St. Paul was the only option left to me, the only place where the temptation to use didn't exist because I had never gotten drunk or high there. So in despair but believing there was still some chance for hope, I fled back to Allison and the city where I had first discovered the freedom and promise of recovery. I had about six hundred dollars in my pocket—that was all that remained of a five-thousand-dollar loan my parents gave me a few weeks earlier when I arrived in Garden City.

They thought they were investing in my recovery, helping me get started on my new life in St. Paul, but I had spent almost the entire loan on cocaine. I had barely enough money to pay the next month's rent on my apartment.

Driving down the tree-lined streets of my hometown, I remembered the way it used to be—running to meet my father as he returned from work, tossing the football in our front yard, playing tag with my brother and sister on the cathedral grounds, sitting in the kitchen with Pricella as she told her stories about growing up in Alabama as the daughter of sharecroppers ("Lord a mercy," she'd always start off), listening to my mother humming as she busied herself around the house. The memories hurt too much, they dragged me down and threatened to pull me under because they reminded me of the way I used to be, the innocent, wide-eyed youth I could never be again.

A few hours later I drove across the Delaware Water Gap and exited Interstate 80 at an unfamiliar town that looked like a picture postcard of colonial America. A small white church sat prominently in the central square. I ate my lunch under a towering pine tree in the church graveyard, and Pricella's fried chicken and homemade biscuits brought the memories flooding back again. Tears streamed down my face. I wanted to go home. I wanted my mother to rub my back. I wanted to talk to my father about God. I wanted Pricella to read to me from the Bible—I wouldn't listen to the words so much as the music of her deep, soft voice. I wanted to be back in Wilmer, walking the black earth of the fields, the wind at my back, the whole day before me with nothing to do and nowhere to go.

Back in St. Paul two days later, I pretended nothing had changed. Allison had returned from Bermuda but within a few weeks she was off again, this time to visit her mother in Toronto, and I tried to get my act together by attending a lot of meetings, jogging every day, and going to bed early. I managed to string together a few months of sobriety and I even landed a job as a reporter in the St. Paul bureau of the *Star-Tribune*, Minnesota's largest daily newspaper. Joel Kramer, the paper's executive editor, was a former protégé of my father's at *Newsday*, and I had worked with the woman who would become my editor, Sylvia Rector, at the *Dallas Times Herald*. When I walked into the newsroom that first day, I looked just fine, and it didn't take long before my byline was on the paper's front page two or three times a week.

"You're the same Moyers I knew in Dallas," Sylvia joked with me one day, "only better."

Everything was getting back on track. I didn't tell Allison, my recovering friends, or my coworkers at the *Star-Tribune* what had happened in New York, and nobody noticed. The mask was good—it fooled people—and for two months I was able to hang on. I tried harder and harder to push the cravings away, but it was an exhausting, never-ending tug-of-war.

Just another hit, that's all, or maybe a few rocks for a few hours one night after work, on the weekend.

No. You can't do that.

Just one more.

You won't be able to stop.

Just one.

The craving became an obsession until one day nothing else mattered and just like that, it seemed, the switch was thrown and the train changed tracks. I could hear the Bic lighter and the sizzle of the crack burning at the end of the pipe. I could see the smoke disappearing into my mouth and filling my lungs. My ears rang. I actually felt high. And it was at that point that I stopped arguing with myself and began planning, plotting. How was I going to find crack in a city where recovery was all I knew? I could walk right into a liquor store, but it wasn't a drink I wanted. I wanted, needed, had to have crack.

My plans fell into place on the day Allison called from Toronto. Problems with her visa kept her stuck on the wrong side of the border, and in tears she told me that the only solution was to go back to Bermuda to straighten out the paperwork. The process, she told me, might take months.

That phone call was like the parting of the Red Sea. With Allison out of the country for at least a few weeks, I was free to do anything I wanted. I hung up the phone and immediately called Ben.

"Hey, man, where the hell are you, where did you go?" Ben said. I could hear his bracelets jangling.

"I'll be there late Friday night," I said. "I'm sending some money today. Get ready for me."

And so began my life as a commuting drug addict. Every three or four weeks I flew back to New York, always taking the last Northwest Airlines flight of the day out of the Twin Cities. I traveled light, carrying a small duffel bag with some underwear, a toothbrush, and one clean shirt. On the flight I'd drink two or three beers, just to calm my nerves and ease me into the weekend. At LaGuardia Airport, I'd rent a car and within an hour I was sitting on the couch across from Ben's throne sharing the pipe. I'd hole up in Ben's basement cave for the weekend and then take the last flight back to the Twin Cities so I could go to work the next morning. I never slept during those weekends, but I also never missed a day of work and I don't think anyone at the newspaper suspected what was happening. When I flew off on my weekend crack binges, I always returned in time to make it into the office. My life was one deep, terrible, devouring lie, but at least the lie was safe.

I kept up the routine all that summer until suddenly, without warning, I couldn't do it anymore. I was sick and tired of the whole thing. Sick of sitting in a dark basement all weekend, smoking crack until I could no longer tell if I was going up or coming down. Tired of peeing in the overflowing bucket in an adjacent storage room, wondering why I never had a bowel movement and glad I didn't need to because there was no toilet in Ben's basement. I was sick with a chronic stomachache that only eased a little when I ate Twinkies to soak up the malt liquor and crack that was chewing away at my insides. Tired of trying to figure out why I had no sex drive when Ben sometimes had sex two or three times a day. Sick every time I thought about Ben's wife and two boys living upstairs. Tired of myself; sick and tired of my life.

I walked out of Ben's basement that Sunday afternoon into the brilliant light of another wasted day. Standing in the driveway, blinking in the sunlight, I waited for my eyes to focus on the shadows and forms in front of me. Everything stayed blurry and unfocused. My ears were ringing and wouldn't stop. I couldn't swallow. The tips of my fingers and toes were numb, and my arms and legs felt disconnected from my body as I walked unsteadily to my car.

Was I dying? Had I overdosed? All I knew was that I had to get out of there. I drove to the airport, leaning forward over the wheel, trying to focus on the road ahead. On the Long Island Expressway, I started perspiring, soaking through my shirt in seconds. I pulled over to the side of the road, got out of the car, and threw up, gagging and choking because there was nothing in my stomach. Terrified now, I got back in my car and kept driving, looking for a place to hide. Somehow I ended up in a hotel room and collapsed on the bed.

The room seemed so bright. I closed my eyes, needing darkness, but the light permeated everything. Somehow I knew at that moment that if I fell asleep on that bed I would die. I tried to stand up but my legs wouldn't carry me so I crawled to the bathroom, my mind filled with one desperate thought—if I'm going to die here, I don't want anyone to find the drugs. Lying on the floor by the toilet bowl, I reached into my pocket, pulled out a lumpy plastic Baggie filled with crack cocaine, and flushed it down the toilet. The thought never occurred to me that if I died, there would be as much cocaine in my body as there was in the toilet.

Afterward I lay down on the cool tiles, willing myself to stay awake. My heart was beating fast, and I was shivering uncontrollably. I didn't feel any pain at all, but it was difficult to breathe. I didn't want to die. I crawled back to the bed and pulled the phone off the nightstand. I started to dial 911 but then I thought about Allison and my parents finding me here, on the floor of a hotel room. I put the phone down. I was too ashamed—I'd rather die than ask for help.

I don't know how long I was in that hotel room or when or how I found my way to the airport, but my next memory is of leaning on the Northwest ticket counter, pleading with the agent to get me on the next flight to Minneapolis/St. Paul. I could barely sign the credit card receipt. At the gate I lay down on the floor and passed out in front of hundreds of people, just a few feet from the spot where my mother hugged me almost exactly a year earlier and sent me off to Hazelden.

I know now that the only reason I survived that day is because I kept moving. If I had stayed in Ben's basement or fallen asleep in the hotel room, I would not be writing this book. Somehow, even as my body began to shut down, I knew I had to surround myself with people, movement, life. The strangers in the airport kept me alive.

For days and weeks after, I remembered the scene in the hotel room and the airport with a feeling of horror. All those years of smoking crack, thinking I was in control and nothing could ever happen to me because I was young and strong and healthy and then one day, without warning, my body simply shut down. It couldn't take any more.

Terrified by the experience, I didn't use again for two months. It wasn't a struggle—even the thought of getting high was repulsive to me. But even though I wasn't using, I was hiding the truth about my relapse from Allison, and when she returned to St. Paul, she knew something was up. You may be able to hide the physical evidence of a relapse, but you can't hide the shame.

One day when I was at work, she went through a stack of papers on my desk and found an airline ticket stub from St. Paul to La-Guardia. When I came home from work, she confronted me.

"What's this?" She was crying as she thrust the ticket in my face. "I want to know what you were doing in New York. You've been there to visit Mary, haven't you? Are you seeing her again? Are you lying to me?"

Allison's questions shocked me. I was never unfaithful to her and my love for her was never compromised, even by the temptations of desperate women in the world of the crack house.

I told her the truth about Ben and the trips back East.

"William, you have to pull out of this," she said. "I can't make you get sober or stay sober—that's your business—but building a life together is my business, too. I love you too much to give up on us."

I came clean with my sponsor, too. "You are only as sick as your secrets," Bob said, "and you can't afford any more secrets, William. They're gonna kill you."

No more secrets, I promised myself. And for a few months I kept my promise, but in late September I went back to New York, this time for legitimate reasons—I had to go back to collect the few items that still belonged to me now that the divorce was finalized. I wasn't happy about the settlement, but I wasn't going to argue about it, either. Still, it rankled me that Mary was getting the house, the china, the silver, the crystal, all the furniture, the computer, and even Dallas, the only dog I'd ever owned. Why did I have to give up everything? The whole thing made me feel sick with anger, but I found comfort in feeling sorry for myself. Once again, I was the victim.

Mom picked me up at LaGuardia and that afternoon we sat in the study of the Garden City house while I bemoaned the utter destruction of my life. I was really feeling sorry for myself, spilling my guts, and my father, good journalist that he is, took notes as I talked. He sent them to me years later, after he found the yellow legal-sized paper with his handwritten notes in a box in the basement. "I will translate the notes because my handwriting is illegible to everyone but me," he typed at the top of the page.

Tears: choked up.

"I can't believe that I'm a thirty-one-year-old man who can't live in his own house."

"I see young couples nicely dressed and with their children and doing normal things and I've always wanted that. Now I'm sitting here in your study reading the paper and the sun is coming through the window and I have all the peace and quiet and space I need and I can't believe that I have to go back to a place called St. Paul."

"I feel like a stranger here. I feel like I have died here."

"The old me will use if I stay here. But the new me can't take the risk."

"I hate this disease. It's pushed me to the edge. It has destroyed my dreams."

The next day Dad drove to Northport with me, and in just a few minutes we had loaded up the boxes of books, the Davidson andirons that belonged to my mother's family, several sweaters and winter shirts, and a framed picture of Dallas and me. When it was time to go, Mary, who had been watching us like a high school hall monitor, gave me a quick hug and wished me good luck.

On the way back to Garden City I couldn't stop crying. Dad kept looking over at me, his face creased with concern. That night, after Pricella served my favorite dinner of fried chicken, biscuits, black-eyed peas, and fried okra, I told my parents I was going to an AA meeting. Instead, I drove over to Ben's house and got high.

Within a week after returning to St. Paul, I had figured out how to score crack on the streets there as well. It was easy, actually—just like in Hempstead, I cruised the streets until I found someone who looked as desperate as me. She was standing on a street corner where there was no bus stop and I pulled up next to her, rolled down the window, and offered her the deal.

"I have plenty of money," I said, "and I don't want sex. All I want is cocaine and a place to use it. I'll treat you well, but don't rip me off, because the first time you do, I'm gone. And we both lose."

Her name was Janette, and she didn't trust me at first. On the street, in her world, men used crack for sex, and women used sex for crack—that's just how it worked. I was offering to take care of her and feed her habit if she'd take me to her dealer and find us both a place to hide. How could she turn down a deal like that? All I needed from her was a connection, and as long as she did her part, I'd supply her with anything she needed including cocaine, beer, food, clothes, or toothpaste. That's how I lived with myself—that's how I convinced myself I was a good person even if I was a crack addict. I never had sex with Janette or any of the other women I knew on the streets, and I never abused them in any way, except the worst way possible—I fed their habits while I fed my own.

We spent a week in a crack house on the corner of Selby and Lexington avenues, at that time one of St. Paul's seediest neighborhoods, with Big Mama and her daughter, Peanut. At least I assumed they were mother and daughter—in the unfriendly environs of a crack house it's better not to ask too many questions. An obese African American woman with a Southern accent who never moved off the couch unless she was combing through the carpet or looking under the furniture hoping to find a piece of lost crack, Big Mama liked to boss Peanut around. "Clean up the living room," she'd suddenly bark out. Every so often she'd tell Peanut, who was as small and shapely as Big Mama was large and round, to "go get some money." Peanut disappeared, sometimes for hours, and she usually came back with a wad of tens and twenties. She always wore sweatpants and a sweater that was much too big for her.

For the week that Janette and I lived with them, I was the patriarch of the group, supplying everyone with crack, Newport cigarettes, cold beer, and, when we felt like eating, buckets of Kentucky Fried Chicken. In exchange, Big Mama let us sleep on the floor and she even gave us a few blankets so we could stay warm. It was February, almost exactly a year after I left Fellowship Club, and bitter cold.

One day Janette and I were sitting around talking and she told me she was seven months pregnant. I stood there, staring at her, trying to comprehend what she was telling me. I just thought she was overweight. Drugs had worn down the edges of my perceptions until all I could see clearly was how to get high, yet at that moment I knew I couldn't sink lower—I was a junkie hiding out in a crack house, feeding drugs to a pregnant woman and her unborn child. What kind of a human being was I? Another hit off the pipe, and the question didn't matter.

I don't know if it was that day or the next that we heard a knock on the door. We all froze, looking at one another, wide-eyed. Someone knocked again, harder. People were talking. I thought I heard my father's voice. How did they find me? Dad told me later that Allison called him in New York when I disappeared and he flew out that night to help her search for me. They drove around the neighborhoods together, keeping each other company, and sometimes Dad went out on his own.

"I drove through the streets with a constant pain in my upper back as if someone had driven a knife between my shoulder blades and left it there," Dad remembered. "When I saw a figure in the shadows or on the sidewalk or crossing the street, my heart seemed to lift against the blade and the pain would burn right up my neck to my head. I drove slowly, leaning into the steering wheel, slowly, so that I could see in every possible direction. I had no idea where to look, was utterly unfamiliar with the area, and didn't know what I would do if I found you and you ran, or were dead.

"At one intersection a car pulled up beside me and two big, tough-looking men stared me down; I thought they were trying to size up whether anyone else was in the car with me, to see if they could take me on. I had deliberately not locked the door or buckled my seat belt because if I saw you I wanted to be able to get out of the car as fast as possible, and I wasn't about to reach up and push the lock because I feared it would be a signal to them. A police car came along at just that moment and they pulled on ahead. I kept driving like a man looking for an unmarked house in a strange neighborhood. I cried some, and prayed some, and I know that I moaned aloud once or twice at the thought you could be dead. I kept telling myself to stay calm. I thought of your mother back in New York, knowing she must be in misery, because the call had come in the middle of the night that you were missing and I had left so quickly for the airport that we had almost no time for a good-bye. I thought of my other children, John and Suzanne, and prayed they were okay. I kept my hands squeezing the wheel, and just kept turning down one dark and empty street after another. I just kept looking."

Dad and Allison looked for two days before they knocked on Big Mama's apartment door.

"We know he's in there!" someone shouted through the door. "Let us in."

I put my finger to my lips, signaling everyone to keep quiet, and tiptoed into the bedroom. I tried to escape through the second-floor window, but it was sealed shut, so I hid in the closet. It was the first closet I had ever seen in a crack house that actually had clothes hanging in it.

I heard a door slamming shut, voices raised, footsteps.

"If he's anywhere in this apartment, we'll find him," someone said. The voice came closer. I pushed myself flat against the far wall of the closet as a hand swept the clothes aside. A box on the rack above my head tipped over. I felt fingers touching the thick cloth of my sweatshirt.

"He ain't in here," the voice said.

"Where else could he be?" My father's voice, confused, desperate. Footsteps retreating, voices fading, the apartment door shutting. I waited, holding my breath, and a few minutes later I came out of that closet feeling like a little kid who had fooled his playmates during a game of hide-and-seek. I was the happiest person in the whole world until I saw the look on Big Mama's face.

"You two are bringing the heat in here," she said, keeping her voice low. Peanut was crying, and Janette just stared at me, stunned. I'd never mentioned any family.

"Time for you to go," Big Mama said.

A steady wind was blowing the snow sideways when we snuck out the back door of the apartment building a few hours later. I must have looked at my watch, noted the date, because I remember thinking that it was February 15, the day after Valentine's Day, and I forgot to buy Allison flowers. I felt bad about that. I should have sent her a dozen red roses.

We trudged through the snow, heading for Janette's house, the only place left to go. On the way we stopped at a corner bar, the green and red neon lights shining through the falling snow and a sign beckoning us to COME ON IN. I needed a drink, and it was warm and safe inside the bar. We ordered two beers, but when I reached into my pocket all I had were a few crumpled dollar bills, so we shared one beer before heading back into the storm. No point in staying there, even if it was warm inside, if we couldn't drink.

Just before dawn, we walked up the steps of Janette's front porch. The windows were covered with plastic in an attempt to keep out the cold, but it didn't work. The apartment was freezing. Janette's mother—she looked old enough to be her grandmother—was in the kitchen drinking coffee, her hands spread around the mug to gather in the warmth. She was my last hope.

"I need to borrow twenty bucks," I said, talking fast, "but I'll give you back forty tomorrow. And I'll bring groceries, too. Just let me have the twenty bucks."

She stared at me for the longest time. Her skin was dark brown, and she was a large woman, but when she looked at me, I saw my mother. She had the same sad, knowing eyes.

"No," she said in a soft voice, just like my mother's. "You're done."

Done. I heard the word and nodded my head.

"Okay," I said. I actually felt grateful. "Can I borrow your phone?"

She pointed at a table in the corner, keeping her eye on me.

Allison answered on the first ring.

"Can you come get me?" I asked.

"Oh, William," she said. She sounded exhausted. "Where are you?"

I gave her the address, hung up the phone, and walked to the front of the house where I stared out the window at the snow falling, feeling the old woman's eyes on my back. I knew what she was looking at because I knew what I was. A bad man, a crack addict who had taken her daughter into the streets, given her money, fed her crack. A down-and-out loser. I felt so lonely. I couldn't run, I had no place to go, I had no money left. I always had money and because I always had money, I was the King of the Streets, everybody liked me, everybody needed me. But when I was out of money, I was useless to everyone. Without money, I was nothing. Nothing.

I was so tired. It was so cold outside.

The Honda pulled up to the curb. I said good-bye but no one answered, and then I walked out into the snow and climbed into the backseat of the car. My father was driving and Allison was in the passenger seat. Neither of them said a word to me. The windshield was all fogged up, and for some reason, that really annoyed me—it really bugged the hell out of me that my father couldn't figure out how to use the damn defogger. I leaned forward from the backseat and pointed out the controls. The whole way home I gave him instructions from the backseat and thought what a fool he was that he couldn't even figure out how to use the damn car controls.

When we got back to the apartment, I followed Allison into our bedroom and shut the door. She sat on the edge of the bed and looked at me, not with judgment or anger, but with something deeper, some mixture of sorrow, pity, grief, and fear. I kneeled down next to her, held her hand, sobbed, begged for her forgiveness.

"I'm a bad man," I kept repeating. I felt so lonely, so terribly, desperately alone.

"You're a good man, William," she said in a voice that was deeply, desperately tired. "But you have a bad problem and you will die if you don't do something about it."

I felt as if I were drowning, and those words were my lifeline. *Good man, bad problem.* Today, I use those same words every time I talk to addicted people and their family members. I look across the table, around the circle, or out across the sea of faces in the church pews, civic auditoriums, or convention halls, and I see my own face staring back at me.

"Good people," I say. "Bad disease." The words sink in, and I know what they are thinking because I thought it once, too. *Maybe there is some hope for me yet.*

Early the next morning, February 16, 1991, my father and Allison drove me to Hazelden.

"All I felt was relief," Dad said, recalling the details of that drive. "You were out of it in the backseat. I could see you in the rearview mirror, gray and dazed like death. But you were not dead and we were on the way to Hazelden and I was overcome with hope. I relived our first experience there, and how I had been so comforted after talking to the counselors and other parents and to recovering people themselves. I remember how my spirit had felt buoyed when I was there, despite my ignorance of the disease and of what was happening to you. I kept telling myself: Once we turn into that driveway, he will be safe and I can breathe again. It was only after you had been checked in and we had said good-bye once again that I went into the men's room near the entrance and broke down. But the fatigue and fear and grief of the previous days were mixed this time with tears of relief. I knew you were safe again."

I remember only this: Hands reaching into the backseat to pull me out, gently, and help me into a wheelchair. Keeping my eyes on the floor, too ashamed to look back at Allison and my father standing in the hallway as a nurse wheeled me into detox.

11

Self-Will Run Riot

I REMEMBER BITS and pieces, like a shaky camera shooting out-of-focus, disconnected scenes. Wheels on the chair, spinning. Bright lights flickering. Doors opening, closing.

"My name is Chris," she said in a voice that was almost a whisper. She looked like an angel. Black hair, hazel eyes, flawless complexion. The blood pressure cuff filled up, emptied out. Gentle fingers on my wrist. Breathing in. Breathing out.

Sleep came fast, but first the plunge, like an elevator cable snapping and the floors of my life rushing by—Allison, Mom, Dad, Pricella, Mary, Dallas, Washington & Lee, Aspen, the Pine Barrens, Garden City, the White House, Marshall, Wilmer. Falling through space, plunging through floor after floor, and then the crash, the cold, rock-solid floor of shame.

I slept for twelve hours and woke up feeling stiff, my stomach knotted from hunger and shame. I was starving. The nurse stopped by—I remembered her name—and took my blood pressure and pulse. We talked for a while—how are you feeling, good, do you need anything, no thank you—and when she left, I propped myself up in the bed and wrote in my journal.

> I slept all day, feeling at times that this whole thing is a dream.
> I know that it is all too real, but I am reluctant to believe it. I
> felt well rested near the end of the day.

Those words seem so strange and ill-fitting now, so out of sync with the reality of what was happening to me. Already I was trying to move ahead, put the past behind me, race past the stark truth that I had suffered a devastating relapse. I had to show everyone that I could get back on track, plug right back into the AA community, and continue on as if nothing had really happened. Ready, set, go! I'd learned a valuable lesson and now it was time to move on.

I always rebounded pretty quickly after a binge, maybe because I was young and still in pretty good shape. Even after bingeing for days, getting no sleep, drinking malt liquor, smoking cigarettes, eating almost nothing, and living in darkness in a dirty, cockroach-infested apartment, I bounced back fast. All it took to feel like myself again were four or five full plates of food, quarts of whole milk and gallons of water, a good night's sleep, and a shower and shave. The next day I'd feel a little nauseous and experience some jittery feelings in my hands and feet, maybe put up with a nosebleed or two, but I didn't suffer through anything like the physical agony of late-stage alcoholics, heroin junkies, or prescription pill addicts. They were the ones who yelled out loud to nobody in particular, vomited without warning, soaked their clothes in sweat, and spent night after night lying in bed praying for just one more drink or one more Valium to ease the pain. They were the helpless ones—not me, thank God.

Oh, but the shame. My body healed fast but my soul was broken and bleeding and the shame was like nothing I had ever known, worse than anything I had experienced at St. Vincent's or during my first stay at Hazelden. On the second day, soon after I was transferred out of the medical unit to Tiebout unit, two friends from Fellowship Club stopped by for a visit. "Big Dave" from New York and "Crawdaddy" from Kentucky offered encouragement, shared their own stories, and honestly and openly expressed what they perceived to be the flaws in my recovery. In AA these visits are called Twelve Stepping, as alcoholics "carry the message" to other alcoholics who are suffering and in that act find their own commitment to recovery renewed and strengthened. I pretended to be truly interested in what Big Dave and Crawdaddy had to offer me.

"Guys, I hate to admit it, but you're right," I said, figuring that if I didn't argue but just agreed with them, maybe they'd leave. I was just so filled with shame. I had relapsed and they were still sober, so we all knew who the loser was. They were clothed in their recovery while I was naked in my relapse, fully exposed and unable to hide what I didn't want anyone to know—William, the recovering alcoholic and drug addict who always ran a Grade A program, the model Hazelden alumnus who had all his shit together and could handle life in the fast lane of the real world, was a failure through and through.

For actively using alcoholics and addicts like me, instinct is one of the tools we use to survive as long as we do when the rest of our world is falling apart around us. Within days of my return to Hazelden, my gut survival instincts took over. Self-will, self-pity, fight or flight, resentment, defiance, and denial were the shields I had learned to use through all the years of my drug use, helping me hide from the truth of my disease. Now they helped me hide from the truth in myself.

When I woke up after that first night in detox, I had one thought: "Oh shit, how am I going to get out of this one?" From that moment on, I was gone. I fled into the isolation of myself and hid there, quivering, defenseless, terrified, waiting for it all to be over. I knew the right things to do and say, I'd been a good student even if I did flunk the course, and so I raised the shields and hunkered down inside Fort Moyers to try to survive the truth. I was going to withstand this bombardment. I could take it. All I had to do was wait them out.

I COULDN'T MOVE fast enough through the next twenty-one days, but I kept up a good front. When Tom the minister visited me in the medical unit on Sunday, the day after I arrived, I told him that I was worried because I wasn't sure where God was or what His role was. I felt like I was trying to pull Him closer to me when it seemed that He should be pulling me closer to Him.

"I know God is there," I said, "but I don't feel like I can turn my will and my life over to Him because the allure of drugs seems so much stronger."

"You will feel God's love and God's power more and more each day," Tom assured me. "You just don't have to try so hard."

Maybe not, but the clock was ticking. I knew the typical stay in treatment at Hazelden lasted about twenty-eight days. If I wanted to make it out on time, then I better damn well find God and find Him quick, especially since it didn't feel like God was looking for me. He was out there somewhere, but where? I needed to track Him down, but where was He hiding?

MONDAY, FEBRUARY 18

When I catch a fish that's too small to keep, I let it go by gently lowering it into the water and simply opening my hand.

When I catch a butterfly and have finished admiring its beauty, I release it with nothing more than a flick of my wrist.

Today I realized what has really been lacking from my AA program, and what I must learn while here at Hazelden.

I *MUST* find the strength to let go of my resentments, my

efforts to control my alcoholism and my way of doing things. My way hasn't worked. Now I must do it God's way.

It shouldn't be that difficult. Like the fish and the butterfly, I should not have to expend much effort to let go of my way and let God and the Twelve Steps do it for me. But it is. Why? Why can't I simply open my hand and flick my wrist?

The strength must come from my willingness to turn all of this over. I've already proved it doesn't work my way, on my terms. That's why I'm back here.

Tonight I prayed to God asking for the strength to set aside my convictions and my agenda and simply follow AA and God. That must be my focus. I won't make it if I don't get out of the way and let it happen.

Why can't I just let it go and let it be? Somehow I must find the strength not to be headstrong.

Another realization that came to my heart while I was walking through the snow in the woods. Like the soil of the garden which must be cultivated before seeds are planted, I've *got* to dig deep inside of me and turn over what I find. I'm stuffed with emotions buried by my alcoholism. It's time to take a shovel and dig that stuff up, turning it over so that all of it can be exposed to the Twelve Steps and God's power. I cannot keep such things buried any longer. I'll relapse again and again.

It never occurred to me during those days that it wasn't God who was hiding from me, but me who was hiding from God. I knew I needed to dig deep inside me if I was ever going to recover from this disease—that's what George, Keith, and my new counselor, Lowell, told me, anyway—but I was terrified to even think about what God might say once I unearthed the rotting, stinking truth that lay hidden in the tomb of my soul. I didn't want God to see those foul secrets that lurked in the hidden reality I was horrified to face and loathe to understand. And what would happen when that tomb was emptied? What would fill the hole inside me?

I felt doubly cursed. I didn't want to live like this, a tormented addict who relapsed over and over again because I wasn't strong enough to face the truth of myself. Yet the very idea of allowing God or anyone else—my counselors, Tom the minister, my peers on the unit, or my friends in AA—to help me exhume my real self was intolerable. Then they would know just how weak I was, and so would I, and what would be left of me, what would I become?

Keith knew I was in trouble, and he did his best to try to help me.

"I'm setting up an interview for you at Jellinek," he said one day, about halfway through the twenty-eight-day stay. I remember looking out his window. Snow fell in fat, wet flakes. I had always loved snowstorms.

Jellinek—just the word gave me the shivers. Jellinek was the extended care unit where the sickest of the sick went to face their inability to stay sober in the world outside the protective cocoon of treatment. At Jellinek time didn't matter because the patients weren't going anywhere, at least not until they faced their demons of rage and fear and shame. But that would take months and months of hard work in treatment, and I didn't have the time, willingness, or patience. Besides, I wasn't that sick.

There was still a way out of this, if I was smart and outmaneuvered the staff. While it was true that I was a hard-headed, relapsing addict, that didn't have to mean I would automatically get sent to Jellinek—first, I had to go through the interview, and then, if the staff agreed I needed extended care, I'd have to show a willingness to "follow the program." That's where I gained control. All I had to do was explain that Jellinek wasn't the right place for me.

On my tenth day at Hazelden I walked out the door of Tiebout along the pathway to the front doors of the stand-alone Jellinek unit.

Anyone who was watching me might have thought I was walking down death row. I had an appointment to see Russell Forrest, the man in charge of the extended care program.

"Why are you here, William?" he asked me when I sat in the chair opposite his desk. He knows exactly why I'm here, I thought. I instantly disliked him.

"I relapsed," I replied.

"Are you willing to do the work?"

I shrugged my left shoulder, a gesture that basically said, "You're full of shit, Russell."

"Of course I'm willing to do the work," I said, staying calm, looking earnest, "but I honestly don't think I need to do it here."

"You've got issues," Russell said. *I really can't stand this guy,* I thought.

"Well, sure I do, we all have issues, but I know what I need to do about them. I have a home group in AA, and a great sponsor, Bob B. Do you know Bob?" Everybody who knew anything about AA in Minnesota knew Bob B., a wise old-timer who had sponsored dozens of men in the Twin Cities. Bob looked a lot like Dick Butkus, the Chicago Bears linebacker once described as "the meanest, nastiest, fiercest linebacker to ever put on a helmet." Bob wasn't mean or nasty, but he sure was fierce—if he didn't love you to death, he'd beat you to death with the Big Book.

Russell wasn't about to get sidetracked. "Tell me about your support network in St. Paul," he said. "How do you know that you can stay sober when you're out of treatment again?"

I stumbled through my response. "Well, I have Bob and my friends from Fellowship Club, and I also have a girlfriend waiting for me back in St. Paul. She went through Hazelden and Fellowship Club. She's been sober for almost two years now."

Russell didn't say anything. "She's an amazing woman." I kept going. "She's written me almost every day, visited every Sunday. She makes cookies for the men on the unit. She's stood by me, and she wants me to focus on the Twelve Steps and my own emotions. When I'm ready, she'll be there."

I didn't say what was really on my mind—if I don't get out of here soon, I might lose her.

"If you come to Jellinek," Russell said, "I'm putting you on female restriction."

Was he suggesting that my relationship with Allison caused my relapse? Did he think I was too dependent on her or that she was an obstacle to my recovery? What right did he have to separate us when we loved each other and she was rock solid in her recovery program? I wanted to stand up and walk out of his office, but I knew he expected that kind of reaction from me. So I just sat there stewing, because he had assaulted my dignity and it hurt that he was challenging my relationship with the woman I loved. Suddenly, I was tired of playing nice to satisfy the teacher.

"You are so wrong," I said. *You're the one who needs treatment,* I wanted to say, *because you don't know anything about me. You think you're so smart, but you've got me wrong just like Keith, George, and Lowell have me wrong. What a bunch of smug, self-righteous, know-it-alls. Get me the hell out of here.*

"We'll see," Russell said, standing up to shake my hand.

You'll see, I thought as I walked back to Tiebout. *I'll show you.*

AFTER THAT EXCHANGE, I settled back into the routine, playing the part of the good patient, doing what I was told, completing all my assignments, and writing in great detail about all the things that were bothering me. "Why can't I stay sober?" I wrote in my journal just hours after my interview with Russell. "What emotions lurk below the surface, waiting to challenge my serenity and sobriety? Will I live a happy and productive life, or will a relapse bring about too much pain to continue living? How is my alcoholism going to impact those who love me, especially Allison?" By asking these questions and opening myself up to scrutiny, I was hoping to prove to myself and the staff that I was serious about my recovery and, at the same time, take the focus off the big, unresolved issue: Would I go to Jellinek or not?

Then my father showed up at Hazelden. It was on short notice; just a day or two before, he called to let me know that he wanted to fly out from New York to visit. I was confused—visitors were strictly limited in the time they could spend with patients and visits were generally allowed only on Sundays during certain designated hours. Dad explained that he was staying at the Renewal Center, a retreatlike program for alumni and other people in Twelve Step programs. It was more like a hotel than part of the treatment environment, and people who stayed there were not required to attend any of the regular Hazelden programming. If anything, I thought Dad should go back through the Family program, especially after the trauma of my relapse. So what exactly was his game plan? Was he going to try to manipulate me into going to extended care?

THURSDAY, FEBRUARY 28
I am growing increasingly nervous about my father's arrival this weekend. In some ways I'm angry, too, because he is coming to the retreat center not the family program. He isn't even in a Twelve Step program, so I don't know how much he can really expect to gain from the retreat center. He swears he isn't coming for me, but for himself. But the family program is where he could gain some significant insights and help for himself.

I'm not certain what I want to talk with him about, either alone or with Lowell. Maybe I'm paranoid, but I'm convinced he will seek to have some input into my treatment, some influence over the course that treatment takes. I wish we could just talk. But that's probably not the way it will be.

There are a lot of areas I want to talk with him about—SOMEDAY. Our intimacy, his brother's death, his attempts to meddle in all my affairs, marriage, how he thinks he succeeded or failed as a father, his career, his fears, and his relationship with his parents growing up. But not now. I need to focus on myself and on determining my issues and how to cope with them. His sudden appearance may upset my delicate cart right now, even though I love my father and have a yearning to see him to say hello and one day have a healthy relationship with him.

I didn't want Dad's visit to interrupt my carefully crafted plans. I didn't want him to trip me up. But at the same time I desperately wanted to talk to him. I had so many questions I wanted to ask him, but they were hard questions, and Dad was so private, I just didn't see how we could close the distance between us. Why weren't we closer? Why did he always write me letters rather than talk to me face-to-face? Why were emotions so difficult for him? How did his brother's drug addiction and death affect him and what exactly were the details of Uncle James's demise? Why did Dad always try to control my life and get involved in my affairs? What was it like to be married for so long to one woman? Was he disappointed in me because of my divorce? How did he think he succeeded or failed as my father? What were his biggest successes and his deepest disappointments? What scared him? What did he love most in the world?

I was dying to ask him those questions, but I knew that now wasn't the time. I was in treatment to focus on myself and try to work out my problems—having Dad there would only confuse me because the spotlight would be on him, not me. Yet I yearned to talk, just the two of us. But why now, why did we have to do this now? My emotions were all over the place.

I called Dad at the Renewal Center the day he arrived.

"Hello, son, it's good to hear from you," he said. "I'm sitting here by the fire. Why don't you come on over for a little while?"

And just like that I was angry. *Well, Dad,* I wanted to say, *I'm in an inpatient treatment center over here across the way, and I have a pretty rigid schedule to follow. It's not like I can just pick up and walk over to the Renewal Center anytime I want. If you had chosen to attend the family program, I'd be able to spend a lot more time with you.*

I told him I had to attend a counseling session, and we agreed to meet the next day. When I hung up the phone, my anger disappeared and I felt a sudden wave of sadness. It would have been nice to sit around by the fire and chat for a while. I thought about him sitting there alone and I felt sorry for him. There he was, longing to be with his son, trying to cope with his confusion over my disease and what he could do to help me. Was he blaming himself? Is that why he was at the Renewal Center, to work on his own issues of grief and guilt? Maybe he decided to go there rather than the family program because he didn't want people to focus on him rather than me. Besides, he'd already been through the family program, and he was entitled to some private time to work on his own issues.

My emotions switched tracks again. What good would one weekend do? Why would anything be different between us this time, when it had always been so difficult for us to talk one-on-one about our feelings in the past? I never could tell what my father was thinking or feeling, what his needs or wants were, what made him happy and what made him sad. Out in the world, he was as public as a person could get, but in private he was reserved and enigmatic. He never talked about his successes with me, the awards he won or the accolades he received, which is why I liked to spend time in the nonfiction section of bookstores looking for books that might mention my father (books about President Johnson, Vietnam, public television, books by liberals and conservatives). Moyers, B., I'd read in the index, and that's how I found out that Dad won more than thirty Emmy Awards and a bunch of Peabodys, Polks, and Silver Batons.

The way he so jealously guarded his privacy from even me, his own son, was a source of torment. Although at some level I understood that my father was trying to protect me from his many successes, knowing how I felt I could never measure up, I deeply resented the fact that he could step in and out of the spotlight whenever he wanted while I had no safe place to hide or cover myself up. Here I was with my life turned inside out for everyone to dissect, and my connection to this famous man made me even more vulnerable. When I broke into the fish market in college and stole $20.06, the story hit the national newspapers and the AP wires. When I signed into St. Vincent's, I used a fictitious name in part to protect myself but also to guard my parents' right to privacy. In every treatment program I attended, the counselors and psychiatrists told me I had "issues" with my father and if I didn't explore them, I'd risk having a relapse. So I bared my soul, spilled my guts, and the whole world, it seemed, knew my most private thoughts and my most vulnerable feelings. And there was Dad sitting by the fire in the Renewal Center, keeping his privacy intact.

Over the years many people have asked me if I became an alcoholic and crack cocaine addict because of the pressures of being "the son of." No, I explain, at least no more than if I didn't have a father or my father beat me or abandoned the family. Sure, I have issues with my father, but my father isn't the reason I'm addicted. The truth is that any unresolved issue—being too poor or too rich, too famous or too unknown, too tall or too short, too smart or not smart enough, too successful or too down on your luck—feeds the discomfort, the sense of not fitting in your own skin, the fear of meaninglessness, insignificance, the sense of shame, the hole in the soul that gives people who are vulnerable to addiction a really good excuse to get drunk or high. And that's why there is always more to recovery than just not taking another drink or hit, because the reasons to take another drink or hit are always going to be there. We can learn to live sober with our "issues," but only if we recognize that it isn't the issue that drives the addiction so much as the addiction that latches on to the issue for a free ride straight into the complicated neurological wiring that underlies the craving and the desire for oblivion.

All addicts and alcoholics have their issues, just as every human being on this earth has issues. My big issue has always been my father. That's not his fault any more than it is mine, but somehow, at some point in time, I would have to deal with it or that neural switchboard would start firing up and eventually I'd give in and give up.

I didn't meet my father by the fire, but the next day, gathering my courage, I called and asked him to go to the evening lecture with me. An AA member told his story that night—our stories almost always follow the temporal format of "the way I used to be, what happened, and the way I am now"—and my father, who possesses extraordinary storytelling gifts himself, seemed to be deeply moved. After the lecture we went to a small private lounge area, just a few feet from where Dad and Allison had dropped me off just two weeks earlier, and spent four hours alone, talking. We talked about the summer before my "crash," as he put it (a word I have never liked because it signifies a violent event, whereas most addicted people experience a slow, gradual decline before finally hitting bottom), and how he feared then that I was having a physical or mental breakdown and he didn't know what to do to help me. Dad talked openly and honestly about his guilt and his shame, and he told me stories that I had never heard before about his childhood, his relationship with his parents, his courtship of my mother, and the joys and sorrows of their thirty-six years of marriage.

I had never felt closer to my father, and I have often wondered if he knew, in his deeply intelligent and intuitive way, that I needed that openness and honesty from him at precisely that point in my life. No miracles happened, no sudden conversion process took place, but the ground shifted imperceptibly. For running like a river through the peaks and valleys of the stories my father told me was the understanding that he loved me just the way I was, all of me, even the addicted parts. Dad said something to me that night that my mother, in different words, would say to me many times in the years ahead. I don't remember the exact phrasing, but the gist of it is something like this: *Although none of us would have chosen this path for you, Cope* (my father still calls me Cope), *our lives have all been changed in ways that have made us deeper, more understanding, more tolerant, and more forgiving people. I am sorry that you had to do most of the suffering, but this disease has been a gift to all of us in so many ways. No matter what has happened, I will always love you.*

After Dad left I read through the Concerned Person Questionnaire that he filled out the day before he arrived at the Renewal Center. In one part of the questionnaire, under "Family Problems that may be related to the drinking or drug abuse of someone that you care about," my father wrote:

> I worked long hours and traveled a lot when Cope was young, perhaps to the point of creating a deprivation in him from my absence. It's possible I also was too involved in his decisions later on, even to the point of intervening when I did not have to do so. Intimacy has always been a problem for me, and I show emotions very little, partly because that is my nature and partly for professional reasons—journalistic objectivity, that is.

In the section titled "In what areas do you feel help will be needed in the future?" Dad filled the page and added an extra typed page.

I believe strongly that Cope needs sustained and intense therapy to help him get at whatever unresolved issues in his life are causing him such deep pain. This is the third time drugs have taken him to the edge—once when he was a senior in college and under the influence he broke into a neighborhood store and was apprehended by police emerging with $20 in coins, for which he was given a suspended sentence that was then erased from the record altogether (and after which he nonetheless offered his younger brother cocaine!); again in 1989 after several months of active use, bringing his marital and financial life to ruin, he went on a binge that led to thirty days in detox in New York and then Hazelden and Fellowship Club; and this most recent episode which ended in his disappearance for several days before his present companion and I could locate him through an intensive search. His behavior in each of these three instances was potentially self-destructive, and his two major crashes put him seriously in harm's way (his mother located him in 1989 in one of Harlem's most dangerous areas; his housemate and I plucked him most recently from one of St. Paul's seediest blocks). It's as if he seeks out the circumstances most degrading to him and potentially destructive. As I have said to him, something within him is eating away at his serenity and self-esteem; cocaine hides but does not heal it. When he is not using he is a wonderful human being who loves life, friends, and family; when he is using, he is not the same person, becoming instead compulsive, moody, and unreachable. "I don't think I've ever seen such pain in anyone as I saw in Cope over the last three moths," his immediate superior said to me after she learned of his recent crash. I am most hopeful that this time at Hazelden he will go deep within himself to discover the cause of that pain, be honest with himself and with us, and deal with it. On a practical level, he quit his job during his recent binge (performing well at it until the final weeks). On his recent binge, he went through several thousand dollars from his mortgage fund, and he has not enough left to meet even his Hazelden charges.

Ironically, there have never been any complaints from his employers. To the contrary, he was an outstanding reporter on three consecutive newspapers and once his addiction carried him away, his editors expressed astonishment that someone could have been so productive while under the influence. Furthermore, he could be hired back at either paper right now, were he to stay sober. That's the kind of reputation he earned. He now says that the stresses of journalism and the endless reminder that he and I are in the same profession make him want to get out of the field altogether.

As for participating in his recovery, I am eager to do so and providing he is amenable, will make myself available out there at any time. I love my son very much and it has been hard for me to accept that I cannot recover for him. But I know he can help me and I hope in some way I can help him, too.

Dad was right, and I knew it, but I couldn't bear to think that he was on to my flaws. For so long I'd tried to be the perfect son—the loving child, the model teenager, and the admirable young man who fulfilled his father's dreams for his first-born child and thus deserved his absolute love and respect. For all those years I desperately needed Dad to be proud of me. "Don't disappoint him" was my mantra growing up, but I did, over and over and over again, and it was like pounding a hammer onto my fingers until they were numb with pain and then striking them a few more times just to make sure the pain didn't come back.

But here on paper were the words that confirmed what I had always feared. Dad knew the truth about those "unresolved issues" that I tried to bury deep inside me where nobody could find them. He could see, or at least imagine, the invisible tormenting demons "eating away" at my soul, from the inside out. The cocaine dulled the pain for a while, but even that wasn't working anymore. Like a skilled drug counselor, Dad knew that, too.

Dad was also the therapist, imploring me to "go deep" to discover the cause of all my problems and deal with it. I felt the sting of resentment when I read those words. Had he gone deep inside himself to confront his own demons? If I needed help, didn't he? Why couldn't he share his secrets with me, since he already knew mine? That was the worst part. Dad had his secrets, but I couldn't have mine.

THREE DAYS BEFORE my scheduled discharge from Hazelden, I announced that I would not be going to extended care. At the time I convinced myself and hoped to persuade everyone else that this was the right path; never could I have imagined that my insistence on doing it my own way would lead years down the road to my self-destruction, for God, I believed, had guided me all along the way. My decision, as I wrote in my journal, came only after intensive prayer led me to accept God's will.

TUESDAY, MARCH 5
Last night I was reading either the Big Book or 12x12 [Twelve Steps and Twelve Traditions] where it claims that some of the original members lost any urge to drink once they turned it over and came to believe in a power greater than themselves. I find it hard to believe ALL urges vanish like that, but I started praying, asking God to remove my urges, to replace those urges with a peaceful confidence that HE will take care of me, and an acceptance I can't do it alone.

Suddenly, the urges melted and since then I haven't felt so alone. I still fear the disease of alcoholism but I don't dread anymore the prospects of having to stay sober by myself. I must never forget that God is with me—if I ask. And right after that confession, which showed more than anything else how much I needed continued treatment, I explained why I had decided not to go to extended care.

I wish I could say my decision came after extensive deliberations and consultations with a multitude of people. Yes, I talked a lot about the pros and cons with friends, including a half dozen who attended Jellinek. Their input and feedback were valuable.

But my decision came following intensive prayer between me and God. Thus, it is difficult for me to accurately describe my reasons for not going. It's just a feeling deep inside that I've made the correct choice. It's a decision based on accepting God's will and putting mine aside. I've witnessed the power of this disease and I'm scared of the consequences of using again. But I've turned my life over to God and trust the process of AA.

I realize my decision means I'll eventually leave here without staff approval. But I hope between now and then that I can work intensively with the staff on some of my issues and develop a strong aftercare program that includes psychological counseling.

Those last three days at Hazelden were not pleasant. The counselors kept challenging me. "You're in denial," they'd say. "You're shortchanging yourself by trying to do this the easy, soft way." The patients were more blunt. They kept telling me I was "full of shit." My anger and resentment grew and seethed under what I tried to project as a calm exterior. What right did these people have to challenge not only my commitment to recovery but my relationship to God?

"I feel as though everybody perceives I'm talking out of both sides of my mouth," I wrote in my journal. "Perhaps I'm heading down the wrong path toward a relapse, but I've been feeling good about letting God do a lot of the work for me."

As I packed my bags that last day, I couldn't wait to prove them all wrong. They thought I wouldn't make it—well, I'd show them. I prayed to God, asking Him to help me with my anger and resentment, and it worked.

I had to admit, it felt really good to have God on my side.

12

Two Dragons

February 19, 1991

Dear Cope:

It seems to me you have two dragons to slay.

One is drugs. Three times now—in your senior year in college, in 1989, and now—drugs have taken you to the abyss. Each time family and friends were around to help you back. What happens when your family is old or spent and your friends exhausted? From here on out you have only your own resources to rely on.

The other lies deeper. Cocaine appeases it briefly but never slays it. I don't know what it is. I know it isn't New York or St. Paul, because you wrestle with it either place. I know it isn't your job or your father's success or cold weather or commuting or any of the other situations that agitate you.

It seems to me you are running from something or profoundly confused about something. Sexuality, perhaps? Mistaken identity? Fear—of what? I honest-to-God don't know and obviously you don't. This is why I think all is for naught unless you submit while you are at Hazelden and, perhaps for some time to come, to deep and sustained therapy, trying to go far into yourself to find the source of your pain. You have so much pain. It is in your eyes and your face. Something is hurting you and hurting you badly. Please get help to find and deal with it.

As one of your editors at the paper said last week, you are "a personable, charming, even charismatic" young man who has so much going for you. But the pain is wrecking your life and will until you bring it into the open and healing happens.

As one counselor told me last week, "There is nothing left for you to do, Mr. Moyers. Trying to help may only enable him. You have to let go and let your son face the consequences of his addiction. Only then can he break through the barrier of denial and rationalization to recognize his illness and seek help for himself."

I pray this is what happens. I pray to God, but in the end only you can make it happen.

I love you with all my heart. But I am emotionally spent, I can't take any longer the dishonesty and deception that accompany your behavior when you are using, and I have a diminished capacity for long nights spent in dreadful anticipation.

I want to be here when you need me. I will know when

that is, not by what you *say* but by what you have *done* to face the realities of your addiction and the demons that drive it.

In the meantime, you are in my thoughts and in my heart and I wish you well. Let me know what I can do, but most important, find out what it is you must do for yourself.

Love,
Dad

13

Lost

LIFE AFTER HAZELDEN was just what I had hoped it would be. Allison and I moved into a two-bedroom apartment in a quiet residential neighborhood of St. Paul, and for the next few months we lived an easy life. We got a kitten from the local county humane society, and I earned minimum wage working as a gardener for a wealthy couple in recovery who often employed newly sober people struggling to get back on their feet. Allison cleaned their house. I cashed my pension from my days as a newspaper reporter in Dallas and New York, so we finally had some money in the bank. We went to AA meetings once or twice a week and enjoyed entertaining our friends in recovery or spending quiet evenings alone curled up with our journals and meditation books and the *New York Times*. I planted a row of tomato and pepper plants along our garage wall, and when I wasn't mowing the couple's lawn or pulling weeds in my own garden, I was attempting to clean up the messes of my relapse, including the details of my divorce, the loans I had to pay back, and the strained relationships with my family and friends.

I learned to fly. Since I was a child lying on my back under the pecan tree in Wilmer looking up at the clouds, I had always wanted to pilot my own plane. High above the distractions and nuisances of the rest of the world, flying offered me freedom and a sense of control over my life. Open the throttle, pull back on the yoke, point the nose skyward, and feel the power in the engine and lift in the wings—there was nothing better than the feeling that I could go anywhere I wanted to go, do anything I wanted to do, and be anything I wanted to be.

"I am happiest when I do what I am afraid to do," I wrote in my journal on September 22, 1991. Three days later I soloed from a small airport just across the Mississippi River from downtown St. Paul, and after that, for a while, I thought about getting a job as a pilot. Then one morning in October the phone rang, and Tom Johnson, the president and CEO of CNN, asked me if I'd consider applying for a job as a writer/producer in CNN's Atlanta headquarters. I was flattered by the call. Tom was a close friend of my father's from the LBJ days when he was a White House Fellow and Dad was President Johnson's press secretary. Although Dad was only a few years older than Tom, he took him under his wing and helped to launch his brilliant career. I'd known Tom my whole life, and ever since my graduation from college, he had shown a keen interest in my career. In the last ten years he'd made phone calls on my behalf, introduced me to editors and publishers, written letters of recommendation, and, whenever I asked for it, offered his advice on both personal and professional issues. Tom also knew I'd been struggling with addiction—when I was living at Fellowship Club in 1989, Tom had a layover in Minneapolis and we talked about my treatment and recovery over dinner.

I was honored by the offer, but wary about going back into a profession that, at least in my mind, was so clearly dominated by my father's success. Over and over again in the despairing aftermath of my sleepless nights, hangovers, and relapses, I knew that if I was going to stay sober, I had to stay away from the newsroom. Dad was the trigger I always pulled when I wanted to get high, and I couldn't take the risk of reentering his world.

But how else was I going to make a decent living? Allison and I had decided to get married and we wanted to start a family, replenish our savings accounts, and maybe, when the time was right, buy a house. We couldn't keep taking out loans to pay our bills. Besides, what an opportunity—CNN! Atlanta! As much as we loved the Twin Cities for its close-knit recovering community, not even the blanket of sobriety could keep us warm against those long, bitterly cold winters. Allison, a native Bermudan, particularly hated the winters in Minnesota, which meant that she struggled through more than half the year. Atlanta was warm and sunny. Maybe it would be the perfect next step.

I flew to Atlanta for the interview with Kim Engebretsen, a copy editor at CNN. I was upfront about my treatment and relapses in part because I had no choice—how else could I explain the fact that I abruptly stopped working at the *Star-Tribune* after only eleven months on the job or the six-month gap that followed when I didn't work at all? Kim didn't seem fazed, and later that day she offered me the job.

Back in St. Paul, Allison and I celebrated my new job and our new life with a steak dinner and a few rounds of our favorite drink— Mendota Springs mineral water with a splash of cranapple juice and a twist of lime. That night we planned everything out: We'd take a few months to prepare for the move, get married in January, and move to Atlanta a few weeks later. We couldn't have been happier. Allison did most of the wedding preparations while I continued flying lessons and brushed up on my journalism skills. One last winter in St. Paul and then on to the next adventure. Best of all, we were both sober.

Just before we left St. Paul, Bob B. stopped by with a reminder. "Keep your head out of the clouds and your feet rooted on the ground," Bob said in his usual gruff, no-nonsense style. "Never forget that people in AA need to see you, and you need to see them whether you're here or in Atlanta or back home in New York."

"I won't forget," I said.

Seven months after we moved to Atlanta, I was standing in the doctor's office looking at an ultrasound screen.

"Where is he?" I asked, trying to figure out the head from the tail of the cloudy, ghostlike image on the black-and-white monitor. What I saw on the screen reminded me of the paramecium I once studied in a drop of water under a microscope in my high school science class. Squirmy. Primal. Eerily alive.

"There's his head coming into view right now," replied the technician, sliding the sonogram paddles across Allison's very pregnant belly. For the first time I believed that this was real, that what I was seeing wasn't a one-celled creature at all but a real live human being that was fifty percent me and, according to the technician's trained eye, one hundred percent boy.

I had tears in my eyes as I squeezed Allison's hand.

"That's him, Allison—that's our baby!"

A moment passed as we stared in wonder at the light and shadows that spoke of life, hope, and the future.

"Wow," I repeated, laughing this time. "That's our baby boy!"

I was going to have a son. Somebody to toss a ball with, to play hide-and-seek, to take fishing on the lake, to help me mow the lawn, to talk to about God, to be my best friend. Pride and a sense of wonder joined forces with new feelings of responsibility. I had duties to fill, values to model, a life to protect. My joy was complex but complete. Life was so good now, after such a long time of being so very bad.

The crack houses in Harlem and St. Paul were behind me and with them the littered pieces of a broken life that I had carefully consigned to the dusty attic where they lingered out of sight but not quite out of mind. The "people, places, and things" of the old days were gone; in Atlanta, there were no ghosts to haunt us. The city represented a drug-free zone, far away from Lexington, Dallas, Northport, Manhattan, and St. Paul—all good places that I had ruined with drugs and alcohol. But the past was behind us now, and we had so much to look forward to in the future.

We were going to have a child. Thank you, God.

Two days after the sonogram, we were sitting in the doctor's office. He showed us several black-and-white pictures of the ultrasound images, pointing to a faint dark spot in the middle of a white mass that he identified as the baby's chest area.

"There's something here that concerns me," he said. "I'll need to take a closer look."

I looked at the images and tried to figure out what he was talking about.

"A closer look—what does that mean?" I said, trying to stay calm.

"We'll need to do more diagnostic scans—another ultrasound, amniocentesis, some blood work," the doctor said, putting the images down and folding his hands together. "Then we'll have a better idea what we're dealing with. In the meantime, I wouldn't worry."

"But what do you think it might be? Why more tests? What are you looking for?" I was getting frustrated. The ambiguity unsettled me because I couldn't get on top of the situation. I needed to know what to do next, what to think, what to feel, how to fix this, right now, instantly, in the snap of my fingers. So I kept pressing him for details.

"We're just not sure yet," he repeated, pushing back in his chair, "and it's best not to speculate until we know more. It may be nothing. In the meantime, my office will set up the necessary appointments, and we'll arrange to talk again next week. At that point we'll know more and we can discuss our next steps."

I couldn't bear the uncertainty. He told us not to worry, but how could we not? Maybe our son had cancer—do developing fetuses get cancer? Maybe there was something wrong with his heart—the doctor had pointed to his chest. What was going on inside our unborn son? Was his condition life-threatening? Were there interventions the doctors could perform, techniques they could use, drugs they could give him? Living in the moment is easy, I thought bitterly, until things don't go the way they're supposed to and the moment becomes impossible.

On August 20, 1992, the doctor told us what was wrong.

"Your baby has a diaphragmatic hernia," he said. "That means he has a tiny hole in the lining around his lungs. This hole failed to close completely during gestation and it has allowed his stomach and intestines to gravitate up into his chest cavity, stunting his lung development. I'm afraid his chances of survival are no more than thirty percent."

Thirty percent. Less than a one-in-three chance our baby would live.

"There aren't many options available to us, short of radical surgery," the doctor was saying. "We could remove the fetus from the womb, repair the problem, and put the baby back into the womb. It's a complicated and risky procedure that could jeopardize not only the baby's life but the mother's life, too. My advice is to wait until the baby is born. Once he can breathe on his own, we'll schedule surgery and put the organs back in their proper place."

We left the doctor's office that August afternoon hand in hand, trying to fathom the implications of a condition that neither one of us could begin to comprehend. We had so much to talk about but neither of us could find the words to express our thoughts or feelings. Allison went into the bedroom and quietly closed the door behind her while I lay down on the couch and listened to a CD by Enya. The dreamy melodies and solemn piano solos seemed like an appropriate background dirge for my thoughts and feelings. Trying to imagine this sick baby in Allison's healthy body, I started to cry. What had we done to deserve this?

A few days later, lying in bed on a Saturday morning, I put my head on Allison's belly and began to talk to our boy.

"This is your Daddy," I said, speaking in a whisper. "Your mum and I love you very much. We are going to help you get better. We can't wait to see you, hold you, tell you how much we love you."

We decided to call him Henry after my grandfathers. Pa Pa Joe's real name was Henry Joseph and Pa Pa Henry's name was John Henry. It was a strong name but gentle, too, just like my grandfathers, and Henry would need their grit and determination as much as he would benefit from their calm inner strength.

Those last few months before Henry's birth were spent in almost unbearable anticipation. Henry's problems, the doctors told us, would begin immediately after the umbilical cord was severed and he began to breathe on his own. We wouldn't know until that moment if his undeveloped lungs could handle the task. If Henry survived that first crucial test, he would be taken immediately into surgery to undergo a risky and extremely complicated procedure in which the doctors would attempt to rearrange his other organs. I imagined the doctor's big hands inside my baby's tiny chest, moving his heart into place, pushing the liver over to the side, adjusting the position of the stomach, the spleen, the pancreas, the intestines.

I felt so helpless. I wanted to fix everything that was broken and perform a miracle that would allow Henry to live, but the only really helpful task I could perform had to be kept secret from Allison—planning Henry's funeral. I talked to my father often, seeking his counsel, and during one of our long talks I asked if he would perform the funeral service.

"No," he said gently but firmly. "My grief won't allow it."

That was the first time I ever remembered my dad turning me down in a moment of need, but I understood. How could he console others when his own grief would be so overwhelming? I grieved alone and in silence, mourning the loss of a child who was much more than a picture on a sonogram, but much less than the healthy child I believed I deserved. I was so sad for this unborn baby and his mother but even sadder for myself. *It's not fair,* I kept telling myself—not to Henry who deserved a chance to live, not to Allison who so desperately wanted to be a mother to this child—not any child, *this* child.

And it wasn't fair to me. I finally had my life together. Hadn't Keith, Lowell, and George, my counselors at Hazelden, promised me everything would get better if I just stayed clean and sober? Wasn't sobriety supposed to make everything easier? And what about those "promises" in the Big Book of Alcoholics Anonymous? Right there on page eighty-three, just one-seventh of the way through the book, was the open window through which the bright light of a happy life beckoned. In treatment, I read that section over and over again until I could recite it in my head.

> If we are painstaking about this phase of our development, we will be amazed before we are halfway through. We are going to know a new freedom and a new happiness. We will not regret the past nor wish to shut the door on it. We will comprehend the word serenity and we will know peace. No matter how far down the scale we have gone, we will see how our experience will benefit others. That feeling of uselessness and self-pity will disappear. We will lose interest in selfish things and gain interest in our fellows. Self-seeking will slip away. Our whole attitude and outlook upon life will change. Fear of people and economic insecurity will leave us. We will intuitively know how to handle situations that used to baffle us. We will suddenly realize that God is doing for us what we could not do for ourselves.

So God would do for me what I could not do for myself? What a joke. Hell, I'd done my part, using all the strength and courage within me. I'd gotten sober, been faithful and loving to Allison, helped other struggling alcoholics and addicts, practiced gratitude and humility every day, and this is what God gave me in return? The counselors at Hazelden, my sponsor, other recovering people had promised me that recovery was all about dealing with life on life's terms. But I couldn't accept these terms, no way. After almost two years of sobriety, in the blink of an eye and the scan of a sonogram, the whole damn thing was falling apart.

Go to AA, everyone kept saying. Talk about your problems, let them out. *No secrets,* my sponsor reminded me over and over again. I did what I was told. I went to meetings and talked about my son's struggle to survive. Everyone listened because that's the way AA works—when you talk, people listen. But when it was someone else's turn to talk, I didn't listen because all I could think about was my own problem. Nobody else was suffering like I was.

I didn't go to AA searching for serenity or for help staying sober. I went to AA hoping to make people feel sorry for me and admire me for my inner strength, my strong values, and my devotion to my family. Sympathy and respect were the drugs that soothed the hurt inside me.

"My name is William. I'm an alcoholic and crack addict," I'd say.

"Hello, William," they responded, as they always did. And then I'd talk about Henry.

"My unborn son has a serious birth defect and might die before he's even born," I announced at one meeting.

"My wife and I need to decide whether to undergo a risky procedure where doctors take the fetus out of the womb and try to repair the damage before placing him back inside," I explained in another meeting.

"Today my son was born by C-section and he's having a big operation in four days," I said on October 24, 1992, just a few hours after Henry was born and rushed from the delivery room to the intensive care unit. I could not get the images of that morning out of my mind. Dad was with me. He had flown down from New York a few days earlier. Allison spent the night in the hospital. The phone rang at the house early that morning, before the sun rose, but I didn't hear it because I went to bed, just as I did every night, wearing earplugs. Dad was shaking me. "Wake up, wake up son, it's the phone, somebody's calling." The woman on the phone told me she was a nurse and to hurry to the hospital, the baby was on the way. When I arrived, Allison was in the operating room sedated but awake. Gauges, monitors, wires were all over the place. The doctor drew the scalpel across her belly and opened her up in a split second. It reminded me of the time I gutted and cleaned my first trout. He reached in and, like pulling a rabbit from the hat, out came Henry. The doctors and nurses huddled around Henry and I tried to look around them, see through them. Was he breathing? Would he make it through the next few minutes? Henry started to cry. He would make it—at least, to surgery.

"I am doing well despite it all," I lied when I told the story. I cried that day. Several times in those meetings, I let myself cry. The tears were real, but they were less about the sadness I felt for Henry or Allison and more about my own self-pity. It didn't hurt, either, that the tears served to showcase my bravery in putting up a good fight in front of my AA audience. I was the hero, and that made me feel almost as good as I used to feel when I drank that first beer or took that first hit.

"He's been in ICU for six weeks."

"He has a feeding tube in his nose and is hooked up to all these machines."

"There's a big flap of skin neatly stitched over a bulging package of organs that are too big to fit back inside him properly."

"He has an infection."

"His infection is better."

"He smiled and opened his eyes today."

"He doesn't cry."

"His breathing is worse."

"He's having another surgery."

At every meeting I engaged in a one-man, play-by-play drama, constantly reenacting and refining my role as the mythic hero who could handle any tragedy life threw at him without falling apart or getting drunk. Because only a few people in the recovering community in Atlanta knew about my previous relapses, it was easy to put on the mask and play the part. My story was anonymous even in AA. Nobody in my home AA group knew about the issues with my father, my failed first marriage, my relapses in New York and St. Paul, or my lifelong fear of anything remotely related to failure. Nobody knew that just two years earlier I'd left Hazelden against staff advice, filled with deep resentment toward the staff for telling me I was sicker than I was willing to admit and bitterly determined to prove them wrong by being the best recovering person that ever existed, without their help. I never told anyone that the real reason I left St. Paul was to distance myself from all those recovering people who knew me too well. In St. Paul I felt claustrophobic because my past still defined me. In Atlanta I was free to be whomever I wanted to be.

A few months after Henry was born, I wrote a letter to Keith Jensen, my counselor at Hazelden. Like so much of the rest of my life, it looked impressive on the company letterhead embossed with the shiny red letters of CNN, but the words revealed the messy truth.

So I've had quite a year. I got married, moved, started a new job, fathered a child and endured his illness. Through it all, I've stayed the course of my recovery. I'll have two years next month. Sometimes it seems I've stayed sober despite my best intentions. There are moments *and* days when I feel the urge to escape reality, if only for an hour or so. At other times, I feel that I stay sober for the *wrong* reasons. The bottom line, I must keep reminding myself, is that I'm addicted and powerless. But it often bothers me that I seem to struggle with acceptance. . . . I do hit meetings here, though I do not feel plugged in like I was up there. In other words, I don't always feel satisfied when I go to a meeting. I've got a ways to go in that department.

Every sentence in that letter warned of trouble. Between those lines I was screaming, *I want to get high!* I just couldn't bring myself to write it because to state that truth was to admit that what I had been doing in my life for two years wasn't working anymore. Failure was my birthmark that I had only allowed Hazelden, through my treatment, to temporarily cover up, making me look and even feel better for a while. Now the cover-up was fading from the inside out, exposing a truth that I had fended off with sheer willpower and giant resentment.

Sometimes it seems I've stayed sober despite my best intentions. I could feel the addiction stalking me, creeping up from behind me. Or was I stalking it, just for the thrill of the hunt, like the old days when half the fun of getting high was the chase and the score?

There are moments and *days when I feel the urge to escape reality, if only for an hour or so.* Life is incredibly hard. Henry's sick, work is stressful, money is tight, the house needs painting, Dad's still famous and I'm not.

At other times, I feel that I stay sober for the wrong *reasons.* I don't like being a recovering alcoholic and addict anymore. The effort to stay clean and sober is like all those other responsibilities in my life— it's relentless. I'm holding on, but I'm not happy. AA tells me I'm supposed to let go and let God, but I'm hanging on for dear life.

The bottom line, I must keep reminding myself, is that I'm addicted and powerless. But if often bothers me that I seem to struggle with acceptance. The Big Book tells me that acceptance is the answer to all my problems, day after day after day. But I can't accept that advice any more than I can the fact that my life isn't turning out the way I expected. Being sober is harder, at times, than being drunk or stoned or fried on crack.

I do hit meetings here, though I do not feel plugged in like I was up there. Meetings aren't working for me, so why should I keep working at them? Yeah, I should stay plugged in, but I'm too busy. I have too many responsibilities. I can't do everything.

In other words, I don't always feel satisfied when I go to a meeting. As I became more entrenched in self-pity, I stopped thinking about what I needed to do to stay alive—it was satisfaction I was after. How many times had the old-timers told me that AA meetings are to alcoholics what dialysis is to diabetics or chemotherapy is to cancer patients—we have to do it to survive. It's not about satisfaction, it's about survival.

And so began my unraveling. The Big Book of AA describes addiction as a disease that's "cunning, baffling, and powerful." Old-timers in AA add one more word: Patient. Addiction waits, lurking in the shadows of a busy life, patiently passing the time until life gets too stressful or too joyous or we stop paying attention or we simply forget how bad it once was. Little annoyances begin to bother us. Life, at times, seems unfair. Peace and serenity are difficult to find and gratitude comes grudgingly.

Not long after I sent Keith that letter, I was driving to work just before dawn when I spotted a group of people loitering on a street corner in midtown Atlanta. I'd probably seen similar gatherings before, but until that moment I had never really paid attention to them. I knew exactly what they were doing, because in the hours just before dawn, street corners are an oasis for drug users—the place where addicts find a solution to their insatiable thirst before the sun rises and they have to scurry back to their caves.

I wonder if I could smoke again, normally this time, just once more and never again? As soon as the thought entered my head, I dismissed it, even chuckling to myself at the insanity of the very idea. Henry was still very sick; just sixteen months old, he had made it through two major surgeries but he faced at least two more. Just a year after Henry's birth, we learned that Allison was pregnant again. We had a mortgage and skyrocketing medical bills to pay every month. I had a good job with a steady paycheck and co-workers who respected me. Why would I even consider risking my career, my marriage, and the future of my children?

Even as I shrugged it off, I continued to drive that same route to work and every morning I'd look for the people on the street corners and every time I saw them, I thought about using again. But the moment I walked into CNN headquarters, I'd forget about the crack heads and drug dealers and immerse myself in the frenetic, unpredictable, deadline-oriented pace of the work, which fit my temperament perfectly. My job was to research breaking news stories, extract the superfluous and unnecessary details, and spin the remaining facts into tightly written scripts that CNN editors and producers matched to reams of raw video footage and then fed to the anchors on the set. The work was exciting and terrifying because if you missed a deadline—and there were at least a dozen deadlines during my shift—the anchors were forced to ad-lib, disrupting the smooth flow of news and information that made it all look so slick and professional. Those deadlines were killers—the word *dead* in deadline has real meaning to a writer—but I felt energized by the fast pace and high expectations. The adrenaline was almost as good as a drug.

I knew how lucky I was to have the job, because working at CNN was getting pretty close to the top of the line in the journalism field. But then again, maybe it wasn't luck at all. While I never mentioned my fears to Allison or anyone else, I was haunted by the thought that I didn't really deserve the job. I was never sure if I was hired for my reporting skills and writing talent or because my father was close friends with Tom Johnson, CNN's chief executive officer, second in line only to CNN's owner, Ted Turner.

"Your dad was my mentor," Tom told me recently. "He taught me about the inner workings of the LBJ White House. He taught me about the White House press corps. He shortened my name from

Tommy to Tom. He said he had been called Billy Don. For him, Bill was a more serious name. He felt Tom would be taken more seriously than Tommy. I changed my name to Tom. He told me to 'stop running everywhere.' He felt that my running back and forth to the East Room, to other parts of the White House grounds, was unbecoming. He said 'walk.' I did."

Tom adored my father, and I couldn't help wondering if he had hired me as a favor, some kind of payback for all the help Dad offered him through the years. If my last name wasn't Moyers, would he have even considered me for the job? The questions gnawed at me whenever I was tired or feeling anxious about making a deadline. I often thought about the summer after college graduation, ten years earlier, when my father suggested that I call Tom for career advice. I did what I was told and Tom, then the publisher of the *Los Angeles Times*, gave me the referrals that led to my first real job in journalism at the *Dallas Times Herald*.

It was no secret that I had a close, personal relationship with the man in the corner office with the big window that looked over the newsroom floor. Tom sometimes called me into his office just to talk, and I would sit in the chair across from his desk, convinced that I could feel the resentful gaze of my colleagues hard at work down below. He gave me prime tickets, just behind home plate, to Braves games and invited me to pool parties at his and his wife Edwina's home in an exclusive Atlanta neighborhood.

One day on the phone I casually complained to my father that the shift I was working at CNN was killing me because I had to get up every day at three a.m. Less than a month later, I was working the prime time slot reserved for writers who had paid their dues after years of hard work. I felt guilty, but I wasn't about to give up that shift.

When O. J. Simpson led the world on his infamous chase in the white Ford Bronco through the streets of Los Angeles, I was assigned the task of feeding the anchors hard facts gathered from reporters in the field that they could mix into their ad-lib descriptions of the events that were unfolding before millions of viewers watching on live television. For nearly two hours I pounded away on the computer, assembling the scripts and sending them to editors who then passed them on to the anchors on the set. Drenched with perspiration, my eyes dried out because I couldn't take the time to blink, my fingers sore and swollen from typing, I was exhausted. When I was finally relieved, Tom bellowed out across the newsroom, "Awesome, Moyers!" Several colleagues shook my hand or offered similar praise, and a note made the rounds recognizing my efforts along with the work of many others in the newsroom that day.

Compliments or criticisms were one and the same, for they felt like fishhooks dragging across my gut, catching on a sharp edge to tear apart my insides. I knew I had done good work that day, and I was proud of myself—but would I have gotten all that attention if I wasn't my father's son? When I was criticized, however, I had no doubt that I deserved every harsh word. One day, just a few weeks after I started at CNN, I screwed up a story about the violent ethnic cleansing campaigns taking place in the Balkans. I don't know how it happened, but somehow I mixed up a video of smiling Muslim peasants with a script describing a mortar attack on a market in which scores of civilians were killed.

When the story aired, the executive producer came charging out of the control room straight to my desk.

"What the hell are you doing?" she yelled. "I thought you were supposed to be a good journalist!"

That was the first time I'd ever met that particular editor—I didn't even know her name, but she apparently knew mine. The only reason she thought I was "supposed to be a good journalist" was because I was my father's son. His reputation supplanted my own. Sitting at my desk feeling like a fool, I was exposed to the entire world as a fraud.

She had seen right through me—I hadn't gotten the job because of any talents or skills I'd developed over the years but only because of the reputation my father had earned and passed down to me.

I couldn't escape my father no matter where I went. His face and his name were everywhere—in popular magazines, on public television, and in his best-selling PBS series and book *Healing and the Mind*. I rarely heard about Dad's success from him or my mother, and in fact I sometimes felt that they tried to protect me by downplaying his fame.

Shortly after Bill Clinton was elected president, CNN ran numerous stories about the president-elect's frequent visits with the nation's greatest minds as he sought advice about how to run the country. I was sitting at my desk one day, working away on a story, when I heard the name Bill Moyers. Surprised, I looked up at the solid wall of television monitors lining the newsroom to see my father with President-elect Clinton at the governor's mansion in Little Rock; when I asked Dad about it later, he told me that Clinton asked him about his experiences with LBJ and sought his advice about how the White House works. Feeling flush in the face and tight in the gut, I immediately looked back down at my desk and pretended to write, counting the seconds until the episode was over.

A year later I was at my desk, laboring to finish a script, when I looked up to see Tom Johnson and Bill Clinton walking across the newsroom toward me. As my editors and fellow reporters watched, Tom personally introduced me to the most powerful man in the world.

"Mr. President," Tom said, "this is Cope Moyers. You know his father, Bill Moyers."

I stood up to shake the president's hand, painfully aware of the reporters and editors who knew that the only reason I was being introduced to the president was because I was my father's son. Clinton had a fierce grip and a genuine smile, and we spent several minutes talking about my job.

"Nice to meet you," he said at the end of our conversation. "Your father is a great man. It's wonderful to see you following in his footsteps."

In everyone's eyes, it seemed, I was the fortunate son following the path blazed by a brilliant, honorable, even heroic man. I was proud of my father, and I wanted to make him proud of me, but every time a comparison was made, whether by the president of the United States or some nameless person I'd just met at a cocktail party, my resentment intensified. When I was working at the *Dallas Times Herald, Newsday*, and the *Star-Tribune*, I would turn to alcohol and cocaine to relieve the frustration and anxiety that flowed every time someone compared me to my father. At least in Harlem and St. Paul I had a respite in the crack house where nobody had ever heard of the famous Bill Moyers, and, even if they had, they couldn't have cared less. Now, sober and leading a respectable life in Atlanta, it seemed there was no place to hide.

One weekend afternoon I was leafing through my address book updating and eliminating the people who had crossed my path over the years when I stumbled upon Ben's name and phone number. Did I just happen to turn to the "S" section in the book or had I planned it somehow, without consciously realizing it? I'll never know.

Old Ben, I thought, remembering all those silver bracelets and backgammon games. *I wonder how he's doing?* I hadn't seen him for more than four years. Was he still alive? Was he still using? Only drug addicts like me think fondly about other drug addicts whom they once used with but would never call friends. Stinkin' Thinkin', they call it in AA. Euphoric recall. *Good old Ben. Maybe I should give him a call, just to see what he's up to.* In the next second I talked myself out of that foolishness. No way was I going back there.

Two days later I called Ben from the break room at CNN. Just hearing his voice on the other end of the line brought back memories of the taste and smell and sound of the rocks in the pipe that we shared so long ago. We picked up the conversation as if no time had passed.

"Heeeyyyy, my man William, how the hell are you?" Ben said. *Oh man,* I thought, *I miss the old days.* I quickly recounted the highlights of the four years since I'd seen him and told him about my job at CNN, Henry's birth, and Allison's pregnancy with our second child. His news wasn't as good. His wife left him a few years earlier, taking the twin boys with her.

"So, my man William, do you ever come by this way?" I knew what he was really asking: Do you want to get high sometime?

"I've been clean for three years," I said. He sighed appreciatively.

"And what about you, Ben?" I said, asking the question I'd been dying to ask, even though I didn't realize I was going to ask it until I did. "Are you clean?"

He knew what I was asking. There was a long pause on the other end of the line.

"Yeah, well, sometimes," he said. "I'm not drinking anymore, but now and then, you know, I do a little bit when I can get some money."

I had my answer, and it was just what I had hoped to hear. I arranged to meet Ben during a quick business trip to New York, and several weeks later we renewed our friendship sitting in his bedroom at his mother's modest house on Long Island. He brought out a few rocks of cocaine and I handed him a wad of cash. I could barely catch my breath as I watched him load the pipe and take a hit. Three years of sobriety, hard time added up one long day after another, and I was about to throw it all away. I didn't think about Henry and the feeding tube sticking out of his belly, or about Allison who was eight months pregnant with our second child. I didn't think about anything but how I was about to feel.

Ben passed the pipe, still hot, and I dropped a fresh rock into the barrel. We smoked and talked, taking it easy, staying in control. Ben's mother was in the kitchen down the hall and I had a train to catch back to the airport. But in the hour or so Ben and I spent together smoking, talking, and playing backgammon, everything I loved faded away. Nothing else mattered to me except when and where I was going to get high again.

How can I explain that obsession to anyone who hasn't experienced it? Researchers say that addictive drugs, when used in large enough amounts or for long periods of time, "hijack" the brain, like Trojan horses that sneak into the nerve cells and take control. That explains the biochemical process, but it doesn't get close to describing the desperate hunger, the consuming thirst, the unbearable craving, the furious yearning, the excruciating need that grabs you and shakes you and won't let you go. A "physiological imperative," some have called it, evoking a howling internal torment that overrides the need for food, for water, for sleep, for love. And then the calm that replaces the fury and the rapture that arises when the convulsions cease.

I flew back to Atlanta and didn't tell anybody what had happened that day. I looked and felt okay, nobody knew, the secret was safe. I was in control, and I had a simple, foolproof plan. I sent Ben three hundred dollars in cash by express mail and told him to buy the cocaine and get the package ready, but to wait until after Allison had the baby. Two weeks after Thomas was born on June 28, 1994—we named him after Tom Johnson—the package arrived by Federal Express. When Allison and the boys were safely in bed and sound asleep, I tiptoed down to the basement where I stayed for the rest of the night. Peaks of ecstasy were followed by plunges of utter despair. I rode the rollercoaster for hours, loving and hating it all at the same time. I couldn't get enough and I couldn't stop. Three years clean and now it was all gone.

The next morning I walked up the basement stairs to a world that looked exactly like the one I'd left the night before. Allison was sitting in the rocking chair while Thomas slept in the playpen next to her and Henry laughed, throwing Cheerios at me from his high chair.

"William," she said. Dry-eyed. Stunned. "What are you doing?"

I told her everything. It was a slip, I promised her. It won't happen again.

We tried so hard to convince ourselves that this was a minor deviation, a bump in the road, a small accident rather than a head-on collision. Everything would work out as long as I was honest with her. We promised each other that we'd go to AA every day, stay in daily touch with our sponsors, go to church, and somehow get through this rough spot. That's what we told each other.

Years later Allison told me that she was actually relieved after that confrontation. "After we talked about it and the secret was out, I thought it couldn't hurt us anymore," she remembered. "I knew you were using again, but all the anxiety left me after we talked that day. I felt so much better. I thought everything would be okay because now that I knew the truth, you wouldn't be able to use again. How could you? With two little kids? How could you?" Sometimes I ask Allison why she stayed with me. Other people have asked her, too, and her answer is always pretty much the same. "You have a disease," she explains, "and relapse is part of this disease. Would I have left you if you were recovering from cancer and suddenly got sick again?"

Ten days later I sent Ben two hundred dollars by express mail. When I got the package, I promised myself, I would make it last. And for a while I did, using one day, skipping a few days, using, skipping a day, using, skipping a few hours, using. But getting through a whole day at work became impossible. One day I walked out of the CNN headquarters building to smoke a few rocks in my car, forgetting all about the scripts that needed to be written for the evening news program. When I returned to my desk, sweat pouring through my clothes, shaking and unable to look anyone in the eye, my producer was frantic. I told him not to worry because I'd get the assignment done on time. I didn't.

One day Allison left me alone with Thomas while she took Henry with her to run errands. I couldn't wait for her to leave, because I had a few small rocks hidden away for just this kind of opportunity. As soon as she was gone, I lit up the pipe and seconds later Thomas woke up from his nap. He needed his diaper changed or maybe he just needed me to hold him. I had no idea. I raced into his room, patted his head a few times, and told him to be quiet. Then I left him alone to load the pipe for another hit. He kept crying. I went back into his room, the smoke still in my lungs, and bent over his crib to pat his back, instinctively exhaling. I watched the smoke drift over him, horrified, but the moment passed and I left him once again to load up the pipe.

How could I have done that? How could a father smoke crack when he's supposed to be taking care of his newborn child? I have only one answer to those questions and, God forgive me, it doesn't make any sense at all, but I wonder if that is the point. My answer is another question: How couldn't I?

Soon enough the crack was gone, and Ben was too far away. I started cruising the inner city along the path I knew so well from my predawn commute to work. This part of Atlanta was like every other street in every other poverty-stricken section in every other city in America. Trash littered the sidewalks and front yards. Ratty old couches and broken chairs sat in the weed-filled front lawns. On every block, it seemed there was a car with the hood or the trunk raised parked by the curb. Squad cars cruised the neighborhood but never seemed to stop for very long. Hanging out on the street corners were the people I saw on my way to work, not doing much, smoking cigarettes, watching, waiting. Waiting for somebody like me to come down the street.

I belonged with them. My need defined me now and I no longer had to pretend to be anything other than what I was—a junkie desperate for dope.

"Hey man, come over here for a minute," I said, pulling up to the curb and motioning to a middle-aged man who looked like he was the center of the action.

He stared at me in disbelief. Who was this guy behind the wheel of a new Honda Accord, wearing a polo shirt and waving a fifty dollar bill in my face?

I felt confident, fearless, untouchable. "I'm not looking for sex," I said as he approached the car. "And I'm not a cop. I just want to score some crack."

I felt a sudden thrill of fear. Running down the left side of his face, from just beneath his left eye to the corner of his mouth, was a thick, jagged scar.

"Get in," I said, opening the door. "What's your name?"

"Scarface," he said. I almost laughed out loud. Of course, what else?

"You're not a cop?" he asked again.

"I'm no cop, and I'll prove it to you," I said, handing him the money and launching into my rap. "I've got a lot more where that came from. If you play by the rules, I'll take care of you. Burn me and you're done."

Scarface pointed down the street, and we drove to a dilapidated apartment building that looked just like every other apartment building on the block. I parked my car around the corner and followed him into the ground-floor apartment. It took a few minutes for my eyes to adjust to the light. Old Venetian blinds, the thick kind, covered all the windows. Bicycles, clothes, stereos, junk were stacked up along one of the walls. The only furniture was a rocking chair and a table and bench pushed up against the kitchen wall. An old man sat in the rocking chair and there were people smoking crack at a table in the kitchen. The smell of urine was everywhere, just like the cigarette butts and empty beer cans.

Scarface introduced me to BJ, who ruled the roost in this crack house. Thin, with short, wiry hair, she always wore flip-flops and a loose blouse and skirt. She was in her thirties, like me, but she could have been fifty or seventy or ninety. Over the next few weeks we'd become good friends. We often sat alone in her bedroom, talking and getting high, finding solace in each other's sad company.

"Are you scared of dying?" I asked her once.

"No, just scared," she said.

"If we get better one day, then maybe we can overcome the fear," I said. I wasn't sure what I was talking about, but the words sounded good.

"Anything is better than this," she said, "but this *is* this."

I took another hit. She took another hit. We sat there for a minute or two, knowing that everything was coming to an end. Even getting high wasn't enough anymore, and we feared that truth as much as we knew it.

I tried to pick up our spirits with conversation again.

"Let me tell you my real story," I said. "It will blow your mind."

I was sprawled out on her filthy mattress, acting like it was just another Sunday afternoon on the couch in my living room in the house where I no longer lived with my wife and two baby boys. I told her about them and about my job, my parents, the places I'd been, the people I knew.

"Hah, you're crazy," she laughed. Her teeth looked huge in her emaciated face.

"But you don't understand," I said. "They'll be looking for me. I work at CNN. I have a good job and a family that cares about me. See, I'm important."

"Now let me tell you my story," she said. "I'm dying of AIDS."

We talked about AIDS and dying for a while, and at one point I mentioned that my father was an ordained Baptist minister. She leaned back away from me, horrified.

"You're the product of a son of God and you're here in a crack house?" she said, her voice raised high. "What's the matter with you, boy?"

"The same thing that's the matter with you and everyone else in this place," I said. "I'm a drug addict."

She nodded her head, a faraway look on her face. "Yeah," she whispered.

BJ wanted to get clean. She talked about it all the time. Every morning she walked out of her bedroom with a small green gym bag packed with her few personal belongings.

"I'm going to treatment today," she proudly announced to anyone who would listen, and she meant it. She would sit down across the table from me, we'd start talking, and when I fired up the pipe, inhaled, and raised my eyebrows to see if she wanted to join me, she'd reach over with a sad little smile on her face. Inhaling the smoke, her eyes closed and her cheeks pulled in so deeply that for those few seconds she looked like a dead person.

I'd been at the crack house for three days when I heard Allison's voice outside. She was standing on the sidewalk, pleading with me to come out. How had she found me? Hiding inside, crouching low to the floor, I frantically tried to figure it out. She had found me in St. Paul and now she'd found me in Atlanta. My car—she must have spotted my car parked in the lot adjacent to the apartment building.

"William, please come with me, I need you!" she called out. "Henry is asking for his daddy. Thomas needs you."

I didn't move from my place on the wood floor. "Go away," I whispered.

She kept calling out to the house, which was deaf, dumb, and blind to her with all the windows darkened and the doors locked and bolted. Nobody in the crack house said a word. We were all just waiting for her to go away.

"I talked to Tom," she said. "He said you're fired if you don't get help." Then she was gone.

To this day, I'm not sure why those parting words got through to me. Maybe I realized that if I lost my job, there truly was no hope left for me. Maybe I convinced myself that Allison and the boys would always be there when I needed them. Perhaps I had sunk so low that people no longer mattered to me but the prestige and respect associated with my job still did. I can't explain it, and I'm not proud of it, but the thought of losing my job was more important to me at that moment than the thought of losing my family.

Two hours later I was sitting in Kim Engebretsen's office. She was my supervisor and she knew about my addiction because I had told her about it the day she interviewed me.

"I need help," I said.

"Let's go get an ice-cream cone," she said.

We walked to the food court in the CNN building, and we both ordered two scoops. We ate our ice cream in silence.

"Here's the deal, William," she said on the way back to her office. Her voice was kind, and I saw compassion in her eyes, but she was absolutely clear about my choices. "Either you get treatment and get sober, or you're fired."

I drove home, tried to reassure Allison that everything would be okay, and packed a bag. A few hours later my sponsor Bob C., a CNN colleague who had been sober for more than a decade and who had agreed months earlier to be my sponsor, drove me to Ridgeview Institute, an inpatient addiction treatment center in suburban Atlanta. I don't remember saying a word on that hour-long drive. I was consumed with shame. Once again, I had failed. I was a failure.

I spent twenty-eight days at Ridgeview and the whole time I was there I had one consuming thought—I had to bounce back as fast as possible and regain control of what I had almost lost. That thought governed everything I did at Ridgeview. I lied to the staff knowing that if I told the truth, they'd try to make me stay there or send me somewhere else for a long time. I admitted that I'd been to treatment once before, at Hazelden in 1989, but I never mentioned that I relapsed and went back, nor did I tell them that during my second stay at Hazelden the staff had recommended long-term treatment and I was discharged against staff advice. Nobody at Ridgeview knew the whole story because I didn't tell them and I didn't sign the release forms that would allow them to talk to my family.

To tell the truth would have been to admit that I was sicker than I appeared to be. Telling the truth would mean I'd have to stay in treatment for a long time, and I had a wife and two babies and an important job to get back to as soon as possible. I knew how to work the program and I had a proven track record of success—three whole years of sobriety. So this relapse wasn't really all that significant—it was a skinned knee rather than a mortal wound.

I didn't get along with any of the other patients, either. "They're just not really like me," I told my mother and father in a long phone call over Labor Day weekend. Allison and the boys were spending the weekend with them at their house in New Jersey and I ached to be with them all.

"Most of them don't know anything about the Twelve Steps," I said. "They don't have a sponsor like I do. Shoot, my sponsor even drove me to treatment after I reached out for help! Virtually everyone here was forced into treatment against their will and this is their first time in a treatment center."

"Try to find things in common with them," my mother advised. "You really aren't different at all, no matter what their circumstances. There are ways you can help them, son, and they can help you, too. Isn't that what treatment and AA are all about?"

"Yes," I said, "you're right." But the clock was ticking, and I had become so good at lying that I was starting to believe my own lies.

Halfway through treatment I received a letter from Allison.

Dear William:
I love you so much and am missing you. We've got some (maybe) tough days to go through but we'll make it. I really

want us to make it as a family. I'm proud of you for choosing to go to the treatment center—it must be hard to start over but you can do it. I feel like I'm starting over in my Al-Anon program too, and it feels really good right now. I think if we are going to make it, I need to go to meetings also. I really got a lot out of today's meeting.

I hope you get to come to New Jersey—if not, we'll have *many* more times to be together—the rest of our lives.

You are a wonderful Dad—and Henry loves you so much—Thomas will in time. Henry was calling your name a lot tonight—I said I was sad Dad wasn't with us and Henry said "yeah!"

I really miss you—I feel like you've been gone a year.

I love you,

Al

A few days later I opened a letter from Dad.

Dear Cope:

You have no choice but to get well and conquer your disease. Allison, Henry and Thomas have need of you.

Young Henry adores you and his world would be shattered without you. On the way from the airport I said, 'When we get to my house, Henry, we'll go swimming.' And he said: 'Dad-dee, Dad-dee,' because he associates you with the good times in the pool. We passed a man mowing his lawn near our house and he pointed and said, excitedly, 'Dad-dee, Dad-dee.' This morning he picked up the unplugged phone on the terrace, pretended to dial it, and said, 'Dad-dee, Dad-dee!' 'Hen-yee. Hen-yee.' He missed you so much and was trying to connect. And little Thomas is in the wings, waiting. Your time to bond with him is soon. They have need of you.

You can do it. You have the stuff it takes. This week I was reading James McPherson's great account of the Civil War, *Battle Cry of Freedom*, and came across this passage about Ulysses S. Grant:

> He may have been an alcoholic in the medical meaning of that term. He was a binge drinker. For months he could go without liquor, but if he once imbibed it was hard for him to stop. His wife and chief of staff were his best protectors. With their help, Grant stayed on the wagon nearly all the time during the war. If he did get drunk, it never happened at a time crucial to military operations. Recognized today as an illness, alcoholism in Grant's time was considered a moral weakness. Grant himself believed it so and battled to overcome the shame and guilt of his weakness. In the end, his predisposition to alcoholism may have made him a better general. His struggle for self-discipline enabled him to understand and discipline others; the humiliation of prewar failures gave him a quiet humility that was conspicuously absent from so many generals with a reputation to protect; because Grant had nowhere to go but up, he could act with more boldness and decision than commanders who dared not risk failure.

So your illness can be an instrument of your service—first and foremost to Allison, Henry and Thomas, each of whom loves you dearly, and in time to others.

I am pulling for you. I know you can do it. To whatever extent our own relationship is one of your issues, I am available at any time to sit down with you and a counselor to explore and resolve it. Nothing means as much to me as your winning this struggle, because I love you, because you are the father of my grandsons who desperately need you, and because I still believe we have things to do together.

And I need you.

Love,
Dad

I read that letter, so full of love and inspiration, and knew I had to get out of Ridgeview as soon as possible so I could prove to everyone that I was the good husband and father my family deserved. I felt overwhelmed by the pressure. I had to prove that I could make it on my own, and I had to prove that Dad could count on me always to be his good son. The last thing I wanted to do was let my father down. I knew he had need of me but never, ever, more than I had need of him.

I was discharged from Ridgeview a week after Labor Day, September 1994. Desperate to hang on, I went to AA meetings and attended the aftercare group at Ridgeview. I held on to Allison and the boys, but it was as if I were falling down the side of a cliff, clutching at branches, clinging to them in misery. I felt myself slipping away, my head spinning, the darkness spreading all around me as the craving grabbed hold and shook me until I let go and surrendered to it.

On a beautiful Sunday afternoon less than a month after I left Ridgeview, I kissed Thomas in his playpen and spent a few minutes talking to Henry as he scooted around the driveway on his tricycle. I told Allison I was going to run some errands but I'd be home soon, in plenty of time for dinner. It was a lie, but I knew it was the last lie I would ever tell her.

In less than five minutes I was in the crack house. Not to get high this time, for like everything else in my life, the drugs had stopped working. I walked in the door, sat down at the table in the kitchen, and fired up the pipe. Again and again and again. Trying, wanting, needing, waiting to die.

14

Found

TIME STOPPED. The seconds, minutes, hours, days, months, and years of my life had nowhere to go, and my existence was confined to a seemingly endless moment on a foam rubber mat on the floor in the hallway of the detoxification unit at Ridgeview Institute. I was placed on suicide watch. The nurses told me later that during those first few days I said only four words. "I want to die."

I only remember lying on the floor curled up under a sheet and a blanket, unable to comprehend anything except that the fluorescent lights in the hallway were always on. They hurt my eyes, and I'd pull the blanket over me, trying to shut out the light. I slept. I didn't feel anything. I wasn't hungry for food or thirsty for water. There was no sadness, fear, or anger. No regrets. No images of Allison's face, no memories of the boys' tears or laughter. No smell of my own rancid breath or itching of the ingrown hairs on my neck and face. No replay of those last hours in the crack house or the ride in the back of the van. No memories, no thoughts, no feelings at all.

Later I had a vague sense of motion and sounds that seemed far-off down the hall, but only gradually did I become aware of other people. They paused just long enough to record my blood pressure and whisper soft words that I couldn't comprehend. I just stared at their ankles. That's how I came to know them, by the shoes and socks they wore on their feet.

For days I slept. I didn't dream because I was empty of all thought and emotion. My arms and legs felt heavy and lifeless, as if they belonged to someone else's body. My stomach cramped. My head pounded. When my mind was able to grab on to images or thoughts, they cut and tore at me like pieces of jagged glass. I pictured Allison in my mind, standing in the kitchen, smiling, trusting me when I said I was going to run an errand and be right back. Images of Henry lying in his hospital bed, tubes in his nose and arms, looking up at me, and Thomas in his crib, crying, reeled through my mind. I saw BJ in the crack house, her cheeks drawn in, her eyes closed, leaning across the table to hand me the pipe, and I saw my father looking at me, his face twisted in pity and revulsion.

"Do you want something to eat?" A woman with white rubber-soled shoes was kneeling on the floor next to me.

"You've been here for four days now." Her voice sounded like music. "You can't just drink Gatorade. You need to eat something solid." She waited a moment. "Are you hungry, William? Can you eat?"

"Yes," I whispered. That was the first word I remembered saying since I'd arrived at Ridgeview. I was starving. Hands reached out to help me up and then held on to my elbows, arms around my waist, gently guiding me to a table. I ate Cheerios with cold milk and sliced bananas. Bowl after bowl. Nothing had ever tasted so good. Hands led me back to my mat on the floor and I fell into a sleep so deep no dream could penetrate it.

Everything seemed cloudy in my head when I woke up again. Had I been asleep for a few minutes or a few days? Where was I? I struggled to open my eyes. I was in the crack house. BJ and the others were running around frantically, trying to hide. I felt the cold rain falling as I walked to the van. I saw my father's face, heard the words *I hate you,* smelled the dusty upholstery against my cheek, felt the floor, hard and cold, beneath me.

I opened my eyes again and for the first time I knew where I was and what had happened to put me there. Seconds later, I asked myself the question I always asked when I was forced to face the consequences of my actions.

"Now what?"

I always had an answer to that question. Get up. Go to work. Keep busy. Run. Buy some crack. Smoke some crack. Clean up the mess. Run. Lie. Hide. Deny that anything is wrong. Keep running. Don't stop.

But now, for the first time in my life, I didn't know what to do. It was all too broken up, there were too many pieces scattered around. I couldn't be fixed because there was nothing left to piece together. The loneliness of that moment was absolute. Shame pressed down on me like a massive weight, pushing me down through the mat and into the concrete floor, breaking me apart, tendon from muscle, muscle from bone. I once heard shame described as an internal hemorrhage, and that's exactly how it felt. Shame was bleeding me dry.

When I woke up the next day, I noticed for the first time that the sun was streaming through a window down the hallway. Still too weak to walk, I half-crawled over to the spot where the light painted the floor. Even through the double-pane tinted window, the sun was warm, and I lay there underneath the window feeling the rays shining through me. I imagined that I was lying outside in the grass, listening to the birds singing, feeling the wind move through me. I was in Wilmer under the pecan tree, looking up at the endless sky.

"Well, look who's stirring," someone said. "We were getting worried about you."

A man was kneeling down next to me. His brown hair fell over his eyes and his walrus-like mustache drew attention to the hollow of his cheeks and his dark, deep-set eyes.

It was Dr. Paul Earley. I remembered him from the last time I was at Ridgeview, just weeks earlier. I didn't like him then because he was always in such perfect control, so confident and self-assured, as if he knew more about me than I did. He had this clipped way of talking, and he'd answer my five-minute monologues with one-sentence prescriptions that always made me feel deflated and defeated. "I think you're full of it." "You screwed up." "Be quiet." "Listen."

Kneeling next to me, he smiled and ran his fingers through the thick piece of long hair that kept falling over his eyes. I could tell he was about to say something important, and I probably wasn't going to like it. Was he going to lecture me? Tell me I screwed up again? I sighed and closed my eyes, wishing he'd go away.

"What do you want me to do for you?" he said.

I was completely baffled by that question. What did he want me to say? He was the doctor and I was the patient—shouldn't he be telling me what to do?

"I don't know," I said. My voice sounded strange after days of not speaking. *I don't know, I don't know, I don't know.* I suddenly felt as if I were in a deep cave, screaming at the top of my lungs, being pounded by the echo of my own voice. *I don't know.* Those words revealed a truth I had never known because I had never stopped long enough to confront it. "I don't know" was the only answer I had now to the question "Now what?" I was out of answers, and that terrified me.

"Is there anything I can bring you?" Dr. Earley rephrased his question. I didn't want him to leave. It was such a struggle to think, to speak. What could I ask for? Another blanket. A book. I remembered my friend Joe, who was in my therapy group at Ridgeview several weeks earlier. A Southern Baptist with an addiction to pain medication, Joe reminded me of a young Mister Rogers with a thick Alabama accent. Everywhere Joe went he carried *The Life Recovery Bible*—"It's written specifically for people like us, William," he told me—and he spent hours talking about how the stories in the book helped him understand the practical, everyday power of the Twelve Steps of Alcoholics Anonymous.

"This is my bridge," Joe told me, patting the book. I wasn't sure exactly what he meant by that but I felt a sudden surge of hope. Maybe it could be my bridge, too.

When Dr. Earley brought me a copy of *The Life Recovery Bible*, I read it slowly, word by word. At first I couldn't focus on more than a few words at a time. I'd read a little bit and think, trying to figure out what the words meant. Then I'd read a few more sentences and think. Read, think, eat, read, think, sleep. The days passed.

I kept reading, and I thought a lot about what had happened between me and God. After the lightning storm I had lost my faith, but over the years I'd patched together an on-again, off-again relationship with God. Allison and I went to church almost every Sunday. We said grace at meals and recited our prayers at night. When I was in trouble, I'd pray to God to help me. In the countless AA meetings I had attended since I first went to treatment in 1989, I listened to people describe their higher power as nature, or love, or goodness, or grace. I just called it "God." But what did I mean by "God"? I read about God in the "How It Works" chapter in AA's Big Book and while the words made sense ("This is the how and why of it. First of all we had to quit playing God. It didn't work."), it was clear from my relapses that I wasn't ready to let God control everything in my life. My faith had become automatic, even mindless, and all too often I'd put words in God's mouth to justify whatever it was that I wanted to do next.

In the weeks that followed I read and reread passages from the book Dr. Earley gave me, searching for a way to understand God. I struggled with the words, trying to keep them in my mind and forgetting them all at once. I stared at the space between the lines, as if the answers were there instead. What did "Almighty" mean? What was "the promised land"? Even the opening words of the Twenty-third Psalm seemed thick and impenetrable: "The Lord is my shepherd, I shall not want." What shall I not want? How should I not want?

Frustrated because I couldn't connect the words on the page to the thoughts in my head, scared because I wondered if the drugs had once and for all short-circuited my ability to think or understand or know anything, I forced myself to slow down, reading one sentence at a time, sometimes over and over again. My eyes ached behind their sockets. The creases across my forehead were like rubber bands tugging at my temples until my whole head throbbed. Read, think, eat, sleep. For days, that's all I did, all I could do, even after I was finally moved out of the hallway and into a real room with a real bed.

One day as I sat on my bed in my sunlit room, I read a story about faith. This time the words seemed to jump right off the page and stick in my head. I asked one of the nurses for a pen (first I had to promise I wouldn't stab myself with it) so that I could underline the sentences.

If we didn't have faith in the promise of a better future for ourselves and our family, we wouldn't put ourselves through the hard work and pain involved in recovery. But as time passes, we may grow discouraged at the length of the process. We may have our spirits dampened by the ups and downs along the road, feeling our faith ebb more than flow. Some people report instant release from their addictions, but for most of us it will take faith and patience to inherit the promise of a new life.

Faith, patience, faith, patience. Over and over I repeated those words, trying to make them sink in, hoping they would reveal a pathway to follow. I knew something about faith, but nothing about patience because I always wanted instant gratification. *I want it and I want it now.* Time was my nemesis. I had lived my life acutely aware that the clock was ticking and to succeed I had to get as much out of every second that I could. It was like that manual juicer my mother had in the kitchen when I was growing up. My job was to squeeze the oranges, and I was never satisfied until I had ground the orange halves all the way to the rind leaving a white outer shell that looked like the dried-out skin of a baseball.

Drugs stopped time. That's one reason I loved them so much, because when I was high, time became irrelevant and the future held no threat. All that counted was the feeling of floating away, rising above and beyond my troubles, being at peace, even if just for a fleeting moment or minute or hour. But now at Ridgeview all I had was time.

I kept reading. The second passage I underlined in red ink had to do with Moses.

Moses persevered through numerous ups and downs. He climbed to many mountaintop experiences—periods of faith and commitment to God that resulted in extraordinary spiritual growth. However, he also had times when his lack of patience and faith or his self-doubt caused him problems.

Who can explain why a word or a phrase suddenly illuminates the darkness inside? If I had read that paragraph nineteen years earlier at my confirmation, or five years earlier at St. Vincent's, or one month earlier during my first stay at Ridgeview, I might have missed the meaning or overlooked it altogether. But on that day, for some reason, the words snagged in my brain, and I understood that Moses struggled on a daily basis with his own imperfections. I'd always pictured him as perfect, almost Godlike, the Charlton Heston character in the movie who parts the Red Sea with a wave of his staff. But that was a myth. Moses wasn't in perfect control—he was flawed, impatient, fearful, anxious, and full of self-doubt. Yet somehow he found the courage to put one foot in front of the other until he reached the mountaintop. His faith sustained him on the journey. Maybe faith was my solution, too.

But where would I find this faith? It wasn't as if I could just grab a bagful of it and head off up the mountain or conjure up a burning bush and a life-changing epiphany. I couldn't force myself to believe or demand that God spend some time with me trying to answer all my questions, and it was those damn unanswerable questions that were driving me insane. Why was I the only person in our family who became addicted? Dad and Mom both drank in moderation. I introduced my brother to cocaine, so I know he tried it and probably more than once, but he never got hooked. I don't know if my sister experimented with marijuana or other illegal drugs in her teenage years, but if she did, I wasn't aware of any problems she might have experienced as a result. Why me? It wasn't fair.

And what about my friends in college who drank and smoked and snorted and dropped with me? They all grew up and got on with their lives. Why couldn't I? Even in Dallas at the *Times Herald* and on Long Island at *Newsday* I'd smoke a joint or go out for drinks with my coworkers and once or twice we even snorted coke. But when it came time to go home, they left and went back to their families while I kept going. Why couldn't I stop? What was wrong with me?

And what about my relapses? Why couldn't I stay sober? Lots of other alcoholics and crack addicts "got it" the first time they went through treatment. Why did I keep relapsing? Why did I always see myself as different, stronger, more in control than everyone else and then prove myself weaker and less capable? Why did I have so much trouble with the whole idea of being powerless?

I couldn't come close to the answers to those questions, yet I couldn't stop asking them. I wanted to penetrate the mystery. I needed the truth to be revealed. And then, one day, I was exhausted. There were no answers, I realized. For all these years, I'd been driving myself insane with unanswerable questions. In that moment, I felt a sudden release. I gave up the effort and the questions faded away.

"I'm done, God," I thought out loud. "Have me."

What followed was no white light experience, as some people have described their spiritual awakening. There were no choruses of angels, no rumbling of the heavens, no transformations, divine presences, or miraculous visions. I just stopped asking questions, the noise inside my head quieted down, and the mystery of it all came through to me. There were no answers to these questions. That was the answer. There are no answers.

Except the One Thing, the one answer I had avoided all these years. Five years earlier when I first arrived at Hazelden for treatment, I was given a book of meditations titled *Twenty-four Hours a Day*. One passage in that book is so critically important that Keith and George and Lowell and all the other staff members repeat it over and over again, hoping the words will sink into even the most stubborn minds.

Keeping sober is the most important thing in my life. The most important decision I ever made was my decision to give up drinking. I am convinced that my whole life depends on not taking that first drink. Nothing in the world is as important to me as my own sobriety. Everything I have, my whole life, depends on that one thing.

That day at Ridgeview I understood for the first time what those words meant. *Everything I have, my whole life, depends on that one thing.* I had to stay sober. Sobriety couldn't just be a part of me—it had to *be* me, become me, take over me. I had to breathe it in like air, for, like air, I could not live without it. It would have to become my breath, my inhalation and my exhalation, my reason for being. If I lost it, I would have nothing because I would be nothing. If I kept it, I would be what I am. An addict. An alcoholic. An imperfect man. A human being. Alive.

That was the truth I had not known before. Perceiving it and understanding it for the first time, my whole world changed. On the phone that night with Allison, I could hear Henry laughing in the background and Thomas squealing like he did when his older brother tickled or teased him. Something about Allison's voice was different—it was as if she'd given up. She had no fight left in her.

"Allison, there's something I have to tell you, something I have to do," I blurted out. "I am going to get well. I promise you that. But I can't be a good husband to you or a good father to Henry and Thomas until I get well. And that means I have to stay here until they tell me it's time to go."

She sounded relieved, almost like she expected it. "You do what you have to do for yourself first," she said. "We'll be here. The boys and I will be okay. We love you. That's all that matters."

In that moment every excuse to leave treatment became the reasons I had to stay. Before I had always argued that the clock was ticking and I had to get back to the rest of my life and my responsibilities as a husband, father, son, employee, and neighbor. Now I finally realized that being a good husband, a loving father, a steady provider, and a decent human being depended on staying in treatment until the experts told me I was ready to go. Everything I had and everything I wanted to hold on to depended on one critical thing—my ability to stay sober—and the black-and-whiteness of it all was liberating. Stay sober and accept life as it is, with both the good and the bad, and live. Relapse again and lose it all. Live or die—that was the choice, and I wanted to live. I was free. I had made my choice.

My treatment at Ridgeview that second time lasted about one hundred days. Every day I learned something new. I became, as the old-timers say in AA, "teachable." The greatest lesson I learned is that I couldn't run away anymore because whatever I was running from wasn't outside of me. I think God might have figured out that He had to do something drastic to teach me that lesson because one night somewhere in the middle of my stay at Ridgeview I broke my foot in a volleyball game. After that, I had no choice but to slow down and ask for help.

"Sit in it," my counselor Richard Morgan told me. "Face it head on. Face the pain, the anger, the fear, loneliness, sadness, and shame. Don't hide. Face it without asking for an answer or a solution. Face it knowing the outcome is beyond your control and what matters is accepting that it hurts and the reason it hurts so much is because you can't do anything about it. It just *is*. Being human hurts.

"Face it, and when you pray don't always expect God to say yes. God answers all prayers but sometimes the answer He gives us is no. Face the no, the negative, the emptiness and nothingness that is at the center, because facing it is the act of faith itself, and it is not something we ever complete but a daily struggle to find peace in the midst of the chaos, relief at the heart of the suffering."

Anger, fear, and loneliness flooded over me as I thought about all the questions I couldn't answer. The shame kept filling me up and emptying me out. I thought about my mother, remembering the sweltering heat of that August day when she showed up at the Harlem crack house. I remembered the look in her eyes when I told her to go away, that I didn't want to talk to her. What did she think when she looked at me, my face broken out in red blotches and sores, my breath rank, my hands shaking, my blue eyes turned yellow? How many times since then had I broken her heart?

I remembered the words I thought I'd heard my father say in the van on the way to Ridgeview. "I hate you."

And my words to him. "I hate me, too."

This was my fourth time in treatment. Why did I think I would make it this time? Where would I find the strength to stay clean and sober when I had given in to my weakness so many times before?

The questions kept coming, and I knew I couldn't answer them so I sat with them, letting them take me over. One night, alone in my room, loneliness flooded over me. My broken foot was throbbing. I ached for my family. I longed for release from the pain and the fear and the shame. I felt as if I was drowning, gulping for air. I couldn't do this. I would never make it.

"Help me," I prayed into the darkness.

I shut my eyes, and then I heard it. It was just a whisper. "St. Paul." Two simple whispered words, but I heard them as clearly as if they had been shouted into my ear. Startled, I opened my eyes and looked around the room, but no one else was there.

"St. Paul." I had no doubt then, and I have never doubted it since, that it was God's voice I heard. God was speaking to me, urging me to go back to St. Paul, the city where I first got sober, the place where I first met Allison and discovered a community of people who loved and accepted me in all my weakness and imperfection. "St. Paul." I felt peace spinning around me, wrapping me tight.

Many, many times in the years that have passed, I have wondered what happened to me in that moment. I know it was real because it changed me in ways that even today I am still in the process of discovering. Did I really hear a voice? I believe I did and that's all that matters, because in that moment I realized that I was not alone and, most important of all, I was worthy of God's attention. And from that realization emerged the awareness that I had work to do and somehow, with God's help, I would find my purpose in life.

I recently found a description of the transformative effect of spiritual experiences in *The Varieties of Religious Experience*, written over one hundred years ago by William James.

> There are only two ways in which it is possible to get rid of anger, worry, fear, despair, or other undesirable affections. One is that an opposite affection should overpoweringly break over us, and the other is by getting so exhausted with the struggle that we have to stop—so we drop down, give up, and *don't care* any longer. Our emotional brain-centres strike work, and we lapse into a temporary apathy. . . . So long as the egoistic worry of the sick soul guards the door, the expansive confidence of the soul of faith gains no presence. But let the former faint away, even but for a moment, and the latter can profit by the opportunity, and, having once acquired possession, may retain it.

That's what happened to me in a treatment center in the suburbs of Atlanta in the month of October, 1994. My sick soul stopped guarding the door, and the soul of faith found its way in. God had been walking alongside me my whole life, but I'd hidden away from Him in shame and fear. Still, He followed me, from the crack house to the treatment center, time and time again, waiting patiently just outside the door until I finally let Him in.

15

St. Paul

I KNEW WHAT I had to do, but my stomach was in knots as I stood outside the corporate office of one of the most powerful news executives in the world, about to tell him that a whisper in my ear had directed me to walk away from my career in journalism.

Tom Johnson was the president and CEO of Turner Broadcasting, my long-time mentor, and my good friend. I'd known Tom since the early 1980s, when he helped me get my first reporting job at the *Dallas Times Herald*. Over the years Tom had invested his personal time and professional expertise to steer my journalism career, much as my father had done for him. Thanks to Tom, I still had my job after spending nearly four months in treatment.

"Cope! It's so good to see you!" Tom pushed aside my outstretched hand for a big bear hug that was almost as smothering as his Georgia accent. "Gosh, you're looking great! We're all so glad you're back. You're needed here."

I sat down in the chair opposite his desk next to the window overlooking the cavernous newsroom. Journalism awards and civic honors covered the desktop and walls, along with pictures of Tom with Presidents Johnson, Carter, and Clinton, a snapshot of Tom and his wife Edwina with Ted Turner and Jane Fonda, and a photo of Tom and General Norman Schwarzkopf. We chatted for a few minutes about world events and at one point Tom took a call from a CNN producer in Beijing who needed approval to set up an exclusive interview with the president of North Korea. During the interruption, I started questioning my decision to leave CNN. I loved everything about this place, especially the unpredictable moments that occur with breaking news, the fast-paced days, the team spirit, all of it a news junkie's dream. I also had the great advantage of a personal relationship with Tom and other senior executives who seemed genuinely interested in helping me learn the ropes and advance my career in broadcast journalism.

What am I doing? I thought at the same moment Tom finished his phone call and leaned across the desk, apologizing for the disruption. I suddenly realized how much he looked like a younger version of my father with his rounded cheeks, dark glasses, steady gaze, and the deep inner kindness shining through.

"Tom, I'm leaving," I said. The words spilled out in a train wreck of derailed sentences. "I have to do this. I love CNN. Atlanta is a great town, but Allison and I have to move back to St. Paul. I don't know what I'm going to do there for work, but I have to go, I just have to do this."

Tom didn't move. He continued to lean across his desk, smiling with the exuberant boyish grin that was his trademark. That smile could disarm a rattlesnake, and at that moment, I felt exactly like a snake in the grass.

"A lot has happened to me since October." I kept talking. "Things I can't explain about my addiction and what I have to do for my recovery." Tom's smile slowly disappeared as he began to grasp the fact that I was serious, despite my unsteady voice. I wanted to leap across the desk and give him a hug, apologize for my impulsive behavior, and run back to my desk in the newsroom. I wanted to make him proud. But I had to go back to St. Paul. I just had to.

"You've been like a father to me, Tom. I know the plan was that I'd go to treatment and then come back to my job, but everything has changed. My whole life has changed."

Finally Tom spoke. "Are you crazy?" The look on his face matched his words. He thought I'd gone over the edge. "CNN is a great place for you, Cope. So is Atlanta. This is your home now. You have a steady job, a good career, people who appreciate and love you. You can't just walk away from all of that."

I had heard a different version of those words just a few weeks earlier, when my parents visited me at Ridgeview for the family program. One evening while we were eating dinner, I abruptly announced that Allison and I had decided to move back to St. Paul. My parents were stunned.

"Are you sure you want to do this?" my father asked. "Have you considered the implications?" Later he told me what was really going through his mind at that moment. "I thought you'd gone nuts."

Dad and Tom were cut from the same bolt of cloth—they were both brilliant, ambitious, internally driven men whose modest upbringings had instilled in them a work ethic that took them to the White House and, afterward, into the world of journalism, where they both rose to the top of their fields. Both men lived to work and worked to live, and life had taught them one cardinal rule: Don't give up one job without getting another one first. Both men were also deeply religious, but I was pretty sure my divine inspiration for leaving CNN wouldn't do much to convince either of them that I hadn't in fact lost my mind. So I didn't mention the fact that one night at Ridgeview God told me to move to St. Paul.

How could I explain to Tom or Dad that the decision wasn't really mine at all? In the Atlanta crack house I hit bottom, a place of such darkness and despair that all hope was extinguished. How could they understand the depth of the shame that engulfed me whenever I thought about how I had abandoned my wife and two young children? How could they even begin to comprehend my decision to "let go and let God"? Those words sounded so trite, and I had struggled against them for so long, yet now they were my only hope. God spoke to me, and I was hanging on to his words for dear life. I didn't know why God wanted me to go to St. Paul, but I didn't need to know. I had no excuses and no explanations. This was just something I had to do.

That's what I told myself, but talking to my parents at Ridgeview and sitting in Tom's office trying to explain my decision, I feared I had disappointed them. Pleasing people had always been my main ambition and the greatest affirmation of my worth. At home, in the newsroom, in rehab, or in the crack house, the motivation was the same: I wanted people to know that I was really a good guy, a generous, kind, thoughtful person deep down, and I wanted them to know that so they'd like me and approve of what I did. That's one big reason why I could never give up on my relentless quest for perfection. And that's why I was terrified about the move to St. Paul, even though I had no doubt whatsoever that it was the right decision, as "crazy" as it might seem.

"I don't want you to make any big decisions right now," Tom was saying. "Let's discuss this when both of us have had more time to think about everything. You know what they say, 'One day at a time,' right? Take some time to think and reflect and then come back to my office in a few days and we'll talk about this again, just the two of us."

At home that night, I told Allison about my meeting with Tom. "I felt like I was in a two-man race and finished second," I said. I was feeling sorry for myself. "For perhaps the first time in my life I stood up for what I believed was my truth—that I must go to any length to stay sober and trust a power greater than me. If only Tom had said something like, 'That's a courageous decision,' or even, 'I'm proud of you,' I'd be able to move forward with confidence and faith in our future. But now I have all these doubts."

Not once in the weeks since I told Allison about God's whisper had she wavered in her support of my decision to return to St. Paul, the city where the terrible winters seemed to last forever.

"Just go and pray about it," she said matter-of-factly, just like she did every time she became frustrated with me because I was confused or anxious. After we put the boys to bed, I went into the living room and stretched out on the couch, replaying the conversation with Tom over and over in my head.

Maybe Tom is right, maybe I'm crazy to give up my job and my house and all the people here who care about me, I thought. Maybe Dad is right, too—it takes a lot of money to feed and clothe and house a family of four. How would I pay the bills without a job and a steady paycheck? Maybe I should stay in Atlanta, at least until I can figure out what I'd do for work in St. Paul. But on the other hand, maybe we should just pack up and go and have faith that everything will work out.

"Stop Shoulding all over yourself." I heard George Weller's voice in my head just as clearly as if he had been sitting there next to me. "Good old George," I thought, reaching for the book of meditations on the coffee table. I turned to the page with the Serenity Prayer.

> *God, grant me the serenity to accept the things I cannot change,*
> *the courage to change the things I can, and*
> *the wisdom to know the difference.*

This simple prayer, adopted decades ago as the mantra for recovering people everywhere, opened or closed just about every AA meeting

I had ever attended. I'd probably spoken those words a thousand times without really thinking about what they meant. But this time was different.

God, grant me the serenity to accept the things I cannot change. Okay, God, you're the one who spoke to me at Ridgeview, and there isn't a darn thing I can do to change what I heard you say, any more than I can persuade Tom to automatically accept my decision. I'm feeling restless, irritable, and queasy in the stomach—the same way I used to feel just before I'd ease the pain by drinking a beer or lighting the pipe. So now I'm asking you, God, please help me find a quiet place inside where I can stop questioning everything. Help me accept what life holds for me next, whatever it is and whenever it happens to be.

The courage to change the things I can. Courage, people say, is one of the classic virtues and is often listed first, because all the other virtues— kindness, honesty, generosity, humility, tolerance, forgiveness—require courage to be put into practice. If I wanted to change anything, I'd have to find the courage within. If I wanted to be an authentic person, true to my own self, I'd need to dig deep for the courage to do what I knew was right even if other people disagreed. Courage and faith, it seemed to me as I read the words of the Serenity Prayer, are intimately connected, because while my rediscovered faith in God gave me courage, I had to keep building up my courage to overcome the doubts and fears that might once again undermine my faith.

The wisdom to know the difference. What little wisdom I might have accumulated so far was the result of all the mistakes I'd made along the way, and in order to hang on to it, I would have to acknowledge and embrace my failure. If I can accept who I am and who I am not, then I am at least on the road to self-knowledge, if not wisdom. That's what I was thinking as I read the Serenity Prayer, and I suddenly remembered a story that I'd heard once, in an AA meeting perhaps, about a man who wanted to change but didn't know how. One night he prayed to God, asking, "How can I change myself?"

God replied, "You are yourself—you can no more change yourself than you can walk away from your own feet."

"But is there nothing, then, that I can do?"

"You can understand and accept this truth," God said.

"But how will I change if I accept myself?"

"How will you change if you don't?" came the answer.

I repeated the Serenity Prayer over and over again until I surrendered to its simple common sense.

AT WORK the next morning Tom's secretary walked into the newsroom and handed me an envelope with COPE handwritten on the front. I tucked it inside my jacket and waited until my shift was over to read it.

In his classic style, Tom got straight to the point:

Cope:
1. *Rebuilding* your personal and professional life. Not a good time to uproot and disrupt the rebuilding.
2. Splendid, caring professional environment for you at CNN . . . and a great future for you.
3. Atlanta has a good environment for your continued recovery.
4. Can you secure paid insurance for you, Henry, Thomas and Allison—includes, for now, the pre-existing "condition."
5. No new professional position. You should not leap from the high bars to an uncertain future (before you *know* you have a new opportunity).

6. "Stabilizing" your life now vs. destabilizing in new city/new job???

—Tom J.

As I read and reread his list of reasons to stay in Atlanta, I felt a faint yearning for the security of the orderly, predictable life he described. But Tom was appealing to my mind, and God was speaking to my heart. That was the difference. If I was going to make it in recovery—a question, really, of life or death—I had to trust that as I leaped from the high bars of everything I knew and loved, I'd land at least somewhere close to where God wanted me to be.

Before Ridgeview, it was all about me, William Cope Moyers—the little boy Cope who couldn't cope, the teenager who adored his father but came to bitterly resent his success, the man who blamed all his problems on others and obsessed endlessly about the hole in his soul, as if he had a birth defect that denied him happiness. Now it was all about God. God was what I needed instead of drugs.

"WHAT HAVE I DONE?" I asked myself as I walked through the century-old home we had bought in one of St. Paul's tree-lined neighborhoods. Thick layers of dust covered everything. Loose wires twisted out from the kitchen walls and hung there in midair. Some of the windows were cracked, others were painted shut. I found two dead bats in the fireplace, and my imagination told me there were more camping out in the massive stone chimney. With no furniture in the empty rooms, the place seemed much too big for a family of four, a cat, and our few possessions. We had a lot of work to do just to make it a livable home, and as I stood in the front hall I realized that it would hardly lend itself to the "Keep it Simple, Stupid" formula that old-timers in AA often repeated to newcomers like me.

In those first months back in Minnesota, there was more than enough uncertainty to make the simplest decisions complicated and keep me constantly on edge. It was easy to let go and let God, as they say, when I was in treatment. The real world was different. From the empty house to the shrinking bank account, mouths to feed and bottoms to diaper, a summer that was way too short and a winter that lasted half the year, I wrangled with what it meant to be powerless even while I hung on for dear life. Serenity? Only when the boys were taking their afternoon nap. Acceptance? That was easy, except when the roof leaked or the eighty-year-old furnace refused to kick in on subzero days. Courage? Draining as fast as my savings. Wisdom? I was beginning to realize that wisdom is all about seeking, not finding, and the more I learned, the less I knew. "The only true wisdom is in knowing you know nothing," Socrates apparently said. I could relate to that.

My friends in the recovering community and my Monday night AA meeting at a church not far from our new house helped me focus on what we all knew was an essential priority—staying in the middle. "You can't fall off the bed if you're in the middle of it," Bob C., my sponsor in Atlanta, liked to remind me, "and you won't relapse if you stay in the middle of the program and the fellowship. Go to meetings, ask for help, call your sponsor, pray, help others—stay in the middle of the bed."

Whenever I seemed in danger of falling off the edge—when I skipped a meeting or sat silently in the back of the room and didn't participate, when I failed to return my sponsor's phone call or found an excuse not to visit an alcoholic in need—it wasn't long before somebody dropped by the house or tracked me down at the local coffee shop to find out what I was up to. No wonder God whispered "St. Paul." The city was thick with people like me who had come to Minnesota for treatment and stayed because of the strength and sheer mass of the recovering community. In a place where AA is as deep and insulating as the snow in winter and recovering alcoholics are as thick as mosquitoes in summer, it was impossible to avoid daily affirmations of why we were all there—even a chance encounter with another recovering alcoholic in the grocery store was a stark reminder of what really mattered.

Addicts and alcoholics love coffee, and places like Caribou, Starbucks, and Dunn Bros along Grand Avenue count us among their best customers. Some of us even end up working there, fresh out of treatment and struggling to rebuild our lives by making cappuccinos and grinding coffee for the people we later see in AA meetings. Whenever two alcoholics spend some time together, it's a reminder of what our lives are all about. It happens to me a lot in Kowalski's, the grocery store where I never fail to encounter somebody I know in recovery. The aisles often become de facto meeting spots where we swap a "How are you doing today?" or "Haven't seen you around, are you going to the meeting tonight?"

Those chance encounters can sometimes be unnerving. I'll never forget the time I took a friend, just out of Hazelden, to his first AA meeting. We sat in the crowded room of a local church waiting for the meeting to start when suddenly in walked the man's doctor.

"You're in recovery! I had no idea," my shocked friend said to his physician.

"You're in recovery." The doctor smiled at his patient. "I had no idea."

St. Paul felt like home, the place where I felt like I fit and belonged, but what was I going to do for a living? There was no way I was going back into the newspaper business, and journalism had been my sole career. After a lot of soul-searching and long talks with Allison and my friends in AA, I came up with the idea to go into business for myself as a "communications consultant," charging one hundred and twenty dollars an hour teaching individuals and organizations how to communicate more effectively. Even though I had no business plan and only a vague sense of what I should be doing, I somehow managed to land a few clients, including some nonprofit corporations and a mutual fund company based in Minneapolis. When potential clients asked me what I might be able to do for them, I automatically responded, "What do you need done?" But I was clueless about the business world, and it didn't take long before my expenses exceeded my income.

Every Sunday I'd scour the pages of the *Sunday Star-Tribune* Help Wanted ads. This was something new for me—I'd never had to look in the newspaper for a job, having spent most of my working life as a newspaper reporter. Every job posting seemed either above or below my skill level. "Dog Groomer Desired." "Senior Legal Counsel Sought." "Nurses Needed." "Seeking Security Guard."

On November 19, 1995, I found what I didn't even know I was looking for.

PUBLIC POLICY SPECIALIST

Hazelden Foundation, located 45 miles NE of Twin Cities, is seeking a dynamic individual to provide assistance to the Vice President for Public Policy with Hazelden's state and national public policy efforts as they relate to Hazelden, the chemical dependency treatment field and related issues. The qualified applicant will have a Bachelor's degree in a related field or equivalent experience; demonstrated successful involvement in previous public policy activities; understanding of the chemical dependency field; strong written and verbal communications skills to influence diverse audiences; flexibility to adjust to changing demands in regard to work hours and locations $32,000-$40,000/yr. Send cover letter and resume to:

Hazelden Foundation
15245 Pleasant Valley Road
Center City, MN 55012
Equal Opportunity Employer

I sat on the living room couch, dumbstruck, alternately staring out the window at the fog and rain and again at those eight words starkly outlined in black-and-white. I knew that something momentous had just occurred, but I wasn't exactly sure what it was. I kept thinking what a coincidence it was that here I was in St. Paul looking for a job at the same time that Hazelden, a place where I had spent two months of my life in treatment, was advertising for someone to help them analyze public policy.

"Individual must demonstrate successful involvement in previous public policy activities," read the ad. That was a problem. I didn't even know what a public policy specialist was let alone what they did. My experience with Hazelden's public policies was limited to my knowledge of the rules and regulations of the treatment program. I had relapsed four times, and my résumé was full of holes that would be easy to explain to people who understood the nature of this relapsing disease but wouldn't exactly instill confidence that I could keep the job, much less stay sober, considering that I had been clean again for all of thirteen months. Undeterred, I sat down the next day and wrote a letter. I must admit I slightly exaggerated the success of my communications company.

November 20, 1995

Dear Hazelden:
I moved back to the Twin Cities this year with one key career objective: to use my extensive skills as a journalist to help nonprofit organizations. But I also returned because I wanted to give away some of what I had gotten as a member of the remarkable community of recovering alcoholics and addicts in the Twin Cities.

Today I am satisfying both goals. My small company (I am the sole employee) develops strategic communications plans for small nonprofits and large corporations. I help them define and refine what it is they want to say, and then determine the most effective way to ensure that message is heard by their targeted audiences.

Equally important is my work with the sober community. I am a Hazelden alumnus. It was in Center City, and then at Fellowship Club in St. Paul, that I began to rebuild my life more than six years ago. Now I volunteer at both places.

I want to build on my experiences as a journalist and as a recovering person in ways that strengthen the mission of places like Hazelden. Your newspaper classified ad for a public policy specialist caught my eye. I would bring a lot to that position because I have strong writing, verbal, and organizational skills, key connections both inside and outside of the recovering community, boundless energy, and an understanding of the issues and challenges faced by treatment centers like Hazelden.

But most important, I need no convincing that Hazelden's public policy is the correct policy. After all, Hazelden helped to save my life.

Please consider my application for the position. I look forward to hearing from you.

Sincerely,
William Cope Moyers

Two weeks later I drove the forty-five miles from St. Paul to Hazelden's five-hundred-acre campus in Center City for an interview. The highways were clear but snow covered the ground, and I couldn't stop thinking about the last time I made that drive in winter, still under the influence of cocaine, slumped over in the backseat, dressed in a grungy sweatshirt and jeans while Dad drove and Allison sat in the front passenger seat. Staff members helped me out of the car into a wheelchair and four weeks later, I walked out of the place in a huff because the same staff told me I was too sick to leave. *I'll prove them wrong,* I told myself, vowing never to return there, but here I was driving down Pat Butler Drive dressed in a suit and tie, hoping to be hired as a Hazelden employee.

"You certainly have some impressive skills," said Jane Nakken as she looked over my résumé. Jane was one of Hazelden's top executives.

"But there's one problem," she added.

"What's that?" I asked, getting nervous but trying to cover up my anxiety with my usual eager, affable style. "I can write, report, communicate, I know people in the recovering field, and I walk the Hazelden walk."

"All of that is true," Jane said pleasantly, "but the problem is that you have no direct experience in public policy." The job, she explained, was designed to help Hazelden advance legislative issues primarily in Minnesota but also in Washington, D.C., and that meant monitoring bills introduced in the state legislature or Congress, communicating with key policy makers and heads of federal and state agencies in the addiction treatment or health care field, and rallying Hazelden's sizable base of alumni and other constituents whenever there was a need to raise a collective voice on behalf of an important issue.

"Without any experience, how do I know that you can convince legislators to believe in Hazelden and what we do here?" Jane asked. "You have to understand, William, that public policy starts with getting people to accept the fact that addiction is a disease, that treatment really does work, people do recover, and when they do, their families and society as a whole benefit. You and I know this because we've been in the trenches, but most politicians don't get it, and neither do their constituents."

In that interview, Jane gave me a crash course on the realities of the uphill fight that kept Hazelden battling to overcome public policies stacked against addicted people. Changing policy, I learned, would mean fighting deep-seated prejudices and misconceptions that alcoholics and other drug-addicted people are weak-willed and suffer from underlying character disorders; that the cause of drug addiction is a lack of self-discipline and moral virtue; that alcoholism is not a true disease but rather a symptom of psychological and/or social problems; and that treatment doesn't work. The stigma goes deep, Jane said, and ends up portraying alcoholic and other drug-addicted people as somehow abnormal and thus less deserving of care.

Each year the federal government spends about twenty billion dollars on the "war on drugs," Jane told me, yet most of the resources are spent on "interdiction" (trying to stop the flow of illegal drugs into the country) and punishment, which means building more prisons to hold more people caught selling and using. What little money is left has to be shared among the researchers studying the science of addiction, the prevention experts teaching schools and communities how to keep the next generation of young people from using alcohol and other drugs, and the treatment professionals who help addicted people into treatment and recovery programs. In the private sector there are precious few resources to help people who can't afford treatment, although Hazelden and many other programs offer millions of dollars each year in financial assistance.

Insurance rarely covers the full cost of treatment, Jane said, and with the growth of the managed-care industry, insurance benefits for chemical dependency treatment have been severely restricted. Benefits are often denied because alcoholism is classified as a mental disorder and thus is not covered under many insurance policies. Insurance carriers often refuse coverage for the more expensive inpatient treatment programs in favor of less expensive outpatient programs, arguing that it doesn't matter what treatment you offer alcoholics because they are all equally ineffective. When coverage is offered, it is, in almost all cases, severely limited to a specific dollar amount with yearly caps.

That day in Jane's office, I truly understood for the first time how fortunate I was to have had my own resources and my parents' help to cover both my Hazelden treatments. My insurance plan at CNN had covered most of the cost of my treatment at Ridgeview, and I was able to borrow money from my parents to cover the rest. What would have become of me, my life, and my family if I hadn't had those resources when I hit bottom and relapsed again and again before I finally got sober? I thought about all the addicted people I knew from the crack houses, streets, and bars of Northport and Harlem, St. Paul and Atlanta: Jack, Jeffrey, Willy, Janette, Ben, Peanut, Big Mama, and Scarface. But most of all BJ, the woman who packed her little bag every day and proudly announced, "I'm going to treatment today" just an hour or two before she spiraled back down into her own desperate world of crack addiction. What if she had showed up one day at the door of a treatment center in Atlanta? She had no money, no family, and no insurance. What would have happened if she had been taken to county detox and then turned away? Would she have concluded that nobody cared, that she wasn't worth the trouble, anyway? I couldn't imagine what was worse—not wanting to get help at all or not being able to get the help she wanted and needed. Where was BJ now? Where were all of them?

"Tell me, William," Jane was saying, "what caused you to leave Atlanta, walk away from your career in journalism, and move here to Minnesota? To be absolutely frank, I'm wondering why you are applying for a position that pays about half of what you were making at CNN. What are you looking for exactly?"

I didn't know Jane's background at the time, and it was a good thing, too, because she was setting me up for the real test. For years

Jane worked as a counselor with drug-addicted teenagers at Hazelden's youth treatment facility in suburban Minneapolis. With adolescents, denial is often encased in a Teflon coating of youthful invincibility, a deep distrust of authority, resentment at being labeled or categorized, and disdain for the treatment process. Skilled counselors like Jane, whose sweet voice and "Minnesota nice" demeanor belie a fiery spirit that matches her head of red hair, know how to drill through those seemingly tough outer layers to the depths of the hurting and hopeful souls hidden underneath.

I knew she wanted the honest truth—everything in treatment and recovery begins with honesty—but I wasn't exactly sure how to explain the events of the past year, from my relapse in the Atlanta crack house to the months I spent in treatment at Ridgeview, and the spiritual awakening that called me back to Minnesota. For the most part I had kept my story private from everyone outside the recovering community in St. Paul. It wasn't that I was hiding anything, it just seemed easier to explain that I had moved to Minnesota for the "quality of life" rather than get into the complicated story of my treatments, relapse, and recovery. But here I was, back at Hazelden, the place that first taught me that recovery is only possible with honesty, openness, and willingness. It suddenly dawned on me that if I couldn't talk about my addiction and recovery in a place like Hazelden, I was doomed to a life where truth was partially if not wholly hidden in the shadows of fear and shame.

I told Jane the whole story. I talked about St. Vincent's and my first stay at Hazelden, followed by the months at Fellowship Club, my relapse in St. Paul, my second stay at Hazelden, and the giant resentment I held toward my Hazelden counselors when they told me I needed more time in treatment and I left against staff advice. I described the three years between 1991 and 1994 when I tried to put my life back together in Atlanta, my marriage to a woman who also started her recovery at Hazelden and was now six years sober, the months when we didn't know if Henry would live or die, my relapses before and after Thomas's birth, the despair I felt when I began to slide downhill, the fear that gripped me when I thought about asking for help, my first treatment at Ridgeview, the final plunge into the abyss at BJ's crack house, my days on suicide watch at Ridgeview, the whisper, and, finally, the decision to leave Atlanta and start all over again in Minnesota. This wasn't a job interview—it was a confessional and I was clearing the record and my soul.

"You've relapsed three times, William, and you're just a little over a year sober," Jane said, being as honest with me as I had been with her. "Do you think you can stay sober?"

"I really don't know," I said truthfully. "But I'm convinced in my heart I can and I know that I have to or I'm going to die. My disease is progressive, I know that, and I know from my most recent relapse that it's progressed into its late stages—if I relapse again, I don't think I'll get another chance. My track record isn't very impressive, I know that, too, but I love being sober. I love my recovery. Getting sober was difficult but staying sober is more important to me than anything else in my life, because I know that everything else depends on it."

We shook hands and Jane told me she'd call me, but there was something she didn't share with me that day. Several years later, after we became good friends, she told me that during the interview she kept thinking to herself, *He's Bill Moyers's son—what if this doesn't work out and I have to fire him one day? How could I fire Bill Moyers's son?* I'm glad she focused on the hiring rather than the firing part, because, for the first time in my life, I believed my last name wasn't relevant to the skills and talents I brought to the position. I had gotten this far in the interview process based on my own merits, including my treatment and recovery history. In a sense, my failures qualified me for the job as much as my successes.

I got the job.

"Go out and change public policy," Jerry Spicer told me my first day on the job. Dressed in Western cowboy garb, complete with snakeskin boots and a bolo tie, Jerry didn't look the part of the president and chief executive officer of one of the world's most renowned treatment centers. But his orders were clear and direct—go out and talk to as many state legislators as possible, give them the facts and tell them the stories that convey the depth and breadth of the problems facing addicted people, and work with them to create legislation that increases access to treatment and recovery programs. I had a clear agenda and a lot of energy and enthusiasm for the job, but it didn't take long before I discovered two major stumbling blocks. The first obstacle was money—simply put, there wasn't enough. When I started working at Hazelden, it was the only treatment center in the country with funds set aside for public policy, but the budget was only $350,000 which included my $40,000 salary. In the world of politics, and especially in a world where the beer, wine, and hard liquor industries spend tens of millions of dollars a year, $350,000 wasn't going to go very far.

The second big obstacle was the absence of a vocal constituency. Without the funds needed to influence county, state, and federal decision-makers, we had to rely on organized groups of people to write letters, make phone calls, sign petitions, and coordinate community coalitions. But few people were enlisting for the job. Not long after I started working at Hazelden I met President Clinton's drug czar General Barry McCaffrey at a drug-policy forum in Washington, D.C. I'll never forget his words that day, which were directed to me and the other recovering people in the audience.

"The problem is that you are invisible," McCaffrey said. "If we're ever going to change this war-on-drugs mentality, then we need to change the attitudes about addiction in this country, and that starts with people like you. You can't remain invisible any longer. You must not be afraid to speak out. You must attack the attitude of hopelessness that most people have today."

I kept thinking about that word *invisible* as I met with legislators and policy makers, drafted position papers on drug policy, wrote op-ed pieces, talked to local civic organizations, and testified before the Minnesota legislature on the nature of addiction and the effectiveness of treatment. I was wrestling with the fact that most recovering people do not stand up and tell their stories but choose instead to live quiet, private lives as hardworking, responsible citizens of their community. Every addicted and recovering person has felt the sting of stigma either publicly or privately, and we all ask ourselves similar questions. What will people think of me if they know I was in treatment for alcoholism? Will I lose my job if my boss finds out I was addicted to cocaine? Will I lose the respect of my neighbors if I'm honest about my past? Will people in my community question my basic character and core values if they discover that I struggled for years with a drug problem?

I had the chance to get some answers to these questions when the St. Paul Downtown Rotary Club invited me to speak in my first public appearance as Hazelden's new public policy specialist. It was a noon meeting in a large hotel ballroom, and the room was packed with about two hundred people, mostly older men, sitting at round tables. Lunch had just ended as the formal part of the program began, but already a few members were snoozing in their chairs and others were looking at their watches, ready to make a quick exit. I stepped up to the podium, shuffled the pages of my carefully prepared speech, and raised my voice above the clatter.

"I want to talk to you today about a disease that has no cure," I began. "It's a terminal disease, one that we know very well at Hazelden, where I work, and it costs our country $168 billion dollars every year.

It's a disease that affects all of us in Minnesota, filling our emergency rooms with victims, our prisons with inmates, our streets with homeless people, and our homes with broken families."

I looked out at the crowd and realized I was losing them before I even got started. It's never easy to give a speech after lunch at an organization where attendance is mandatory, interest diminishes as food gets digested, and people either fall asleep or head for the door. It didn't help, either, that the grim statistics bored the audience to tears. They'd heard all this before. For a moment I considered gathering up the pages of my failed speech, saying a quick thank you, and getting the heck out of there.

Instead, I changed my game plan by ignoring my written remarks. I only had one more chance to recapture their waning attention.

"This disease is alcoholism and drug addiction," I said, leaning forward and speaking forcefully into the microphone. "And I have it. I am a drug addict and an alcoholic. This is what one looks like. Take a good look at me."

The room fell suddenly silent. The whispered conversations and clinking of silverware faded away. One or two people stared at me, their mouths wide open, their forks frozen in midair. A prominent businessman I knew stopped in his tracks as he was making his way out the rear exit. It was as if a collective "huh?" rose from the floor. I sensed that while they knew people like me, they had never before heard anyone stand up and announce it.

They quieted down. The bustling stopped. They were paying attention now. "Addiction is a bad disease that affects good people and families, even mine," I said, still nervous but feeling more confident as I spoke the words that gave life to my experience. This was my story, and I knew it inside out. For the first time in my life, I was owning it, and I wasn't ashamed.

"I didn't grow up thinking I would become an alcoholic or addict,"

I said. "My parents didn't raise me for that to happen, no one expected it to happen, but it did. I had everything I could ever want in terms of being loved and cared for, but I still became addicted to alcohol and other drugs."

My script was out the window. I wanted desperately for them to see that my story could help them and the people they loved who might be going through the same thing right now.

"Two years ago I was on my back in a place in the inner city of Atlanta more horrific than I can describe to you—a place where there was no hope, no help, no love. But even though I had given up on myself, people who loved me did not give up on me and I was able to get back into treatment and get well. I needed treatment not once, not twice, but four times before I was able to take personal responsibility for my illness as a recovering person.

"Treatment works, and I'm living proof. Because I got treatment at Hazelden I am now a taxpayer in Minnesota, a consumer of the products your companies make, a volunteer trying hard to make our community an even better place to live, and a good neighbor who mows the lawn in the too-short summers here and shovels the snow off the sidewalk in our endless winters."

They laughed, and I joined in, feeling relieved, even liberated. The people in the audience were community activists, highly respected business leaders, men and women who I held in great respect. Now they knew me for who and what I really was—William Cope Moyers, recovering alcoholic and crack cocaine addict. I didn't have to hide anymore.

"I've never told this story in public before," I said. "Because of this opportunity at Rotary today, maybe I will again someday. Thank you for listening."

And I sat down. There was scattered clapping, and then applause filled the room. The applause got louder. A few people stood up, others joined them, and suddenly everyone in that room was on their feet. I was surprised and for a moment I thought they were just getting up to leave, but most of them lined up to shake my hand. "Thank you," they said. "Thank you."

I believe that they were thanking me for talking about something they had experienced in their own lives or had witnessed in the lives of people they loved. Something in their eyes, in the handshakes that lingered longer than normal handshakes, in the emotion I heard in their voices convinced me that they had some personal knowledge of this disease.

At work the next morning I answered the phone to hear a man fighting back tears.

"I was at the Rotary meeting yesterday," he said. "I wondered if you might be able to help me with my son." He told me about his nineteen-year-old son who was in the hospital with a serious concussion after getting drunk and falling down the stairs at a fraternity party. "He started smoking marijuana in eighth grade," the concerned father explained, "and I knew he drank heavily at times, but I had no idea how serious his drug problem had become." We talked for a long time. I suggested he call Hazelden's 800 number so he could talk to a counselor, and I gave him the days and times of several local Al-Anon meetings. ("Be sure to tell family members about Al-Anon," my mother always reminds me, "because those meetings are still a lifesaver for me.")

A few days later the owner of a major business in downtown St. Paul called me at home. "The people sitting at my table—many are old friends and customers—were deeply moved by what you said," he told me. "Not one of them knows I'm in recovery, and your speech got me thinking that maybe I should tell them my story, too."

Later that same day Ron Clark, the editorial page editor of the *St. Paul Pioneer Press* newspaper, invited me to write an opinion piece about treatment for publication in the paper.

"I was in the audience at the Rotary Club meeting," Ron said. "Just condense your speech into several hundred words."

"Well," I laughed, "what I ended up saying that day isn't what I had written down on paper. I just spoke from my heart."

"Then write from your heart," Ron advised.

I wrote about the fact that I struggled for years with a baffling inability to control my drinking and drug use. I got well, I wrote, not because I was morally upstanding or a good citizen or came from a well-known family or had parents or a wife who loved me—I got well because I got treatment not once, not twice, but four times, and every time I was treated with dignity and respect, while receiving strong encouragement to accept personal responsibility for my recovery. All chronic diseases carry with them the risk of relapse (addiction is no exception), and while relapses are certainly not inevitable, they are a powerful reminder of the tenacious nature of the disease and represent a potentially life-transforming opportunity to learn from previous mistakes. No individual, no family, no community is immune to the ravages of alcohol or other drug addictions, I wrote, but every individual, every family, and every community benefits when people like me get well. Throughout that op-ed piece I emphasized how my story underscored the need for changes in public policy to help the millions of addicted people who are still suffering.

Dozens of people responded to the article. Several readers accused me of trying to shirk responsibility by foisting the blame on my disease—the old "my illness made me do it" excuse. One person who identified himself only as Joe called me at work and told me I should be ashamed of myself for violating the traditions of Alcoholics Anonymous by breaking my anonymity. Others called to ask for my help with an alcoholic father, a marijuana-dependent son, a husband addicted to methamphetamine, a wife addicted to painkillers.

I was proud of my Rotary speech and I knew Dad would want to know about it, so I sent him a copy of the Rotary Club program and the op-ed piece I wrote for the *Pioneer Press*. His response was addressed to Allison and me.

Dear Cope and Allison:

I want the two of you to know how much I admire you for the way you have put your lives together.

I worried about your leaving Atlanta so abruptly, as you perceived. Hazelden had taught me the first time around that hasty decisions so soon after a crisis are very often wrong decisions. And I was troubled by how you would earn a living to support yourselves if Cope gave up his CNN job. After all the Ridgeview counseling and enlightenment, it seemed to me that it would be disastrous to both of you and to our relationship if you had to turn to us for financial support; I had come to see at Ridgeview that even the modest help we had been providing had been injurious to your self-esteem, autonomy, and sense of responsibility.

So I worried when you announced you were going back to St. Paul, even though I could understand the attraction of the recovering community.

Well, I know now you did the right thing. It took courage and resolution, but those have been qualities you two have in abundance. Going back was the thing to do. Putting down roots there where you met has been a healthy step; you have a rounded life, and the job you have taken on, Cope, seems perfectly suited to call on your inherent talents and to provide you a sense of mission altogether harmonious with your own recovery. Allison, the boys could not have a more devoted or knowing Mom, and I feel fortunate my grandkids are in your care.

I am feeling very good about you. And I love you both very much.

Dad

Of all the letters Dad had written to me over the years, this one touched my heart most deeply. I had done "the right thing," he said. I also loved what he said about my "mission," and as I thought about that word I realized that it had nothing to do with being famous or trying to match his success and everything to do with being true to myself. And who am I? A drunk and a drug addict who stumbled and fell not once but many times, who kept doing the same thing over and over again, even though he promised that he would change, who by all logic should have died but lived only because the people who loved him didn't give up on him and because when he needed treatment, he was able to get it. A drunk and a drug addict who has been given a chance to redeem himself by reaching out, with his life's story, to those who still suffer.

Not long ago I spoke at a conference for doctors and other medical professionals in Chicago. I noticed a man crying in the audience. At the end of my talk he approached, thrust a note in my hand, said "thanks," and disappeared back into the crowd.

Dear Mr. Moyers,

Thank you for speaking to me, the addict. I wanted to speak with you, but because of hearing your passion against the stigma, I am in tears and just can't right now. I would love to speak with you more and find out if I can do anything else. Because of hearing you, I will speak more and more—no matter the risk.

May God richly bless you and yours, and Hazelden.

Sincerely,

Barry

P.S. The stigma is allowing people to die.

I keep that note in my wallet with another note that is wrapped around a laminated wallet-size photo of a smiling young man. His name was Jake Sipe, and his twin sister, Julie, gave me his photograph and told me his story. Jake was addicted to marijuana, alcohol, and prescription drugs. He killed himself when he was twenty-seven. "My pain was unfathomable, boundless," Julie told me, "but I wanted to know, I *had* to know, firsthand, that Jake's death wasn't worthless, that genuine good could come of it."

After her brother's death, Julie, a litigation attorney with a large law firm in Indianapolis, quit her job, sold her house, and took a fifty-percent pay cut to work as a staff attorney at the Indiana Judicial Center, where she works today educating and training judges and judicial officers, providing legal research and technical assistance to the courts, and administering and supporting drug courts as well as other court-related alcohol and drug programs. She also volunteers for the Judges and Lawyers Assistance Program (JLAP), where she helps legal professionals deal with their own alcohol and drug problems.

These are the words Julie wrote that I take with me everywhere I go.

Wherever people are in the black hole of addiction—whether it is at the edge of a loved one's battle with drugs, in a horrifying fight of one's own, or standing amid the devastation caused by death, even suicide—I want them to know that addicts are not monsters. I want them to know that healing and beauty can come from the most destructive forces our world has ever faced. I want them to know that hope still exists.

16

Cancer

In March 1998 the Moyers family went public.

"My wife Judith and I thought we knew about addiction until it came close to home," my father said in the opening scene of the documentary series *Moyers on Addiction: Close to Home.*

"Then we discovered how naïve we had been," Dad said. "Ten years ago our oldest son plunged into a long and painful struggle with drugs and alcohol. Our whole family was swept into the ordeal. It's come to a happy place for us, fortunately, and our son is doing well. Many others are not so lucky. What we have learned from our experience and are still learning prompted this series."

The series, which aired in five parts on PBS, triggered an enormous outpouring of interest in addiction, controversy about how to deal with the problem, and pleas for help from addicted people and their family members. Suddenly it seemed like everyone in America was talking about addiction. Oprah devoted an entire hour to our story and in the hour after the show aired, Hazelden received two thousand phone calls from people asking for help. My parents and I appeared on *Larry King Live* and the *Today* program. The *New York Times*, *Newsday*, and dozens of other newspapers and magazines featured stories. The U.S. Conference of Mayors asked us to speak, Congress held a committee hearing on addiction treatment, and invitations poured in to talk at churches, treatment facilities, schools, and state legislatures. My mother also spearheaded a Web-based program designed to reach into rural communities and neighborhoods in the toughest inner cities from coast to coast.

It was a whirlwind few months but it wasn't long before life returned to normal, whatever that means in a household with three little children. Nancy Judith, born in 1997, was already trying hard to keep pace with Henry and Thomas, who liked going to school almost as much as they liked building with LEGOs in their bedrooms. When Allison wasn't being a mom, she made jewelry and took classes in still life painting. I got a promotion at work and stayed busy there, though we managed to sneak away most weekends in the summer to our little cabin on a seventy-acre lake in Wisconsin, not far from Hazelden. At the lake our neighbors were loons, bald eagles, bears, and bass. I even learned how to fish so I could catch some of those bass, and I taught the kids to fish, too. Life wasn't perfect, but it was pretty close, which is why I kept going to a lot of AA meetings and even sponsored a few newcomers in recovery; the most dangerous time for people in recovery, they say, is when things are going well.

Early one morning before work I was standing in front of the mirror in the bathroom, a towel wrapped around my waist. I'm left-handed and as I raised my left arm to shave the right side of my face, I noticed an odd-looking black spot on my upper arm. *That's funny,* I thought, *I've never seen that before.* I tried to flick it off as if it were a pesky bug, but it was firmly anchored in my skin and didn't budge.

I told Allison about it that night after we put the kids to bed.

"You'd better get that looked at," she said. Unlike the moles and freckles sprinkled over my skin, this spot felt bumpy and thick. The unusual dark color and irregular edges worried us both, and a few days later I was sitting in the dermatologist's office. I figured he'd tell me it was a regular old mole, nothing to worry about or—worse case scenario—he'd say it was a surface skin cancer that he could remove right there in the office and then we'd be done with it.

"I don't like the look of it," he said, taking a biopsy and instructing me to call in a few days for the results. That was Tuesday. On Wednesday I flew to Washington to attend a national forum on drug policy and the next day, October 12, 2000, marked my sixth anniversary of sobriety. I tried to call the doctor several times that day but we never connected. On Friday the thirteenth, while I was waiting at the airport for my flight back to the Twin Cities, I finally reached him.

"It appears the growth is a melanoma," he said. "I've scheduled surgery for you for next Tuesday morning."

The two-hour flight back to Minnesota seemed to last forever. Assuming the worst had always been my first line of defense and the worst, in this case, was pretty bad. I was scared, but more unsettling than the fear was a desperate sense of powerlessness. It was the same sickening feeling I had experienced in detox at Ridgeview exactly six years before. "Now what?" I asked, over and over. There was no answer.

The porch lights were on when I walked up to the front door of my house, and Allison was waiting for me. She took one look at my face and knew. We held on to each other and cried for a long time.

The "whys" rattled around in my brain all weekend until I could barely sit still in the day or sleep at night. "Why this?" "Why now?" "Why me?" I envisioned cancer as an evil intruder into the lives Allison and I had worked so hard to put back together. We had both been through so much together, starting with our own addictions, my relapses and repeated treatments, Henry's surgeries, the move back to

St. Paul, and those early months when we had no idea how we were going to make it. Now I had a steady job that fulfilled me, we owned a beautiful old house on a tree-lined street, our neighbors had become good friends, our finances were secure, and our children were healthy and happy. Since we'd moved to St. Paul our family had grown, and Nancy, now three years old, followed me around the house like a devoted puppy, always wanting to sit on my lap or cuddle next to me on the couch.

In the blink of an eye all those memories and experiences paled against that black spot no bigger than an eraser on the end of a pencil. I was forty-one years old and I couldn't even begin to grasp what this diagnosis meant and how it would affect our lives—how would my children ever make sense of it? Not knowing the answer was the worst part, and to occupy the void, I spent most of the weekend wrestling with the boys in the living room, reading *Goodnight Moon* over and over again to Nancy, and raking leaves into piles in the front yard for the kids to jump in. When nobody was looking I searched the Internet for information on melanoma. Nothing I found gave me any comfort, but I didn't know what else to do.

On Monday night I went to my regular AA meeting at the church five blocks from my house. This was my "home group," made up in large part of old-timers I had known since I first attended a meeting there in 1990, just after I left Fellowship Club. On this particular Monday night we held our annual potluck banquet, handing out medallions marking days, months, or years of sobriety. A thirty-day coin is as important to a newcomer as a forty-year coin is to an old-timer, and celebrating together is a reminder to all of us that one day at a time does add up after a while. Weeks earlier I had signed up to get my six-year medallion, and when my name was called, I went up to the front of the room feeling shaky and uncertain about what I was going to say.

"My name is William and I'm an alcoholic," I said. At once and in unison everyone in the room said, "Hello, William." As always, the power of the spirit of the fellowship in that room instantly enveloped me. But this time the feeling was even more intense because I was vulnerable in a way that went beyond any need I had ever experienced as a recovering alcoholic. I had a new and equally deadly illness, one that made me feel afraid, adrift, and plenty angry. While I had no desire to drink or take a drug, I knew that nothing is more lethal in recovery than those raw emotions, with a big resentment thrown in, too. This whole cancer thing really seemed unfair to me. Hadn't I already suffered enough?

"It's hard to believe I have six years, and for that I'm truly grateful." My throat tightened, and I paused to take a deep breath. "But I've got cancer, too, and tomorrow I'm having surgery. I don't know what else to say except I need your help."

A hush fell over the room as people stared at me in disbelief, and at that moment I knew I had to be careful. The scene was eerily reminiscent of the AA meetings in Atlanta in the summer of 1994 when I focused attention on my role as the resilient, courageous father with the critically ill newborn son. Back then, it wasn't help I was after—I wanted to be a hero. This time, with cancer, I just wanted to be like everybody else, because stripped down, that's exactly what I was—an alcoholic and a drug addict faced with the challenge of living life on life's terms. I didn't have to like it, but I had to be honest about my anger and resentment, and I had to openly admit and accept that I needed help dealing with it all. If I wasn't honest, and if I didn't ask for help, I'd be in big trouble. I knew from experience that it wouldn't happen suddenly—it would be a process stretching over a period of weeks or months, starting with one secret and then adding secret upon lie upon secret upon lie until I was so full of secrets and lies that they would destroy me.

I took my medallion back to my seat at the table and listened to dozens of other people express their gratitude for their medallions.

One speaker after another reminded the rest of us why we were gathered to celebrate recovery—we were sober for this many days or that many years, and for that we were all grateful. After the meeting friends and strangers alike hugged me, patted me on the back, and offered words of support. Several friends called the house that night to check in, including my sponsors Bob B. and Paul L. Like always, Paul reminded me that after four decades of continuous sobriety, the best he had ever done is "a day at a time, for twenty-four hours." And, like always, he was quick to add: "I'll worry about tomorrow later."

I had surgery the next day. Under local anesthesia, I was awake but felt no pain, although I was uncomfortably aware that the growth seemed to fight back as the surgeon worked to remove it. I imagined that it was connected all the way to the bone and wasn't going to let go without a fight, but I was wrong. The doctor was able to remove all of it, and while I was still lying on the table he gave me the good news that the cancer had not spread to my lymph nodes.

"You are very lucky, my friend," he said.

My luck continued. Every month I drove to the Mayo Clinic in Rochester, Minnesota, for blood screenings and checkups, and month after month, the tests came back negative—no recurrence of cancer. Almost exactly ten months after the diagnosis, Allison and I heard the words we hoped beyond hope that we would hear someday.

"Mr. Moyers," the oncologist said, "you are cancer-free."

Walking down the long hallway of the Oncology Department at the Mayo Clinic, past the anxious faces of other patients and their families in the waiting room, we were barely able to restrain ourselves. Only when we reached the lobby did we dare grab on to each other in tearful relief. Driving home we found it difficult to put our feelings into words—over and over again, I asked myself, "Why me?"

A wise person once said that we have no right to question or argue when bad things happen if we don't also question the good things that come our way. No one in the waiting room of the Mayo Clinic that day deserved cancer any more than I did, and nothing I had done put my cancer into remission. I was simply one of the fortunate ones who got well. "Why me?" That night I went to an AA meeting to remind myself that the unanswerable question didn't really matter. What mattered was staying sober today.

I am forty-seven years old as I write these words, and I'm twelve years sober and six years cancer free. I've had a lot of experience with two deadly diseases in my relatively young life, and I've spent some time thinking about the differences between them. Both diseases are chronic, progressive, and life-threatening. Nobody deserves to get either one. Continuing care is an essential part of treatment, and reoccurrence of the disease is always a possibility. Yet public attitudes toward the victims of these diseases are as different as night and day. That's the gap we must understand and attempt to bridge; until we do, millions of addicted people will suffer needlessly.

When my doctor told me I had cancer, he didn't raise his eyebrows or wag his finger at me. I felt no shame or humiliation. When I told my family and friends that I had cancer, no one ever suggested that I gave myself the illness or that it was in any way my fault, though I suppose people could have pointed a finger of blame at my parents for allowing their blue-eyed, blond-haired, fair-skinned child to swim every summer without sunscreen, go to the beach without wearing a hat, and play outside in the hottest and brightest part of the day. Such carefree and voluntary behavior over the years had resulted in many severe sunburns, but thirty or forty years ago people didn't know a whole lot about skin cancer and because we didn't have the knowledge, we didn't make responsible choices. Nobody was to blame—I just happened to get it, and when I did, everyone stepped in to help.

During the diagnosis, treatment, and recovery stages of my cancer, I was overwhelmed by offers of sympathy and support from family, friends, and even strangers. "Get Well" cards and "How ya' doing?" phone calls affirmed that I was surrounded by people who cared about me and were pulling for me to get well. When I needed emotional support, I didn't hesitate to ask for it, and friends and strangers immediately responded. People told me they admired my strong spirit, and some even called me "courageous." Having cancer never eroded my self-respect, compromised my morals, or challenged my belief in God. I felt more loved and accepted during that difficult period than I have ever felt in my life.

With cancer I never doubted that the medical advice and continuing care I received were the best possible treatments available. From the moment my dermatologist examined the growth in his office to the checkups I continue to get all these years later at the Mayo Clinic, not once did anyone or anything get in the way of my treatment. My health insurance plan was my ally. Every time I pulled out my insurance card and presented it to a doctor, a specialist, or a clinic, I felt absolutely confident that I had the financial safety net I needed for my care. It never crossed my mind that the billing person might hand the card back to me and say, "I'm sorry, Mr. Moyers, your card is no good here. We'll need fifty thousand dollars up front before we can treat you."

Even when I called my insurance company with a question, the faceless and nameless customer service representative on the other end spoke to me with dignity and respect. Because my insurance covered most of what I needed, I never had to beg, borrow, or steal to get the care I needed and deserved. In that sense, my treatment for cancer was no different than my son Henry's treatment for a life-threatening birth defect—we both got everything we needed to give us the best chance possible to live. Without that treatment and continuing care, neither of us would have made it.

Of course, it helped that I did my part, too, and strictly followed the oncologists' orders. I never once challenged the diagnosis, the treatment regimen, or the aftercare plan. Sure, I asked for second and even third opinions, but not to confirm my own theories or attempt to discredit one of my doctor's opinions. I trusted the experience and expertise of my doctors, even if I didn't like what they had to say about the cancer or my chances of surviving it. And my desire to get well and be healthy again was anchored in a sober, clear-headed brain that reminded me every moment of every day what I needed to do to get well. If my doctors had advised me that I might improve my chance of a cure if I stood on my head fifteen minutes a day while singing "Twinkle, Twinkle Little Star," I would have done it without a second thought, and happily, too. If other melanoma patients had told me that eating liver for breakfast increased my odds of recovery, it wouldn't have mattered that I hate liver because I would have eaten it for breakfast, lunch, and dinner. If I'd thought running down the street naked on a subzero Minnesota day would slow the growth of the tumor, I'd have been out there in the buff without pausing to hang up my clothes.

When I did overcome the disease of cancer—through luck and the skills of my doctors rather than anything I did on my own—I took the aftercare plan seriously. All these years later, I continue to get annual cancer checkups, wear sunscreen, a broad-brimmed hat, and oversized sunglasses, and I avoid spending too much time in the sun. Once I knew I had cancer, I vowed to go to any length to avoid a recurrence.

It was a completely different story with my addiction. From the beginning, we all thought the disease was partly if not wholly my fault. I'll never forget the time a family friend, a doctor at St. Vincent's, confronted me in my room at the psych ward.

"How could you have done this to Mary? Why did you do this to her?" she asked, her tone angry and incredulous. *What's wrong with you?* she was really saying, and that sentiment was secretly shared by everyone, including me. What was wrong with me that I would willfully choose to use drugs and destroy my marriage and my life? How could I be so weak, so thoughtless, so self-centered? Why couldn't I just exert some willpower and strength of character and stop this self-destructive behavior?

When I checked into St. Vincent's, I didn't use my last name but instead identified myself only as William Cope. I don't know exactly who made that decision, but we were all complicit in it. We decided not to notify my insurance company for fear that I'd forever be tagged with the label of exactly what I was. My parents told only a few close friends what had happened to me and everyone else was left to wonder why I suddenly disappeared from the neighborhood, from work, and from church. Even the handful of people who knew the truth weren't sure how to reach out in response. I got one or two "Get Well" cards and a few visitors from the outside, and that was it. In truth, I didn't want to see anybody because I was so tortured by shame and guilt.

We didn't even tell my grandparents. When I was at Hazelden in the fall of 1989, my father wrote to me after visiting his parents.

Dear Cope:

I was in Marshall this weekend. Mimi and Pa Pa Henry are holding their own. Their spirits are good but the flesh is weak. Each time one of them gets out of a chair I hold my breath for fear they will fall . . .

They asked about you. I told them you were "getting along busily." It seemed best not to say more, as they have all day to sit there and worry. As it is, they assume you are home and working away. Anytime you think it is time to tell them, I'll do so. But for the moment they just seemed so fragile that I didn't want to disturb them further, all the more so since their views of substance abuse run no further than what they see on television and their experience with my uncle Ralph, who never went through treatment and never tried to recover. When you leave Hazelden, you can go by Marshall to see them and they'll witness in your presence what it means to be the very opposite of Ralph.

Love,
Dad

Addiction separated us in life and in death. I never spoke to my grandfather again. He died a few months after I left Fellowship Club. Mimi and I never talked about my addiction, either; by the time I was solidly in recovery she was in a nursing home. With all my heart I regret not being able to tell them what happened to me during those years when I should have been calling them, writing to them, flying to Marshall to see them. I can't imagine what they must have thought about my behavior. What happened to the devoted grandson who loved them so much? Where did he go? Did they ever fear that I would turn out like Uncle Ralph, my grandmother's alcoholic brother, who drank until the day he died, sometime in his sixties or seventies?

I wish I could have said to them, "I disappeared from your lives because I am addicted to drugs, and it took a long time to get well. I was not in my right mind for the last ten years, but now I'm in recovery and I'm getting back to myself. I love you more than I can say. Will you forgive me?" But I will never be able to say those words, to try to make right what was so terribly wrong, and that is one of my deepest regrets.

As the truth about my addiction painfully unfolded during those early days at St. Vincent and later at Hazelden, my parents and I felt deeply ashamed. "Why didn't we see it coming?" we asked ourselves. Everyone else wondered the same thing. How could this problem have gone undetected? Why didn't anyone step in and stop the madness? How could I have ended up in a crack house in Harlem when just days before I was working a full-time job and sleeping at home with my wife? Surely there were signs—by the time I was thirty, I had uncontrollable nose bleeds, a hacking cough, a beer gut, and my behavior was erratic, even appalling.

"You were rude and disgusting," my father said, referring to the summer evening when I slobbered lobster all over my face at the dinner table. Another time I fell asleep and started farting repeatedly while Mary and my parents were watching television. My insides were a roiling mess, bubbling, boiling, overflowing, but I slept right through the whole thing. I was more than the proverbial elephant in the living room—I was the flatulent elephant snoring and loudly passing gas on the living room floor.

"You offended all of us," my dad remembered, "but we didn't know what to say any more than we knew what to think."

My family didn't "see" the addiction and neither did my friends, my pastor, my coworkers, or my therapists because my face wasn't anything like the face of the stereotypical drug addict who stumbles around city parks begging for quarters or the whiskered alcoholic who passes out in the subway station still clutching a bottle wrapped in a paper bag. I had a job, a car, a home, a wife. I paid taxes, helped the needy, volunteered at church. How could I be an alcoholic and a drug addict?

My family's inability to face the truth was grounded in ignorance about the causes, signs, and symptoms of addiction. Experts sometimes label that ignorance *denial,* as if the progression of the disease was somehow our fault—yet that term was never used to describe why I had gotten cancer or why it wasn't detected any earlier. I never felt that I was to blame for my cancer, but for many years I believed I was responsible for causing my addiction. I never felt ashamed of having cancer; with addiction, shame filled me up and emptied me out over and over again.

Just a week after I arrived at St. Vincent's in 1989, I wrote this entry in my journal:

One week out of the rest of my life has passed. That is terribly scary. It's not like a broken arm that needs healing. I almost wish I had cancer. Then I'd either beat it or die from it. But my disease, even if successfully treated, will never go away. And it might not kill me. But it will hang over me like the blade of a guillotine, more threatening inert than if the blade suddenly slips and mercifully turns out my lights. This is my war to end all wars.

I felt the blade touching my neck, threatening my life, but even that grim reality didn't inspire me to follow the treatment plan, even though I was paying a lot of money for the expertise of doctors and counselors who knew much more than I did. From my very first days at St. Vincent's, all the way through my relapses in Atlanta five years later, I refused to follow the treatment plan and prescriptions for care that were designed to keep me alive. *Don't use, go to meetings, pray, stick with the winners, ask for help, give away as much as you receive.*

Not a cure, certainly, but a solution with a proven track record that tens of millions of addicted people had used to get and stay sober. Not for me, though—I had to do it my way, and not just once but over and over again. From my embarrassment over being addicted in the first place to the secret search for the gardening glove, the insanity of believing I could control my use again, the dishonesty and the pain of it all, I convinced myself that my way was the only way. And I chased that sentiment to the gates of my own destruction.

Addiction is a disease so cunning and baffling, they say, that when it tells you that you don't have it, you believe it. Then, when it tells you that you can beat it on your own with no help from the experts, you believe that, too. In its ability to take over your mind and destroy your very will to survive, addiction is unlike cancer or any other chronic, progressive disease in the world.

THE DISEASE OF addiction and the disease of cancer—I've been intimate with both, and my experiences help to frame my public advocacy work and inform every conversation I have and every issue I raise. In comparing the two, I ask (and attempt to answer) these questions:

Why do we continue to whisper about addiction like earlier generations did about the "long illness" that too many people died from?

Because people who are addicted are too sick to know it and those of us who have recovered are too ashamed to admit we ever had it.

Why is addiction the only disease without a ribbon of hope to wear out in public?

Because it's noble to fight breast cancer and courageous to fight for the rights of people with HIV/AIDS, but the stigma of addiction, in many ways similar to the stigma of mental illness, envelops all those who are suffering (including family members) in secrecy, silence, and shame. Shame fosters stigma and stigma promotes shame, and in the meantime the tradition of anonymity in Alcoholics Anonymous often prevents people from standing up and speaking out. Somehow it still remains against the rules of Twelve Step anonymity to be seen or heard standing up for a cause like recovery. We hide behind our recovery, but did we worry about going out in public and making fools of ourselves when we were drunk or stoned? That behavior was a symbol of everything that was wrong with us then—what is the symbol of what is right with us now?

We should take hope from the struggles and strides of people with diseases such as HIV/AIDS or mental illnesses. They've fought hard to improve public understanding and to change public policy around their illnesses, and they've been successful. We will be, too.

Why do so many people with addiction receive censure and punishment, which do nothing to solve the problem, rather than understanding and treatment, which do?

Because the myths and misconceptions about addiction tell us that addicts and alcoholics are somehow "bad" (lazy, self-centered, immoral, weak-willed) and being bad means breaking the law, and breaking the law means crime followed by punishment. Besides, the country would have to stop building more jail cells in favor of more treatment beds, and how many politicians are willing to risk the label "soft on crime"?

And another question along these lines to ponder: Why is it that people with cancer, diabetes, or hypertension are considered "victims" when their own behavior or lifestyle sometimes contributes to their illness—but we never attach the same sympathetic label to people with my disease?

Why do most insurance companies refuse to pay for chemical dependency treatment when they so generously cover expenses associated with other illnesses?

Because not enough people have called to complain. Imagine the outrage if insurance companies systematically denied women with breast cancer or children with congenital birth defects access to the medical expertise they deserve to overcome their problems? I wonder: Where is our outrage?

Why does society continue to spout the old line that treatment doesn't work when research shows that quality treatment is even more effective for addiction than it is for other chronic diseases?

Because people like me don't stand up and speak out as often as we should, proving with our faces and voices that treatment does work and recovery is possible. Too many of us just want to be "normal" again. We don't want to talk about our past with people who may think less of us or somehow make our lives more difficult. We also take for granted that the treatment options we had when we needed them will be there for the next generation. But there are not enough treatment programs available to help the people who need help—that is the bottom line. Treatment facilities are dying in America, and so, too, are the people who need them.

THE QUESTIONS and answers can be argued forever—and, in truth, they have been—but more than anything else, I believe ignorance and age-old misconceptions about addicted people are to blame. Even where I live in St. Paul, known nationally for being the "crossroads of recovery," the stigma prevents people from thinking about alcoholics and other drug addicts as "good people with a bad illness." A story helps to make the point.

Last year, with my oldest son in tow, I went to the neighborhood bank where I've had an account for more than a decade. I filled out the appropriate paperwork to open a savings account for Henry, and a young bank officer courteously offered us seats across from his desk while he reviewed the information.

"Oh, you work for Hazelden," he said with an odd smile on his face. "Isn't that the place where you fix those crooked people?" He bent his index finger into a grotesque little "r" shape.

I took a moment to respond. I was shocked, but I knew this was a teachable moment for this young man. I slowly raised my eyebrows and frowned.

"What do you mean, 'crooked people'?" I replied.

"You know, the ones who aren't right," he said, the smile still on his face. "They're 'crooked.' "

"You mean people like me?" I said quietly.

"Oh no, not the people who work there; I'm sure they're all good people like you," he said, getting a little flustered. "I'm talking about the ones who go to that place to get fixed."

I leaned forward across the desk. "Before I worked there I went to treatment at Hazelden," I said. "I am one of 'those' people. And I was never 'crooked.' "

He fumbled for a reply. "Right, well, let's move on," he began, but I interrupted him.

"Alcoholics and other addicts look just like everyone else who comes into this bank," I said. "Recovering people, including me, live and work in this neighborhood, using your bank's services to spend and save their money."

He didn't apologize. The next time I visited the bank, I told the manager that it might be a good idea for his young employee to visit Hazelden, just to see what goes on there. I doubt that he ever did but if he had, he would have seen men and women, young and old, educated and uneducated struggling not only to overcome their disease, but to understand it, too, so they can learn how to live with their shame. Once a month or so I talk to patients at Hazelden. Some of them have been sober for a few days; others have been in treatment for months. I tell them my story because it is their story, too.

I used to think that the worst thing in the world that could happen to me was to become an alcoholic. There was a time when I couldn't imagine being an alcoholic and a time when being labeled an addict hurt so much that I hid away and kept my disease a secret from everyone I loved.

There was a time when I was first in treatment that I wished I had cancer instead. Be careful what you wish for, they say. When I got cancer, I was afraid—I didn't want to die. So I went to meetings and there I was reminded that the only thing that really matters is staying sober.

I was a victim of cancer and now I am cancer free. But I still need to go to meetings, because no matter what life throws at me, I am an alcoholic and a drug addict and that fact will never change. Unlike the nasty growth on my arm that my doctor called melanoma, surgery can't rid me of my alcoholism any more than radiation, chemotherapy, or an antibiotic could offer me a cure.

My recovery from addiction began when I stopped using

alcohol and other drugs, but the only solution to my disease is to stay stopped. And, as you know too well, anyone can quit—it's not starting again that's the hard part. For while researchers and scientists tell us that our disease originates somewhere in the brain, it also lingers in the deepest regions of the human soul. And as the Big Book reminds us, we are not cured of alcoholism. What we really have is a daily reprieve contingent on the maintenance of our spiritual condition.

"The spiritual life is not a theory," the Big Book reminds us. "We have to live it."

We have a disease that cannot be cured, and recovery requires that we work hard every day to be humble, honest, tolerant, forgiving, and, always, teachable. Every time we go to a meeting, answer a cry for help, or ask for help ourselves, we witness the necessity of this daily work, but even more important, we are reminded that we are not alone.

Reading through the Twelve Steps not so very long ago, I noticed that the words *I* and *my* are not mentioned once, yet the words *we* and *our* each appear seven times. At its heart and in its soul, recovery from addiction is about fellowship—becoming part of a bigger whole. We are all broken, and the only "cure" for our brokenness is to be broken together.

17

Scarface

IT'S A HUMID July day in Atlanta, and I've just finished speaking to three hundred addiction treatment professionals at a regional conference on addiction, mental illness, and co-occurring disorders. It's dinnertime, but I'm not very hungry. I'm tired but my brain is racing from the events of the day. What I really need, I decide, is a long walk before going back to my hotel room and getting ready for my flight home in the morning.

Walking along the streets of downtown Atlanta I think about Allison and my three children, waiting in St. Paul for me to come home to them. Nancy has a piano recital coming up, and she told me on the phone she is excited to play for me. Thomas and Henry are getting ready to spend two weeks at a summer camp. Allison is preparing for a dinner party this weekend. After three days alone with the kids, she's ready for me to come home.

I think about the time we lived in Atlanta and how far away that seems now. I recall the details of that day, almost exactly ten years earlier, when my father found me in the Atlanta crack house. I want to go there, suddenly, and see the old neighborhood.

I hail a cab and ask the driver to take me to the intersection of Ponce de Leon and Boulevard streets. For ten minutes or so I wander the neighborhood, walking up and down the block several times trying to figure out exactly which building used to be the crack house. After a decade, the neighborhood has been transformed and the decrepit buildings of my time have been renovated and turned into middle-class apartments and condos. While Boulevard and Ponce de Leon will always be a street corner in Atlanta, the crack house is now a four-unit condominium building with a fence and iron gate around it. The parking lot where I bargained with gun-toting crack dealers is now a lush community vegetable garden. I struggle to get my bearings, for I barely recognize the place that is indelibly tattooed in my memory.

A man approaches me on the sidewalk. His shoulders are slumped, and he keeps his eyes firmly fixed on the pavement. In one hand he grasps a brown paper bag with a bottle of booze hidden inside and in the other hand he holds a box of chocolate Girl Scout cookies. As he passes by me, I notice a long scar running from his left ear across his cheek to the corner of his mouth. He doesn't recognize me, but I immediately know who he is. It's Scarface, the crack dealer I first met in the insanity of that summer in 1974.

"Hey, I know you, do you remember me?" I say, reaching out to shake his hand. But how can he know me? I'm William, clean and sober, living in Minnesota. And he's Scarface, still addicted, still struggling to survive.

He looks confused. He's trying to size me up while casting furtive glances at the cell phone attached to my belt. Does he think I'm a cop out to arrest him? A street preacher hoping to save him? A social worker intent on helping him?

I keep talking. I don't want to lose him. There's an urgency in my voice that borders on desperation. I want him to remember who and what I was so he can see who and what I am now. I need him to see that I made it, because if I made it, he can, too.

"I'm the guy who smoked crack with you ten years ago," I say. "Don't you remember me? You took me around this neighborhood and introduced me to BJ, right here in one of these buildings. You helped me find the crack dealers. I gave you money, and you gave me crack. Do you remember?"

He looks perplexed now. For a moment his eyes try to focus, not just on me but on that time and place a decade earlier. But nothing has changed in his life, and so he can't imagine that the crack addict he knew back then is the man in the suit who he's talking to now. For Scarface, and for millions of other addicted people, time is just one long series of moments spent trying to get high or stay high. He doesn't remember me.

"What's your name?" I ask.

He keeps staring at me, clutching his bottle of booze and his box of cookies.

"I'm William," I say. "You're Scarface, aren't you?"

He chuckles and smiles nervously. He glances over his shoulder, then slowly his eyes meet mine. He nods. It is Scarface.

Coincidence is God's way of remaining anonymous. Here, in Atlanta's inner city, I realize that it isn't by chance that I've crossed paths again at this moment with a man who is at the center of my story, the link between the way I used to be and the way I am now.

Talking fast, I try to condense the last decade of my life into a few sentences. "I live in Minnesota now. I got clean, and I haven't had a drink or used a drug since I left this neighborhood in 1994. I went to treatment, and now I work for a treatment center."

These simple facts seem to impress him. "Man, you been clean that long," he says. He gives me that sideways look and adds a respectful "Hmmmmm."

"And how about you, how are you doing?" I ask.

"I'm still drinking," he says. "Sometimes I smoke crack, but not as much as before. I been to prison twice since '94."

He still doesn't remember me, but I can tell that he's trying to make the connection. I don't look anything like I did back when I lived in BJ's house, and there were always so many of us, coming and going. Scarface looms large in my memory, but to him, I'm just one of hundreds of crack heads that he has known over the years.

"Have you ever been to treatment?" I ask him.

"A man's got to want it in his heart," he says, holding the brown bag against his chest. "Ain't gonna work if a man don't want it in his heart."

"Would you mind if I ask your real name?"

"Tony," he says with a big smile. "Tony Alexander."

"Tony," I repeat. "Nice to meet you, Tony."

A young man, probably in his early twenties, approaches us on the sidewalk. "Hey, what's happenin', whaddya want?" he says to Tony.

"Get outta here," Tony growls at him. "This ain't no crack deal."

The young man moves off, grumbling to himself.

I find myself thinking that this is probably the first time Scarface has ever turned down a drug deal. I look at my watch and realize twenty minutes have passed. The cab is still waiting at the curb. It's getting dark.

"I have to go," I say. I scribble my name and phone number on a scrap of paper and hand it to Tony, who thanks me and tucks the note in his sock. I say good-bye and start walking back to the cab.

"Hey, Mister," Tony yells after me. "I don't got no place to stay, no place to go. Got no money, either. Help me out."

I know what kind of help Tony wants, and I also know that any money I give him won't help at all because he'll use it to buy another bottle of booze or a handful of crack. Instead, I tell him to call me. I offer to get him into treatment. That's all I can do. That's everything I can do.

18

E-mailing the Dead

I'LL NEVER FORGET the moment when Larry King asked me on his television program, "So, William, how do you *stay* sober?"

Nobody had ever asked me that before. The question is always, "How did you *get* sober?" Most people want to know why I finally stopped using after so many relapses, how I got into treatment, and what happened once I got there.

I could have spent the rest of the show answering Larry's question. But this was a moment that required nothing more from me than the simple truth, an explanation anyone who was watching could understand. It took only a second or two to think about it.

"Well, Larry," I said, "I lean on the collective wisdom of thousands of people who have come before me."

He didn't ask me to elaborate, but I've often thought about the central importance of that question and what my answer really meant. I can't stay sober by myself—I tried that approach, once upon a time, and it didn't work. To stay sober I lean on people like Bob B., Paul L., and Bob C., who never failed to be there when I needed their help. I lean on strangers I meet once and never see again in meetings in St. Paul, Atlanta, Dallas, and New York. I lean on the stories I read in the Big Book and the casual conversations I have with patients in the hallways at Hazelden. I lean on the wisdom and experience of people who have "been there, done that" and survived their own struggles with alcohol and other drugs.

My sponsor in Atlanta, Bob C., the CNN colleague who drove me to Ridgeview in 1992, finally helped me understand this point about the fellowship. One afternoon not long after my final treatment at Ridgeview, I drove to his house for my "fifth step." This was the moment when I was going to tell another human being my whole life story, admitting every flaw and "defect of character," as AA puts it, holding nothing back. I had many imperfections, of course, and I had confessed most of them in my previous journeys through recovery, but with Bob C. that November day in Atlanta, I decided to reveal certain pieces of the puzzle that I had never admitted to another soul.

I rang the doorbell and panicked. *I can't do this,* I thought. In the next instant I said to myself, *But I must.*

Bob greeted me with a smile and a hug. He offered me lunch, but I wasn't hungry. We sat in his living room, and I started reading through my long list. An hour passed, and another, and I kept going, into the harder stuff, drilling down into the deepest core of my shame. Every flaw in my character, every indecent, reprehensible thing I had ever said or done or thought or felt flowed out of me until it seemed the room was filled with it all, and I was empty. Bob just sat there listening, smoking one cigarette after another. Finally, there was nothing left for me to say.

Bob leaned back in his chair, took a deep drag off his cigarette, let it out slowly. Then he said the words I had been waiting my whole life to hear.

"You too, huh?"

IN OCTOBER 2005, as I was finishing this book, Allison became seriously ill with depression and an eating disorder. For sixteen years she had been the bedrock of our relationship and our family. Never once did she complain through all my relapses and treatments. After Henry was born and required one surgery after another, she slept on a sofa bed in his hospital room, day after day, for months. When the whisper in my ear sent us back to St. Paul, she never questioned my decision or my faith. During my cancer scare she kept her fears to herself, afraid to burden me, always helping me keep my spirits up. Not once has she ever objected to the pace of my frenetic travel schedule, the long hours I work at Hazelden, or all those weekends, holidays, early mornings, and late nights I have spent in front of the computer writing speeches and position papers or answering e-mails from people who need help. For all these years together, her solid, steady support made everything right even when it seemed, at times, so hopelessly wrong.

I always believed that Allison could handle anything that came her way. I took her for granted until one day I was forced to realize how blind I was to the person I love most in the world. She needed expert medical attention far from where we lived, and overnight, it seemed, she was gone. The short-order cook was out of the kitchen. The chauffeur stopped making the daily roundtrips to and from school. The maid ignored the laundry. The gardener neglected the flower beds. The artist stopped painting. The lover didn't get into bed. An enormous void filled our house and our lives. The kids desperately missed their mom, and I longed for everything about her until I was so raw with emotion that I could barely stop myself from breaking down in front of friends and strangers alike.

Allison had been gone eleven days when I wrote her a letter. It was October 13, 2005 (the day after my eleventh year of sobriety).

Eleven years ago yesterday, I finally understood what recovery is all about. Sitting still, experiencing the pain, anger, fear, sadness, joy, freedom, and peace. Not on my agenda or my timelines. It only happened for me when I stopped trying to make it happen, when I gave up looking for it and allowed recovery to find me. God played a big role in that. So did the counselors and the Twelve Steps. And so did you, by giving me permission to stay in treatment until I got well.

Let me return as a gift to you the time you need to heal. If you "get out of the way and let it happen," as George Weller used to tell me, it will. Just remember that it takes time. In the meantime, we'll be okay here.

I love you, Al.
William

I was a mess inside for the five months Allison was gone. Life was out of balance. But I stayed sober through those long days and nights of Allison's illness by never forgetting that old axiom that had come to mean so much to me during my stay at Ridgeview. *Nothing is more important than my sobriety. My whole life depends on this one thing.* The first week she was gone, I went to two or three meetings a week, and then I started going to meetings every day. One day, during one of the toughest periods of Allison's absence (between Thanksgiving and Christmas), nine-year-old Nancy asked me a question.

"Why do you go to all those meetings, Dad?" Her simple child's question required an equally simple answer.

"Because I want to be your daddy," I said.

In those meetings I was never alone. On good days and bad days I found what I needed, even at those times when I forgot that I needed it—the strength of fellowship and camaraderie shared by men and women who, like me, were once desperate but now had hope. In every meeting I was reminded by imperfect people living in an imperfect world that the only thing harder than living life sober is living life drunk or high.

One year later, with Allison home again and healthy, I continue to go to meetings every day. I talk to my sponsor and my friends in recovery, I do what I can to help others, and I do not hesitate to ask for help myself. The mornings begin like the evenings end, with prayer and meditation to get me through the good days and the bad days, sober.

I stay sober by staying connected to the living, who remind me that the stakes are high. I stay sober, too, by remembering the dead. On the dresser in my bedroom I keep a picture of a group from Fellowship Club playing football on a fine fall day in 1989. I'm in the picture, and so is Billy M., who grew up in my hometown, Garden City. Billy was ten years older than me, so we didn't really know each other growing up, but our parents had always been close friends. In fact, when I was at St. Vincent's and my parents weren't sure where to send me for inpatient treatment, Billy's mother recommended Hazelden because that's where Billy went for treatment. We met at Fellowship Club not long after I arrived there. Later, Billy moved to San Francisco, and I lost touch with him.

In 1993, four years after the picture was taken, Billy died alone in his apartment from a heroin overdose. I keep that picture where I can't ignore it, and every day when I reach into the drawer for underwear or a pair of socks, Billy reminds me what's at stake.

I remember the dead on my morning jog when I run past the

house where four men, all graduates of Fellowship Club, once lived. They were "Old Man Joe," a corporate executive; "Crazy Ray," a gay musician from South Carolina; Chris, an all-star football player for the University of Wisconsin; and a guy whose face I recognized in meetings but never found out his name. Three of the four roommates died within a year of one another, because they couldn't stay sober. When I run past the house, I always tip my baseball hat, letting them know that I haven't forgotten them.

I keep running. A mile away, I tip my hat again when I pass the apartment building where Andrew C. died from a heroin overdose.

"I was once right where you are," I told Andrew after an AA meeting in St. Paul, when he was relapsing and desperate to get back into recovery. "Someone told me back then to get my head screwed on right. I'm passing that advice along. Your wife and your boys need you."

Andrew couldn't let go of his craving for heroin any more than he could hold on to another addict's offer of help. Two weeks later he was dead.

At the AA meeting where I last talked to Andrew, I always pause for a moment to talk to my friend Clark. Standing in the foyer at the back of the church, closing my eyes for a moment to gather in the memories of our time together, I whisper, "Hello, Clark." I last saw him in that spot back in 1992 when he had relapsed and was struggling to get back into recovery. A few days later he climbed into the backseat of his car in the garage of his home and left the engine running. He died of carbon monoxide poisoning, leaving behind a wife and three-year-old daughter.

"You may very well be one of only two people living in St. Paul who knows where Hallsville, Texas, is located, and that is an accomplishment that should not be taken too lightly," John K. e-mailed me after I met him at the Monday night AA meeting. He grew up in eastern Texas not far from Marshall where my dad lived, and our familial roots gave us a strong connection.

"Give me a call and let's have lunch," John wrote. "I look forward to seeing you."

He promised to bring me a container of Neely's Brown Pig BBQ sauce from Marshall the next time he went home to visit, but it never happened. A few months after I got his e-mail he drank himself to death. But I still have that e-mail stored on my computer and every once in a while I write to him.

"Hi John," I type into my computer. "Wherever you are, I want you to know I am thinking about you. I'm sorry we never got a chance to dip into that barbecue sauce." Off the e-mail goes, and within a few minutes back comes an automated reply: "Undeliverable."

I e-mail Paul F., a brilliant graduate student at UCLA who worked for Hazelden as a consultant on public policy issues. The last time I saw Paul was at a Hazelden benefit in New York in 2003. He looked elegant in his tuxedo, but as so often happens with addicted people, the outside didn't match the inside. He was relapsing but was too scared to admit it. Ten days later, he was dead.

"Damn you, Paul," I write. "Why didn't you ask for help?" My e-mail bounces back with a "fatal error" message.

I e-mail Mike R., whom I met at Fellowship Club in 1989. On Father's Day two years ago, Mike wrote me a long, chatty e-mail about his new job as a high school teacher and his thirteen-month-old daughter, who was taking her first steps. "Sobriety makes possible all the joys of my life," he wrote. Three days later he was shot dead in his car by a stranger who was allegedly under the influence of drugs.

"Dear Mike," I write, "I miss you." The e-mail returns to me a few minutes later. "User unknown."

I e-mail the dead, and they remind me that when we are gone, we can't hear the cries for help any more than we can reach out to touch and be touched by the people we love. We are "undeliverable." "Unknown." Our addresses have "permanent, fatal errors."

I feel the emptiness. I listen to the silence. And I am reminded once again that recovery is my life.

I want to live.

Epilogue

ADDICTION NEARLY KILLED ME, more than once. Recovery saved my life. Poles apart, the pain, desperation, liberation, and gratitude of all my experiences collided head-on to forge what I am at the end of this story: an advocate who is dedicating my life to unmasking the dark stigma of addiction by speaking out about the promise and possibility of long-term recovery.

It's a story I share everywhere I go—from Rotary clubs in Moline, Illinois (the Midwest hometown of John Deere tractors), to the fast-paced Diamond District in midtown Manhattan. From a Jewish community center in suburban Minneapolis to a Baptist faith-based treatment program in the Texas Hill Country. From international AA conventions to professional conferences for doctors, lawyers, nurses, social workers, business executives, and human resource directors, many of whom are in recovery too. From legislative hearings in Congress to student assemblies at private academies and inner-city public schools, from radio interviews to Internet chat rooms to newspaper op-ed pages, wherever I speak, my message is the same:

> My name is William Moyers and I am in long-term recovery from the disease of addiction to alcohol and other drugs. This is what an alcoholic and a drug addict looks like. I'm proof that addiction doesn't discriminate. And neither should recovery.

Carrying this message is what I do for Hazelden, whose mission is to help people recover from alcoholism or drug dependence. That means working to eliminate obstacles that prevent people from asking for help, and getting them the help they and their families need and deserve.

According to the National Survey on Drug Use and Health (NSDUH), about 22 million Americans required treatment for alcoholism or drug dependence in 2003. Yet only 3 million people received it. More than eight of every ten Americans who need services for addiction to alcohol and other drugs are not receiving the professional help that they need to get well. Without help, most of them are doomed to lives filled with hopelessness, despair, and fear. Without help, many will die. These are the millions of moms and dads, sons and daughters, brothers and sisters, wives and husbands who are the real victims of the failed war on drugs.

A severe shortfall of federal and state dollars, discrimination in private insurance plans that don't cover addiction like other chronic illnesses, and rigid public policies that criminalize addiction are just some of the obstacles addicted people face. But the biggest obstacle of all is stigma. Too often, policy makers and their constituents view addicts and alcoholics as degenerates who somehow deserve their problem—helpless and hopeless souls who lack willpower or religion, who are the by-product of broken homes with abusive or absent parents, who are unemployed or unemployable, who live under bridges, in flophouses or homeless shelters, or across the tracks in somebody else's town.

The truth is that almost two thirds of Americans have friends or family members who have struggled with addiction. Millions of people are in recovery. We live in your town, on your block and in your home, but still many people don't know that treatment works, and that long-term recovery is a common reality.

To break down the wall of shame, stigma, and discrimination that keeps people from finding their paths to recovery, I invite my audiences to take action in their own communities. Here's the challenge:

• If you are a person in recovery, share your story with a friend, a neighbor, or another person in your life who doesn't know it. Let them know how you were broken, how you healed, and why your life has changed for the better.

• If you are the family member of somebody who has struggled with alcoholism or drug dependence, share that with somebody who doesn't know. And if your loved one has recovered, make sure to share that, too.

• If you are a professional who works to help addicts and alcoholics turn their lives around, start talking to people in your community about your successes.

• If you are on the board of an organization that helps people with addiction, explain to your friends or colleagues why you donate your time, energy, and money to support access to treatment and recovery.

• Engage the media. The media drives public perception, and public perception drives public policy. Write letters to editors, call radio talk shows, and get to know local reporters who write about health-related issues so you can be a resource for them on their next story. Invite the media to events and to see what you're doing to make recovery a reality.

- Get to know your local, state, and federal elected offi-cials. Tell them you and your family vote and that you care about legislation and regulations that support recovery.
- Finally, do all these things using your first and last name and address.

When I first made this challenge the cornerstone of Hazelden's call to action in the late 1990s, I thought I was one of just a handful of people who were willing to speak out and publicly share their stories of addiction and recovery. I was wrong. As I traveled the country speaking out, I met other recovery advocates who were doing the same thing, some who had been doing it for a lot longer than I have been.

Today there are tens of thousands of people involved in this re-markable grassroots effort, represented by such organizations as the National Council on Alcoholism and Drug Dependence (NCADD), the Johnson Institute, and most recently, Faces and Voices of Recovery (FAVOR). A not-for-profit based in Washington, D.C., allied with community-based groups all over the country, FAVOR (www.faces andvoicesofrecovery.org) is changing the debate for the sake of those who still suffer from alcoholism or drug dependence now and for fu-ture generations of children and families who may face it someday, too. (I serve on FAVOR's board.)

My hope is that today's advocacy efforts will result in a treatment center in every community; prevention programs taught in every ele-mentary and high school; sufficient private and public funding so that scientists and other experts have the resources to research and under-stand the complexities of addiction and put that research into practical use in our communities; halfway houses and recovery homes in all kinds of neighborhoods; revamped insurance policies offering cover-age for inpatient treatment, long-term treatment and recovery support services; and drug courts in every community. Most of all, my hope is that help will be available to anyone who needs it, even if they need it, as I did, more than once.

The war on drugs must shift from an obsessive focus on trying to reduce the supply through interdiction and criminal justice to promoting what works the best—recovery. Perhaps someday that will happen. In the meantime, people addicted to alcohol and other drugs, their loved ones and the communities where they live, are desperate for help. And that's the real reason those of us in recovery and our families must stand up and put our faces on the solution. This misunderstood disease still thrives in the shadows of public intolerance and private shame. When we speak out, we become beacons of hope and pathways to help for addicts and alcoholics who don't know where else to turn. I've learned this over and over again. From e-mails, letters, and phone calls at work to unannounced visits on the front porch or in the living room of my house in St. Paul, in my story people find the permission they desperately need to open up and tell their own stories, taking that first step on the road to recovery. For many of them, it's the first time they've ever known of an alcoholic and drug addict they can relate to, and they rarely stop sharing until they've squeezed out every ounce of pain, anger, fear, and frustration. Most of their stories end with the question, "Can you please help me?"

Many years ago, when I was a patient at Hazelden, our morning group meditation always included somebody reading aloud a long passage from a chapter buried deep in the back of the Big Book of Alcoholics Anonymous. It's unofficially called "Acceptance is the Answer." I can still hear those words in the back of my mind: "And acceptance is the answer to *all* my problems today." In those early days of trying to understand what my newfound sobriety was all about, I assumed its only relevance to me was in the importance of embracing the reality that I was an alcoholic and a drug addict.

But all these years later I have discovered an even deeper meaning in that passage, which has more to do with my life today than I could have ever imagined.

"For years, I was sure the worst thing that could happen to a nice guy like me woud be that I would turn out to be an alcoholic. Today, I find it's the best thing that has ever happened to me."

Like this memoir, my public advocacy is a window into my self. And so it's my own life that has benefited from the work I do today. Helping people helps me. When I hear their stories I'm reminded of mine. In their brokenness I see the depths of my own despair so many years ago. Then I realize the distances I've traveled and how far there is still to go.

Acknowledgments

Dear Mr. Moyers:

    I'm just going to jump in and say it: I would like to write a book with you.

    I've been thinking long and hard about the book I'd like to write and the general idea is to feature real-life stories of adolescents who are struggling with drug addiction.

For a moment I was taken aback by the letter I found at the top of a stack of mail on my desk at Hazelden one day in March 2004.

    What did I know about addicted kids, I thought, except from my own experiences growing up? I'd never written a book before. And, besides, just who was this stranger who signed her name to this out-of-the-blue pitch to me?

    Intrigued, I called the author of that unsolicited letter. I had a better idea.

"Would you help me with *my* book?" I asked. And with that, Kathy Ketcham and I began this collaborative effort called my memoir.

Along the way some people have asked me why I needed another person to help me write a book about my life. As you've read in these pages, I learned the hard way that, left alone, I easily get myself in trouble. And I owe what I am today less to what I've done and more to the insights and feedback of the people around me. Kathy's credentials as an author are obvious. What is even stronger is her remarkable wisdom, patience, and ability to get beyond my head and into my soul. Many were the moments when she pushed me to "go deeper, William, and open that vein." Because of her, I have.

But the genesis of this book began long before I got Kathy's letter. In 1998 another woman who knew of me before I ever met her suggested I write about my life. Amy Williams had seen me on television with my parents, talking about our family's struggle to deal with my illness. "I'm not ready to tell my story," I told her, "because my story isn't done yet." Still, from time to time she'd pester me with a quick e-mail: "Now?" It didn't hurt, either, that Amy knows a thing or two about the literary world. Finally, when the time was right Amy Williams, now my agent, helped birth this endeavor. I am forever grateful.

Memories alone don't just become a published memoir. As a first-time author, I've learned that a story worth telling is only worth reading after a lot of hard work to develop themes and structure, then mating them to words and sentences and chapters to become this book. Molly Stern, my editor, and associate editor Katherine Carlson made this happen. So did all of their colleagues at Viking, especially Clare Ferraro, who believed my story really was a book even before I was convinced. And to Pamela Dorman, formerly of Viking, now I understand why there's much more to your wisdom than what meets your literary eye.

To Mike Rudell, thanks for helping me navigate the unexpectedly choppy waters that threatened to swamp this project at the moment it was launched.

To Nick Motu, Jill Wiedemann-West, and Ivy Bernhardson, my colleagues at Hazelden, I will always respect not just your professional expertise but your inherent willingness to trust that in the end this story was all about Hazelden's heart and soul, and nothing less.

Peggy Fisher, my assistant at Hazelden: How in the world did you put up with me long enough to help me see this through? And you still managed the whirlwind of details of everything else to allow me to meet my day-to-day obligations at work!

Pat Spencer, thanks for your supreme patience and understanding during all those difficult times when your wife, Kathy, was immersed in turning this story into the book. Ben, Alison, and Robyn, your mother's dedication to this project was exceeded only by her commitment to you, her children.

I can't imagine how books were written before there were computers, e-mail, and laser printers. Just the same, I can't see how this book would have been created if not for Michael Jurayj, my down the street neightbor. He's the IT guy who kept it all running and prevented me from short-circuiting.

I suggest that any aspiring author spend a couple of days on the front porch or at the breakfast table of the Green Gables bed-and-breakfast inn in Walla Walla, Washington. Margaret and Jim Buchan made me feel right at home away from home whenever I visited Kathy to work on this book.

Gracias, Queralt Pinto. En esos días aparentemente sin fin, de agotamiento y desesperación confusa, nunca habría podido ver la luz sin tu incansable compromiso con mi familia. De hecho, fue el momento más oscuro justo antes del amanecer. Pero lo conseguimos.

At a critical moment, my friend Dwight Vick at the University of South Dakota looked over my shoulder and offered his professional feedback on the manuscript. His personal perspectives on the journey he and I share are even more invaluable to me. And to Ashley Stanley, who channeled her energy and passion for this story into the extra boost needed to make sure we got it right, don't forget to pace yourself now.

Kathy's agent, Sarah Jane Freymann, helped to successfully guide this project from start to finish. We thank you.

Many of the other people who I owe so much to are mentioned by name in this story. But if not for Bob Bisanz, Paul Lawson, Bob C., Keith Jensen, Richard Morgan, and Jane Nakken, there would have been no story at all.

Thanks to Mel Schulstad and Ernie Kurtz for reminding me that there's a heck of a lot of spirituality to be tapped from all my imperfections.

The experience, strength, and hope of my "fellow travelers" helped pull me through the toughest moments, especially as the deadline for this book approached and life became unmanageable.

To my children, Henry and Thomas and Nancy, you are a true reward of my recovery and an affirmation that sustains me every single day, no matter what.

Allison, what more can I say: I love you, one day at a time, forever.